The Optical Unconscious

OCTOBER Books

Annette Michelson, Rosalind Krauss, Yve-Alain Bois, Benjamin Buchloh, Hal Foster,
Denis Hollier, and John Rajchman, editors

Broodthaers
edited by Benjamin H. D. Buchloh

AIDS: Cultural Analysis/Cultural Activism
edited by Douglas Crimp

Aberrations
by Jurgis Baltrušaitis

Against Architecture: The Writings of Georges Bataille
by Denis Hollier

Painting as Model
by Yve-Alain Bois

The Destruction of Tilted Arc: *Documents*
edited by Clara Weyergraf-Serra and Martha Buskirk

The Woman in Question
edited by Parveen Adams and Elizabeth Cowie

Techniques of the Observer: On Vision and Modernity in the Nineteenth Century
by Jonathan Crary

The Subjectivity Effect in Western Literary Tradition:
Essays toward the Release of Shakespeare's Will
by Joel Fineman

Looking Awry: An Introduction to Jacques Lacan through Popular Culture
by Slavoj Žižek

Cinema, Censorship, and the State: The Writings of Nagisa Oshima
by Nagisa Oshima

The Optical Unconscious
by Rosalind E. Krauss

Rosalind E. Krauss

The Optical Unconscious

An OCTOBER book

The MIT Press
Cambridge, Massachusetts
London, England

First MIT Press paperback edition, 1994

This book was set in Sabon by DEKR Corporation and was printed and bound in the United States of America.

Library of Congress Cataloging-in-Publication Data

Krauss, Rosalind E.
    The optical unconscious / Rosalind E. Krauss.
        p.   cm
    Includes bibliographical references and index.
    ISBN 0-262-11173-X (HB), 0-262-61105-8 (PB)
    1. Visual perception.   2. Optical illusions.   3. Artists—
Psychology.   I. Title.
    N7430.5.K73   1993
        701—dc20   92-28978
                                                                                CIP

For Denis Hollier

Contents

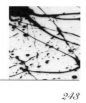

Acknowledgments

The logical extension of work begun over a decade ago, on Giacometti's connection to "primitivism" as that was being rethought by the group around *Documents* and on surrealist photography, this book owes much to the two instigators of those early projects: William Rubin, who invited me to contribute to the catalogue of his *"Primitivism" and Twentieth-Century Art,* and Jane Livingston, who had the vision and the persistence to transform research on surrealist photography into an exhibition and thus to collaborate with me on our joint *L'Amour Fou: Photography and Surrealism.* The issues generated by those two projects seemed to demand further investigation and I therefore embarked on the present work.

In this I have been aided by the many people, most particularly my students at The Graduate Center, City University of New York, who listened to this material as I tried it out in lecture form. I am also grateful to the University of Southern California's Getty Lectureship, which gave me the opportunity to present the early chapters of the book to a perceptive and questioning audience. Help in the writing of the book was further provided by a CUNY Research Fellowship. The encouragement and advice offered by friends and colleagues who read the manuscript have been extraordinarily important to me. I want to thank them here, although many of them will see how often I have stubbornly held out against their counsel: Leo Bersani, Yve-Alain Bois, Anne Boyman, Benjamin Buchloh, Robert Cornfield, Hubert Damisch, Teri Wehn-Damisch, Georges Didi-Huberman, Ulysse Dutoit, Hal Foster, Anne Hollander, Denis Hollier, Martin Jay, Molly Nesbit, John Rajchman, Margit Rowell, Julia Strand, Mark Strand, Holly Wright. And to Roger Conover, my editor at the MIT Press, my thanks here are only a token of what I owe to his support of my work.

The Optical Unconscious

The optical arts spring from the eye and solely from the eye.

—Jules Laforgue, "Impressionism"

one

And what about little John Ruskin, with his blond curls and his blue sash and shoes to match, but above all else his obedient silence and his fixed stare? Deprived of toys he fondles the light glinting off a bunch of keys, is fascinated by the burl of the floorboards, counts the bricks in the houses opposite. He becomes the infant fetishist of patchwork. "The carpet," he confesses about his playthings, "and what patterns I could find in bed covers, dresses, or wall-papers to be examined, were my chief resources." This, his childish solace, soon becomes his talent, his great talent: that capacity for attention so pure and so disinterested that Mazzini calls Ruskin's "the most analytic mind in Europe." This is reported to Ruskin. He is modest. He says, "An opinion in which, so far as I am acquainted with Europe, I am myself entirely disposed to concur."

Of course, it's easy enough to laugh at Ruskin. The most analytic mind in Europe did not even know how to frame a coherent argument. The most analytic mind in Europe produced *Modern Painters,* a work soon to be known as one of the worst-organized books ever to earn the name of literature. Prolix, endlessly digressive, a mass of description, theories that trail off into inconclusiveness, volume after volume, a flood of internal contradiction.

Yet there's still the image of the child, with his physical passivity and his consuming, visual fire. I think of him squatting on the garden path, knees and arms akimbo, staring at the ants swarming along the cracks between the paving stones, fixating all that miniaturized activity into purest, linear ornament. It's the stare's relation to pattern, and its withdrawal from purpose. His boyish connection to the sea is just one more example of what we could only call the modernist vocation of this stare.

Listen to him saying, "But before everything, at this time, came my pleasure in merely watching the sea. I was not allowed to row, far less to sail, nor to walk near the harbor alone; so that I learned nothing of shipping or anything else worth learning, but spent four or five hours every day in simply staring and wondering at the sea,—an occupation which never failed me till I was forty. Whenever I could get to a beach it was enough for me to have the waves to look at, and hear, and pursue and fly from." And of course he does not forget to assure us that there's nothing useful, nothing instrumental in this look; for right away he adds, "I never took to natural history of shells, or shrimps, or weeds, or jelly fish."

Is it possible, I imagine someone asking, to think of Ruskin—who could never produce a thought about art that was not at the same time a sermon—in the same universe as modernism? Ruskin, who held that High Renaissance painting was bad because its makers could not have been very moral; who could never stop badgering and preaching and thinking about instruction.

Yet for all that, Ruskin cannot take his eyes from the sea. And it functions for him in the same way it does for Monet in *Impression: Sunrise* or Conrad in *Lord Jim*. The sea is a special kind of medium for modernism, because of its perfect isolation, its detachment from the social, its sense of self-enclosure, and, above all, its opening onto a visual plenitude that is somehow heightened and pure, both a limitless expanse and a sameness, flattening it into nothing, into the no-space of sensory deprivation. The optical and its limits. Watch John watching the sea.

And then there's the moment when Ruskin is four and sitting for his portrait. "Having," he says, "been steadily whipped if I was troublesome, my formed habit of serenity was greatly pleasing to the old painter; for I

Frank Stella, *Louisiana Lottery Company*, 1962.

"So he hits the ball right out of the park. That's why Frank thinks he's a genius . . ." (p. 7)

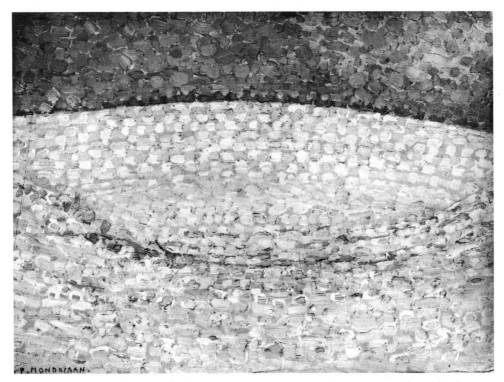

Piet Mondrian, *Dune III*, 1909.

On the site of the rationalization of painting around the laws of color
theory . . . (p. 11)

sat contentedly motionless, counting the holes in his carpet, or watching him squeeze his paint out of its bladders,—a beautiful operation, indeed, to my way of thinking;—but I do not remember taking any interest in Mr. Northcote's application of the pigments to the canvas." The obligatory comment about the stare's detachment from the field of purpose is there, of course; but added to it is the final, perfect touch, where the whole thing comes full circle and the motionless, silent, disembodied subject of the stare becomes its equally disincarnated object, becomes, that is, himself an image: "My quietude was so pleasing to the old man that he begged my father and mother to let me sit to him for the face of a child which he was painting in a classical subject; where I was accordingly represented as reclining on a leopard skin, and having a thorn taken out of my foot by a wild man of the woods."

So here is this little boy, no toys, beaten if he cries or is "troublesome," no sweets of any kind, not even soft white bread—though his father is in the sherry trade and is quite exacting about matters of table—his every movement restricted lest he happen to hurt himself, his days an untiring cycle of reading scripture from one end to the other and of memorizing the verses set for him by his mother. And his one release: the family pleasure, the exquisite luxury of travel. Mamma and Papa in the beautifully fitted coach, with little John in the dickey, and Salvador riding courier. Paris, Brussels, the Black Forest, the Bay of Uri, the Bernardine Pass, Lake Como, Milan. It's the courier of course who books rooms in the inns, arranges for the fresh teams of horses, orders the meals, and bargains over the fees. For beyond a smattering of French, the Ruskins are strictly limited to English.

Travel is thus not a release from but a luxuriating into the same rapt stare that is the medium of John Ruskin's daily life. And he glories in it, calling their style of passing through foreign lands a mode of "contemplative abstraction from the world." Naturally he has nothing but praise for the advantage of this abstraction. "There is something peculiarly delightful— nay delightful inconceivably by the modern German-plated and French-polished tourist, in passing through the streets of a foreign city without understanding a word that anybody says! One's ear for all sound of voices then becomes entirely impartial; one is not diverted by the meaning of syllables from recognizing the absolute guttural, liquid, or honeyed quality of them: while the gesture of the body and the expression of the face have the same value for you that they have in a pantomime; every scene becomes a melodious opera to you, or a picturesquely inarticulate Punch."

I think of the Bergman film *The Silence,* the one where they are traveling through a foreign city where there seems to be a revolution going on but they don't understand a word of the language. It's like Ruskin's using the old, shopworn, novelistic image of the theater—with the unfolding of the drama before him a metaphor of the unity of the world's great stage—except that he's a deaf-mute and can only see the scene as patterns and colors and lines. The theatrical continuum gets splintered and the senses go off each in its own direction. And for each sense there's an image. And each image is independent, freestanding: autonomy in practice.

Here's how the passage ends, then. "I don't say that our isolation was meritorious, or that people in general should know no language but their own. Yet the meek ignorance has these advantages. We did not travel for adventures, nor for company, but to see with our eyes . . . and even in my own land, the things in which I have been least deceived are those which I have learned as their Spectator."

Even now I can hear the objection, not only "theirs" but my own. All of this is well and good; Ruskin's view-hunting is a means of transforming the whole of nature into a machine for producing images, establishing in this way an autonomous field of the visual—characterized, indeed, by those two qualities onto which the optical sense opens uniquely: the infinitely multiple on the one hand, and the simultaneously unified on the other. A field that is both continuously divisible, into smaller and smaller parts, more and more detail—the impossible limit of every single leaf on the Fontainebleau aspens—and at the same time structured into pattern. *Modern Painters* sets out to prove the superiority of landscape painting over all other art because its field is precisely this domain of the purely visual. But the sticking point—is it not?—is that it's not just form that enters the field of contemplation through this grasping of aesthetic coherence as lawlike. It's God that enters the abstracted, contemplative field. For Ruskin insists that the coherence is the manifestation of His law, and that therefore what is to be derived from the field of the visual is grace.

I remember reading Michael's last sentence—"Presentness is grace"—with a dizzying sense of disbelief. It seemed to shake everything I thought I'd understood. The healthy, Enlightenment-like contempt for piety, the faith instead in the intellect's coming into an ever purer self-possession, the oath that modernism had sworn with rationalism. And to show that that final sentence was no accident, Michael Fried had prepared for it from the first, with the passage about Jonathan Edwards's faith that each moment places us before the world as though in the very presence of God in the act of creating it. It didn't seem to me that anything about this could be squared with the robustness of most of Michael's earlier talk about modernism. Like the time we were speaking about Frank Stella and Michael asked me, "Do you know who Frank thinks is the greatest living American?" Of course I didn't. "Ted Williams." And Michael covered my silence with his own glee. "Ted Williams sees faster than any other living human. He sees so fast that when the ball comes over the plate—90 miles an hour—he can see the stitches. So he hits the ball right out of the park. That's why Frank thinks he's a genius." This was by way, of course, of inducting me onto the team, Michael's team, Frank's team, Greenberg's team, major players in the '60s formulation of modernism.

To see so fast that the blur of that white smudge could be exploded into pure contact, pure simultaneity, pure optical pattern: vision in touch with its own resources. And fast, so fast. In that speed was gathered the idea of an abstracted and heightened visuality, one in which the eye and its object made contact with such amazing rapidity that neither one seemed any longer to be attached to its merely carnal support—neither to the body of the hitter nor to the spherical substrate of the ball. Vision had, as it were, been pared away into a dazzle of pure instantaneity, into an abstract condition with no before and no after. But in that very motionless explosion of pure presentness was contained as well vision's connection to its objects, also represented here in its abstract form—as a moment of pure release, of pure transparency, of pure self-knowledge. In Michael's hilarity was all his admiration for Frank. For the dazzling aptness of Frank's metaphor. Because of course the image of Williams's heightened vision conjured those very aspirations toward what Clement Greenberg had, at just about the same time, outlined as modernist painting's self-critical dimension: its participation in a modernist culture's ambition that each of its disciplines be rationalized by being grounded in its unique and separate domain of experience, this to be achieved by using the characteristic method of that discipline both to narrow and "to entrench it more firmly in its area of competence." For painting, this meant uncovering and displaying the conditions of vision itself, as these were understood, abstractly. "The heightened sensitivity of the picture plane may no longer permit sculptural illusion, or trompe-l'oeil," he wrote, "but it does and must permit optical illusion. The first mark made on a surface destroys its virtual flatness, and the configurations of a Mondrian still suggest a kind of illusion of a kind of third dimension. Only now it is a strictly pictorial, strictly optical third dimension . . . one into which one can look, can travel through, only with the eye."

one

7

Georg Lukács, deploring this technologizing of the body, this need to abstract and reify each of the senses in a submission of human subjectivity to the model of positivist science, would have found nothing to argue with in such an analysis. He would only have objected to its tone, to its assumption, which Greenberg shared with Adorno, that in this withdrawal of each discipline into that sphere of sensory experience unique to it there was something positive, something utopian. For a utopian modernism was insisting that this sensory stratum newly understood as discrete, as self-sufficient, as autonomous—this very stratification—permitted an experience of rescue and retreat, a high ground uncontaminated by the instrumentality of the world of labor and of science, a preserve of play and thus a model of freedom. Perhaps the pleasure for both of us at that moment in the '60s in the idea of a high-cultural ambition's being allegorized through a baseball player was just this insistence on the seriousness of this very sense of play.

But from the secularity of the baseball player to the metaphysics of grace is a leap indeed, a leap that performs the peculiar feat of folding all of utopian modernism into the arms of the writer of Sesame and Lilies, *showing that the visual speed that produces the disincarnated look is not an athlete's but an evangelical Christian's, or God's. It produced a shudder, like a lining ripping open so that the ideological seams showed through.*

So there's the sea, Conrad's sea, the sea, for example, in *Typhoon* where the storm is gathering:

> At its setting the sun had a diminished diameter and an expiring brown, rayless glow, as if millions of centuries elapsing since the morning had brought it near its end. A dense bank of cloud became visible to the northward; it had a sinister dark olive tint, and lay lower and motionless upon the sea, resembling a solid obstacle in the path of the ship. She went foundering towards it like an exhausted creature driven to its death. . . . The far-off blackness ahead of the ship was like another night seen through the starry night of the earth—the starless night of the immensities beyond the created universe, revealed in its appalling stillness through a low fissure in the glittering sphere of which the earth is the kernel.

Piet Mondrian, *Pier and Ocean*, 1914.

Two immense horizontal fields broken only by the projection of a small jetty . . . (p. 12)

Piet Mondrian, *Pier and Ocean (Composition No. 10)*, 1915.

Translated into the plus and minus of a moment not of sensation but of cognition . . . (p. 12)

When he's describing the impressionism of Conrad's style, of Conrad's peeling sense data away from the world and refashioning them into pure image, Fredric Jameson is led to quote that passage. "At its most intense," he says, "what we will call Conrad's sensorium virtually remakes its objects, refracting them through the totalized medium of a single sense, and more than that, of a single 'lighting' or coloration of that sense. The possibility of this kind of sensory abstraction is, to be sure, at first given in the object—the unearthliness of the sea—but then returns upon that object to remake it anew as something never dreamed on heaven or earth."

But would be dreamed anew—I want to interject—by Mondrian. That other, limitless space, beyond even the waves and the stars, the total stillness of that space, and its stunning transparency, would be the lining of nature turning inside out in the *Plus and Minus* pictures in Holland. And the rage for abstraction that would appear there would be a passion to remake the object, shaping everything about it in the lens of the optical continuum, all of experience condensed into a single, luminous ray.

Or. Rather. A single, colorless ray.

If Mondrian began with divisionism, with that positivist notion of making the picture a mosaic of color sensations—each dot the marker of a point of light reflected off the field of objects—so that the painting became a recreation of the surface of the world only because it was first and foremost the reconstruction of the surface of the eye, he started off from late nineteenth-century optical theory. His entry into modernism took place on the site of the rationalization of painting around the laws of color theory and physiological optics, at the point where composition and pictorial harmony were at last to be demystified by science and to find their grounding in a set of abstract theorems—theorems that bore the names of great physiologists and physicists like Fechner, Young, Helmholtz, Hering. Simultaneous contrast, nerve tissue response-time. The two planes—that of the retinal field and that of the picture—were understood now to be isomorphic with one another, the laws of the first generating both the logic and the harmonic of the order of the second; and both of these fields—the retinal and the pictorial—unquestionably organized as flat.

But the *Plus and Minus* paintings would take the pared-down surface of the color mosaic and abstract it one step further. The color mosaic, after all, still presupposes the empirical field "out there" as its sensory stimulus; if the mosaic abstracts the world into the "pure" relationships of optics, it is nonetheless empirically founded in the naturalism of color and—no matter how finely grained its text—the point-by-point stimulation of a perceiving eye. Like Seurat at Honfleur, Mondrian would start his *Plus and Minus* from an expanse of sea and sky, two immense horizontal fields broken only by the projection of a small jetty. But he would not transcode the optical moments of this vastness into points of color. He would imagine optical law as something that is itself submitted to a code, digitalized by the higher orders of the intellect, translated into the plus and minus of a moment not of sensation but of cognition, the moment, that is, of pure relationship. His field would thus be structured by these signals—black on white—these signs for plus and minus, these fragments of an abstract grid that would intend to throw its net over the whole of the external world in order to enter it into consciousness. To think it.

The whole of the external world. That, I can imagine the social historians saying, is a bit of an exaggeration. It's sea and sky, or dunes, sea, and sky, that have been segmented off from the rest of the world, from everything political, or economic, or historic, and themselves made into an abstraction of that world. In 1916, after all, the Great War was being fought not too far away from that very sea and sky.

And they would be right, of course. The sea and sky are a way of packaging "the world" as a totalized image, as a picture of completeness, as a field constituted by the logic of its own frame. But its frame is a frame of exclusions and its field is the work of ideological construction.

Your modernism, they would continue, not only walls off art from every- thing else in the historical field, but even within its closure it involves the most arbitrary of selections. It chooses to include this and this but not that and that. And those very things it deals with are themselves submitted to the test of *its* concepts. Your modernism, they would say. Yet, saying that, what would they be saying? They would be saying that "modernism" names an ideology, a discursive field whose occupants believed that art could stand alone—autonomous, self-justifying. Occupants consisting not only of artists but of ideologues as well: theorists, critics, writers, histori- ans. Historians not just contemporary with the artists in the field, but those historians who, even today, continue to talk of modernism's "autonomy," thinking they can bracket it off from the world, from its context, from the real.

And I am saying nothing different. "My" modernism is, of course, another name for a discursive field that, like any other such field, is structured. The set of concepts that grids its surface not only organizes the facts within it but determines what, by their lights, will even count as facts. Thus in being the name of a historical period it not only points to the series of events that will figure within that period—"modernist" artists, "modernist" works of art—but to the self-understanding of the practitioners as they participated in those events, as they made their choices in relation to those concepts and not others. It is only because a field *is* so structured that, for example, it can be attacked by its fellow opponents. As when dada can say: "No more cubism. It is nothing but commercial speculation!"

And how do we understand that attack? Is it coming from outside the field? Or from within?

It struck me one day that it was more interesting to think of modernism as a graph or table than as a history (the history that goes from impressionism to neoimpressionism to fauvism to cubism to abstraction . . . ; the history of an ever more abstract and abstracting opticality), that there was something to be gained from exploring its logic as a topography rather than following the threads of it as a narrative. Without speaking here of what later occurred to me as all the advantages of this graph, I will simply sketch it now.

I start with a square. In its upper right corner I write figure *and in its upper left I write* ground. *I want this square to represent a universe, a system of thinking in its entirety, a system that will be both bracketed by and generated from a fundamental pair of oppositions. This of course is the universe of visual perception, the one that is mapped by a distinction between figure and ground so basic that it is unimaginable, we could say, without the possibility of this distinction. The Gestalt psychologists have told us that: if no figure-detached-from-ground, then no vision.*

But the universe I am mapping is not just a binary opposition, or axis; it is a fourfold field, a square. And its logic is that the generating opposition can be held steady over the whole surface of the graph, extending into its other two corners. To do this, I need only exercise the logic of the double negative. The symmetry of the square will then be maintained, as the product of a four-part mirror inversion. I could write the narrative of these double negatives—of how not-not-figure can (in this universe where not-figure is the same as ground) *be just as easily written as* not-ground; *and how not-not-ground can be (following the same logic) expressed as* not-figure—*but it's both less tiresome and clearer just to show it:*

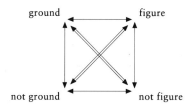

And what we then see is the completeness of the symmetry. Figure *versus* ground. *And* not-figure *versus* not-ground. *But also,* figure *versus* not-figure *and* ground *versus* not-ground. *So that every side of the graph maintains the same opposition—only rewritten. All around the square we find the same thing stated over and over—*figure *versus* ground—*except not stated exactly the same way. It's in the not-exactly-the-same-way that the square's beauty lies.*

The graph is, of course, a Klein Group. For Lévi-Strauss, for Greimas, for the structuralists generally, the interest of the Klein Group was precisely in this quality of rewriting, so that what might seem the random details of cultural practice—as in the wildly varied aggregates of episodes that make different versions of the same myth into barely recognizable tangles— emerge as a set of ordered transformations, the logical restatements of a single, generating pair of oppositions. What the rewriting made clear to them is that for every social absolute—marriage, yes; incest, no—there is its more flexible, shadow correlate: the kind of maybe, maybe of the not- not axis; of the way in the traffic system the absolutes of red for stop *and green for* go *are rendered into* maybe *by the possibility opened by yellow. The structuralists call the top axis of yes/no the "complex axis," using the term "neutral axis" for the* maybes.

Figure *versus* ground, *then. The fundamentals of perception. The opposition without which no vision at all: vision occurring precisely in the dimension of difference, of separation, of bounded objects emerging as apart from, in contrast to, the ambiance or ground within which they appear. The modernist logic is a visual logic, and so it must be contained by the terms of visual perception. But it must also contain them.*

Thus not-figure *versus* not-ground *as the statement of this containment. The* not-figure/not-ground *of the "neutral axis" is that peculiar conversion of empirical vision's* figure/ground *distinction that can be seen to have generated one modernist icon after another: the grid, the monochrome, the all-over painting, the color-field, the mise-en-abyme of classical collage, the nests of concentric squares or circles. And while each is its own version of the neutralizing of the original distinction, none is an erasure of the terms of that distinction. Quite to the contrary. The terms are both preserved and canceled. Preserved all the more surely in that they are canceled.*

Empirical vision must be canceled, in favor of something understood as the precondition for the very emergence of the perceptual object to vision. To a higher, more formal order of vision, something we could call the structure of the visual field as such. For the structure of the visual field is not, cannot be, the same as the order of the perceptual one. The perceptual field is, after all, forever behind *its objects; it is their background, their support, their ambiance. The modality of the visual field—vision as structure, vision "as such"—has nothing, however, of this behind, this afterward, this successiveness. For, as the matrix of an absolute simultaneity, its structure must mark it with the perfect synchrony that conditions vision as a form of cognition. Beyond the successiveness of empirical space's figure/ground there must be this all-at-onceness that restructures successiveness as* vision.

Vision as a form of cognition. As a form, then, it reworks the very notion of ground. The ground is not behind; the ground is what it, vision, is. And the figure, too, is reworked. Perception marks this figure that the eye singles out by labeling it "pure exteriority": set off from the field on which it appears, it is even more surely set off from me, the beholder. But cognition—in vision—grasps the figure otherwise, capturing it in a condition of pure immediacy, yielding an experience that knows in a flash that if these perceptions are seen as there, *it is because they are seen by* me; *that it is my presence to my own representations that secures them, reflexively, as present to myself.*

No figure, then, either; but a limit case of self-imbrication.

The perceptual terms are rejected thus, and marked by this rejection as not-figure *and* not-ground. *But in being canceled they are also preserved. And the logic of that preservation is made transparent by the graph. The graph's circumference holds all its terms in mutual opposition:* figure versus *ground; ground* versus *not-ground; not-ground* versus *not-figure; not-figure* versus *figure. Its diagonal axes yield, however, to mirror relations, or rather to mirror restatements (the structuralists' inverse-of-the-opposite, their double negatives), with* figure *in this case being the "same" as* not-ground.

And this is how the graph's logical unfolding captures the form of the modernist logic. For at the moment when the background of perceptual space—with its former status as reserve or secondariness—is rejected by modernism, in favor of the simultaneity that is understood as a precondition of vision, the logic of this inversion into not-ground *already determines that new condition according to its mirror—or to use the structuralist term, deixic—relation to the diagonally opposite pole:* figure. *Which is to say the* not-ground *does not become available to the modernist painter in a whole range of random ways, but in a logically conditioned, single way: as the new order of "figure." The modernist* not-ground *is a field or background that has risen to the surface of the work to become exactly coincident with its foreground, a field that is thus ingested by the work as figure.*

In 1919 the *Plus and Minus* paintings would give rise to the lozenge pictures which Mondrian would now organize by means of complete and regular grids. The scatter and gaps of the natural field would finally be closed by the seamless regularity of the arithmetic order. Now for the first time he would encounter vision as fully abstract. And the grid would succeed in drawing successiveness off this space like water evaporated from a dry lake. Leaving behind only the marks of the infrastructure of the field, scoring and crossing its surface like so many restatements of its geometrical givens. Its simultaneity would be figured forth in this brilliant, obsessional hatching. It would be his first truly systematic reinvention of the ground as figure.

And were we to project the other term—where determination to resist the alienating "figure" of empirical, realist vision generates the *not-figure*, itself however logically invested with *its* mirror condition, as "ground"—we have only to think of Matisse's *Windows*, or any other structure *en abyme*: some of Picasso's collages, say, where the front face of the guitar or the piece of sheet music becomes the figure for the whole of the sheet onto which it is pasted, or Stella's nested squares as in *Jasper's Dilemma* or *Hyena Stomp*. The frame-within-a-frame is a way of entering the figure into the pictorial field and simultaneously negating it, since it is inside the space only as an image of its outside, its limits, its frame. The figure loses its logical status as that object in a continuous field which perception happens to pick out and thereby to frame; and the frame is no longer conceived as something like the boundary of the natural or empirical limits of the perceptual field. As figures of one another, outside and inside take on a deductive relation to each other, the figure of the frame turning the

Piet Mondrian, *Composition in Lines (Black and White)*, 1916–1917.

*To throw its net over the whole of the external world in order to enter it
into consciousness. To think it . . . (p. 12)*

Piet Mondrian, *Composition 1916*, 1916.

The modernist not-ground *is a field or background that has risen to the surface of the work to become exactly coincident with its foreground, a field that is thus ingested by the work as figure . . . (p. 16)*

painting into a map of the logic of relations and the topology of self-containment. Whatever is *in* the field is there because it is already contained *by* the field, forecast, as it were, by its limits. It is thus the picture of pure immediacy and of complete self-enclosure.

And the graph itself is also a picture of pure immediacy, of complete self-enclosure.

First advantage of the graph. It dispenses with narrative. It captures the inner logic of modernist art on its own grounds—that of the terms of vision. It gives one the logic in the form of transparency, simultaneity, and the containment of a frame. As a logic of operations it already accounts for its closure; has always already enframed it.

That totalizing aspect of the frame comes from how the relations between all four of the terms are conceptually accounted for. But it is generated as well from that pole on the lower axis of the graph where the not-figure *forms itself as the "figure" of the deduction of the frame. Thus the second advantage of the graph. It puts the dynamic of the logic on display. It shows the difference between the two axes—upper and lower—as two different forms of vision. The upper axis is the simple form of the opposition:* figure *versus* ground. *For the Klein Group it was the complex axis; I have been calling it, here, perception. The lower axis—the* not-figure *versus the* not-ground, *or structuralism's neutral axis—functions in this, modernism's visualist universe, as the demonstration of vision in its reflexive form: the terms not just of seeing but of consciousness accounting for the fact of its seeing. It is the axis of a redoubled vision: of a seeing and a knowing that one sees, a kind of* cogito of vision.

The two poles of this axis are, however, distinct. On the one hand, the pole of the not-ground *will be the place of this seeing, the place where the empirical viewer is entered into the schema, marked by the way the empty mirror of the pictorial surface is set up as an analogue to the retinal surface of the eye opened onto its world. On the other, the* not-figure *is the totalizing viewpoint of "knowing that . . .". It marks the place of the Viewer as a kind of impersonal absolute, the point at which vision is entered into the schema both as a repertory of laws and as a relationship to those laws which is that of the transcendental ego. The* not/not *of the lower axis is not, then, a cancelation of* figures *and* grounds *but a sublation of them. Not an* informe *but an accounting for form.*

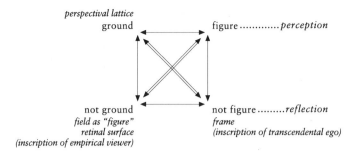

perspectival lattice
ground   figure ....*perception*

not ground   not figure ....*reflection*
field as "figure"   *frame*
retinal surface   *(inscription of transcendental ego)*
(inscription of empirical viewer)

The second advantage of the graph was that it released for me something of the triumphant, rational energy in operating the modernist logic—in the derivation of those spare, nearly airless, self-abnegating reductions: the grid, the monochrome, the all-over painting, the concentric figures. For the excitement there—the sense of breakthrough, of discovery—was enough to support a lifetime of reworking this logic. Several lifetimes. The elegance of the model. The thrill of its manipulation.

Third advantage of the graph. It makes clear why the system is finite. The reflexive relations of its terms can generate only so many solutions, only so many transcodings. More than one or two, of course, but not a very large number. Grid, monochrome, all-over, mise-en-abyme. . . . It is finite in the historical sense as well. For all its inner dynamism it is a graph in stasis. Its inner possibilities can be explored, filled out. But its system admits of no evolution. You can simply come to its outer limit, and then stop.

The graph's relation to time is nonhistorical. History appears only when you stand outside it and see how it maps a certain set of real preoccupations and you say, "So that was what modernism was." But inside there is only repetition. The solution to the same puzzle taken up over and over again, worried, reworked, refigured.

Which brings up the fourth advantage of the graph, the one that is personal, to me. By showing me the system whole, it showed me my own outsideness to it. But it also gave me a way of picturing what it had been like to be inside, where its choices seemed to compose a whole universe: the universe of "vision." It's only from inside, after all, that I could have taken pleasure in understanding why Frank Stella thought Ted Williams a genius. And that I could have been deaf to the assumptions about virility in that metaphor. Deaf to the fact that inside the logic of that metaphor everything material falls away, so that, just like the effect it proposes, the physicality of bat and ball and of the nature of their contact had simply vaporized, had become all the more dazzlingly rational in that they had been rendered ephemeral, the limit conditions of vision.

The semiotic square, or the structuralists' graph, is a way of picturing the whole of a cultural universe in the grip of two opposing choices, two incompatible possibilities. Cultural production is the creation of an imaginative space in which those two things can be related. The conflict will not go away. But it will be, as it were, suspended. Worked and reworked in the space, for example, of myth. The imaginary resolution, as Lévi-Strauss projects it, of conflicts in the real. And Althusser follows him. And Jameson follows him. The structuralists' graph becomes the self-contained space of ideology. And cultural production the impossible attempt to construct an imaginary space within which to work out unbearable contradictions produced within the real field of history. These contradictions, which are repressed, are the site of Jameson's *The Political Unconscious.*

The fifth advantage of the graph only came to me later. After I had begun to fill in the space of an alternative history, one that had developed against the grain of modernist opticality, one that had risen on the very site of modernism only to defy its logic, to cross the wires of its various categories, to flout all its notions about essences and purifications, to refuse its concern with foundations—above all a foundation in the presumed ontological ground of the visual. When does this other history begin, this refusal of the optical logic of mainstream modernism?

It's hard to set a date, to bring forth the monument, the event, the specific demonstration. Should we speak of Duchamp, of that moment in Buenos Aires in 1918 or 1919, when the whole mechanical metaphor of The Large Glass *would suddenly lose its interest for him, and he would trade in the bachelor machine for an optical contraption, a lesson in optics that he would chase for the next fifteen years? "Precision Optics" he would call it parodically, a counter to modernist, rationalized vision. Or perhaps Max Ernst's overpaintings, his dada collages that would so stun Breton, made around the same time?*

Whatever the beginning might be, the terrain of this counterhistory soon became guideposted with various conceptual markers, ones that did not map it—for this would be impossible—but only pointed to the way the foundations of modernism were mined by a thousand pockets of darkness, the blind, irrational space of the labyrinth. Concepts like informe, *mimicry, the uncanny,* bassesse, *mirror stage,* Wiederholungszwang; *figures like the* acéphale, *the minotaur, the praying mantis. The terrain broadened into the 1920s and '30s, with players like Giacometti, and Dalí, and Man Ray,*

and Bellmer. *The theorists of this refusal were Bataille and Breton, Caillois, and Leiris, with, in the background, Freud. And in the foreground, Dalí linked through one arm and Caillois through the other, there was Jacques Lacan.*

Lacan, it struck me, provided a key to this refusal, a way of giving it a name.

Then it's language, one might say, it's text that's the refusal of vision. It's the symbolic, the social, the law. But that makes no sense, one would have to add, because modernist visuality wants nothing more than to be the display of reason, of the rationalized, the coded, the abstracted, the law. The opposition that pits language against vision poses no challenge to the modernist logic. For modernism, staking everything on form, is obedient to the terms of the symbolic. No problem, it would say.

I started calling the hare I was chasing over this historical terrain antivision. *But that* anti *sounded too* much *like the opposite of a* pro *the all too obvious choice for which would be* pro-text. *Which was not at all the case of what I was tracking. The name that gradually took over was the* optical unconscious. *Which begins to suggest the fifth advantage of the graph.*

Structuralism's graph, the graph I adopted, is written:

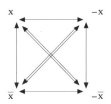

When Lacan constructs his L Schema, his graph of the subject as an effect of the unconscious, he writes:

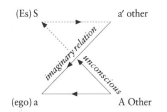

Lacan's L Schema, a meditation on the structuralists' graph, is a manifestation of his delight in sowing the psychoanalytic subject over a field organized by a set of terms of which the subject can be no more than the effect, the outcome of the structure's own dynamic of internal contradiction. So the L Schema, rhyming with the Klein Group, is isomorphic with the graph I had made to display the logic of modernism.

It contains, for example, the complex axis: S on the left, objet a *on the right: the subject on the one hand and its objects on the other. And on the neutral axis, below the subject comes the* moi, *and below the* objet a *comes the* Autre. *Another version of inside/outside, this axis plots the ego's submission to the social, the Law. Further, the Schema displays the diagonal, mirroring relationships—structuralism's deixic axes—that map the way the ego identifies with its objects: a as the "same" as a', the ego reflecting and reflected by* objet a. *There's no mistaking it, for it is spelled out in the L Schema as the "rélation imaginaire"—the mirror connection.*

With this mirror connection, however, Lacan performs what we have to see as a peculiar slippage between two rather different structuralist terms: the deixic *and the* deictic. *The first he takes from its move in logic to express "sameness" as the inversion of the opposite, the double negative. The ego is the "same" as its objects. But the second implies the beginning of an explanation of how this "sameness" is constituted, how* deixic *is, for the formation of the subject, derived from* deictic. *Taken from the linguistic (rather than the logical) part of structuralism,* deictic *refers to a form of verbal pointing: to the fixing of meaning through a set of existential coordinates—*I, here, now. . . . *These terms, sometimes called* shifters, *are designated "empty signs," since they function as place-holders within language, vacant seats that await being filled by a subject who steps forward to speak them—"I," "here," "now." So language can be imagined as a kind of card game, all of whose rules are fixed and unchanging, but for which places are prepared at the table for a succession of players. In stepping up to that table and becoming a player, the speaker becomes a subject: what structural linguistics calls a "subject of enunciation," the one who gives "I" its (existential) meaning in the act of speaking it. Now, Lacan takes this "subject of enunciation" and understands it as a subject* tout court. *He sees that identity in all its power and resonance comes from being able to break into this circuit of impersonal rules and to join it by saying, and meaning, "I." But he also believes—and here is the slippage between* deictic *and* deixic—*that the pointing gesture, the "this," which initially singled out the subject as unique and instituted it as the one who* *can identify itself as "I," this gesture comes from outside the subject. It is a primary pointing to the infant by someone or something else, a pointing constituted for example by the look of the mother, a look that names the child to itself, for itself. The child's identity is to be found in that look, just as its terror of identity's loss is prefigured in its withdrawal.*

In this slippage between deictic *and* deixic *there is built, then, both the logical relation of the double negative and the causal one of the history of the subject. And so this is where the isomorphism between the L Schema and the Klein Group begins to dislocate.*

For the L Schema is not conceived as a static picture, but instead as a cycle: first the subject, then his objects, then his ego, then . . . The relationships are in permanent circulation, continuous flow. Their dynamic is productive, producing repetition. And the circuit interrupts the perfect symmetry of the graph. For the imaginary relation, transecting the square by crossing it diagonally with a channel of visibility, reflecting the subject back to himself in the smooth surface of its mirror, plunges the other half of the graph into darkness. The ego's traffic with the unconscious goes on out of sight. Something dams up the transparency of the graph, cuts through its center, obscuring its relations one to the other. Ruskin sees the pattern in the carpet, in the sea, in the aspens. Sees their form, their "picture." What he does not see, cannot see, is how he has been made a captive of their picture.

The optical unconscious will claim for itself this dimension of opacity, of repetition, of time. It will map onto the modernist logic only to cut across its grain, to undo it, to figure it otherwise. Like the relation between the L Schema and the Klein Group, which is not one of rejection, but one of dialectics. Lacan pictures the unconscious relation to reason, to the conscious mind, not as something different from consciousness, something outside it. He pictures it as inside consciousness, undermining it from within, fouling its logic, eroding its structure, even while appearing to leave the terms of that logic and that structure in place.

The advantage of the graph as a picture of modernism and its visualist logic is that it is perfect. Both a perfect descriptor and a perfect patsy. Its frame which is a frame of exclusions is oh so easy to read as an ideological closure. Nothing enters from the outside, there where the political, the economic, the social, foregather. But neither does anything rise up into the graph from below. Its transparency, the logic of its relations, creates a pellucid field, all surface and no depths. The problem of this book will be

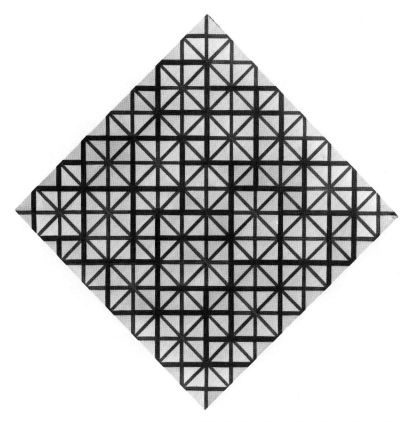

Piet Mondrian, *Composition with Gray Lines*, 1918.

And the grid would succeed in drawing successiveness off this space like water evaporated from a dry lake . . . (p. 16)

Frank Stella, *Hyena Stomp*, 1962.

The figure of the frame turns the painting into a map of the logic of
relations and the topology of self-containment . . . (p. 16)

to show that the depths are there, to show that the graph's transparency is only seeming: that it masks what is beneath it, or to use a stronger term, represses it.

The relation between the L Schema and the Klein Group could configure this repression. Not because the L Schema shows an elsewhere, an "outside" of the system. But because it shows the repressive logic of the system, its genius at repression. It can, that is, figure forth the "beneath" of the system; although the figure of that beneath is peculiar of course. It can't simply take the form of a figure because it is a form under attack, a form qualified by the logical illogic of that beneath, an impossible quality that Jean-François Lyotard wants to track when he names the unconscious's relation to the visual image through the chiasmatic term he invents: "fiscours/digure." In so doing this relation can account for two things at once: both the structure of operations of the repressed material and the reasons within the historical period of modernism for its repression. It therefore helps to map the objects—The Master's Bedroom, the Rotoreliefs, Suspended Ball, and so forth—and to explain why a hegemonic modernism had to evacuate them from its field.

And so this book will be called *The Optical Unconscious.* Does the title rhyme with *The Political Unconscious?* It's a rhyme that's intended; it's a rhyme set into place by a graph's idiotic simplicity and its extravagant cunning.

The passages from John Ruskin's autobiography, *Praeterita*, 1885–1889 (Oxford: Oxford University Press, 1979), are: Mazzini's opinion, 49; Ruskin's early deprivation of toys, 14; his sitting to Mr. Northcote, 16; his early thirst for looking, 60; his life-long relation to the sea, 86; the advantages of traveling without knowing foreign languages, 138.

"Presentness is grace" is the final sentence of Michael Fried's essay "Art and Object-hood," published in 1967 in *Artforum* (reprinted in *Minimal Art,* ed. Gregory Battcock [New York: Dutton, 1968]). Clement Greenberg's articulation of a "strictly optical third dimension" is in his "Modernist Painting," 1965 (reprinted in *The New Art,* ed. Gregory Battcock [New York: Dutton, 1966]).

Georg Lukács analyzes the compartmentalization of the human sensorium in relation to rationalization and reification in "Reification and the Consciousness of the Proletariat" (*History and Class Consciousness,* trans. Rodney Livingstone [Cambridge: MIT Press, 1971], part I, section 3). For Adorno on art's opening onto freedom, see "Commitment," in *The Essential Frankfurt School Reader,* ed. Andrew Arato and Eike Gebhardt (New York: Urizen Books, 1978).

Fredric Jameson discusses the becoming autonomous of the various senses in relation to the rationalization of life and labor under capital in *The Political Unconscious: Narrative as a Socially Symbolic Act* (Ithaca: Cornell University Press, 1981). With special regard to Conrad's style, see pp. 225ff.; his quotation from *Typhoon,* p. 230.

For a presentation of the Klein Group, see Marc Barbut, "On the Meaning of the Word 'Structure' in Mathematics," in *Introduction to Structuralism,* ed. Michael Lane (New York: Basic Books, 1970). Claude Lévi-Strauss uses the Klein Group in his analysis of the relation between Kwakiutl and Salish masks in *The Way of the Masks,* trans. Sylvia Modelski (Seattle: University of Washington Press, 1982), p. 125; and in relation to the Oedipus myth in "The Structural Analysis of Myth," *Structural Anthropology,* trans. Claire Jackobson and Brooke Grundfest Schoepf (New York: Basic Books, 1963). In a transformation of the Klein Group, A. J. Greimas has developed the semiotic square, which he describes as giving "a slightly different formulation to the same structure," in "The Interaction of Semiotic Constraints," *On Meaning* (Minneapolis: University of Minnesota Press, 1987), p. 50. Jameson uses the semiotic square in *The Political Unconscious* (see pp. 167, 254, 256, 277), as does Louis Marin in "Disneyland: A Degenerate Utopia," *Glyph,* no. 1 (1977), p. 64. Jameson further discusses Lévi-Strauss's concept of myth as the imaginary resolution of contradictions in the real (*The Political Unconscious,* p. 79) and Althusser's notion of art as a presentation of ideology stripped of its internal contradictions (p. 56). For Althusser, see "Letter on Art," in *Lenin and Philosophy,* trans. Ben Brewster (New York: Monthly Review Press, 1971). For Lévi-Strauss, see *Tristes tropiques,* trans. John Russell (New York: Atheneum, 1971), pp. 176–180.

I have dealt with the grid as one of the modernist compositional paradigms that have been structured by repetition in "Grids," *The Originality of the Avant-Garde and Other Modernist Myths* (Cambridge: MIT Press, 1985). In my own work the background of an interest in the contestation of modernist opticality includes "Anti-Vision," *October,* no. 36 (Spring 1986); "No More Play," an essay on Giacometti's surrealist sculpture and its relation to primitivism, in *The Originality of the Avant-Garde* (originally written as a chapter of *"Primitivism" and Twentieth-Century Art,* ed. William Rubin [New York: Museum of Modern Art, 1986]); and "Corpus Delicti," a study of surrealist photography, in *L'Amour Fou: Surrealism and Photography* (New York: Abbeville Press, 1986).

Lacan has published two versions of the L Schema, the one in the 1955 "On the Possible Treatment of Psychosis" (*Ecrits: A Selection,* trans. Alan Sheridan [New York: Norton, 1977], p. 193), in which the position of the ego is given as *a'* and the objects are given as *a;* and another set up for the 1966 "Introduction" to the 1955 "Seminar on 'The Purloined Letter'" (*Ecrits* [Paris: Editions du Seuil, 1966], p. 53), in which the ego is designated *a* and the *objet a* is represented as *a'*. The axis *aa'* he has characterized as an "alternating doubling" (ibid., p. 55).

Just so does the purloined letter, like an immense female body, stretch out across the Minister's office when Dupin enters. But just so does he already expect to find it, and has only . . . to undress that huge body.

—Jacques Lacan

two

And how do we imagine Theodor Adorno as he "looks back at surrealism," looking back in 1953, even though André Breton, very much alive, is still looking forward? For it's true that very few people in 1953 are looking Breton's way. Surrealism's import lies, now, in the past. Even so, Adorno's glance is somewhat jaundiced, we notice. He can't quite share Walter Benjamin's old enthusiasm for those "energies of intoxication" that Benjamin saw surrealism placing in the service of freedom. Adorno finds much of surrealism's claims, Breton's claims, absurd. "No one dreams that way," he snaps.

And yet. A dialectical image begins to form for him. Its ground is a series of white, geometrical planes, the stark, streamlined architecture of Bauhaus rationalism. *Sachlichkeit.* The new objectivity. Technology as form. "Ornament," Adorno remembers Loos having said, "is a crime." And gleaming and new, this architecture will admit of no crime, no deviation. It will be a machine stripped down for work, a machine to live in. But there, suddenly, on the stretch of one of its concrete flanks, a protuberance begins to sprout. Something bulges outward, pushing against the house's skin. Out it pops in all its nineteenth-century ugliness and absurdity, a bay window with its scrollwork cornices, its latticed windows. It is the house's tumor, Adorno thinks. It is the underbelly of the prewar technorationalism, the unconscious of the modernist *Sachlichkeit*. It is surrealism, connecting us, through the irrational, with the other side of progress, with its flotsam, its discards, its rejects. Progress as obsolescence.

Perhaps this is why Adorno looks back at surrealism with a copy of *La femme 100 têtes* spread across his knees. He muses over these images collaged "from illustrations of the later nineteenth century, with which the parents of Max Ernst's generation were familiar," but which Ernst as a child must already have sensed as archaic, and strange, and wonderful. And if the child stirs in the images, if the memory of having been so little is nudged into being by them, then that is something potentially powerful working against the abstracted, flattened uniformity of a technologized world, a world from which time is all but erased. Adorno has no patience for the psychoanalytic conception of history—with its constant refrain of Oedipus. The history he is interested in is not that of the privatized individual but instead the history of modernity, or the fact that it even had a history, that it too was young. History working against the grain of an abstracted, bureaucratized uniformity, of a technologically rationalized world. surrealism's shock, Adorno muses, while he looks at these pictures, is to put us in touch with that history, as our own.

"One must therefore trace the affinity of surrealistic technique for psychoanalysis," Adorno decides, "not to a symbolism of the unconscious, but to the attempt to uncover childhood experiences by blasting them out. What surrealism adds to the pictorial rendering of the world of things is what we lost after childhood: when we were children those illustrations, already archaic, must have jumped out at us, just as the surrealistic pictures do now. The giant egg out of which the monster of the last judgment can be hatched at any minute is so big because we were so small when we for the first time shuddered before an egg."

Adorno is looking at the first plate of *Femme 100 têtes,* or perhaps, since they are identical, the last. "Crime or miracle," the initial caption reads, "a complete man." In its second, final, appearance the image is titled simply "End and continuation." But in each of the two identical plates, Blake's angel Gabriel, minus his trumpet, collaged against a stormy sky, is falling from the center of the large, egglike form of something that could be an ascending balloon. Or is he, too, like the souls he is calling forth on the last judgment, rising? The tiny men huddled below, in the windswept space of the nineteenth-century wood engraving, resemble indeed the populations of awakened dead from medieval tympana. At least in the grip of Adorno's associations, they do.

And in the grip of the art-historical imagination? That imagination is determined to "read" Ernst's novel, to narrativize it, to give it a shape, a story line. It has chapters, after all, does it not? It is a Bildungsroman, *goes one explanation. Conception, infancy, childhood, adolescence, adulthood, senescence. The life cycle patiently traced, elaborated, returned to its beginnings. Each of Ernst's novels is mined for its "compositional principle."* Une semaine de bonté *is seen as following Sade's* 120 Days of Sodom *or Lautréamont's* Les chants de Maldoror, *all of this itself woven on the loom of the seven days of creation. "It's an alchemical novel," one of them insists. To which another rejoins that the only alchemy in question is Rimbaud's "Alchimie du verbe," since the designation of a different hue for each section of the book recalls the poet's imperious coloristic baptism of the vowels—"A noir, E blanc, I rouge, O bleu, U vert."*

The art historian thinks with the mind of a scholastic. Typologies. Recensions. The world seen through old men's eyes, looking with that fixedly backward stare that intends to find ladders of precedent, ladders by means of which to climb, slowly, painfully, into the experience of the present. Into a present that will already have been stabilized by already having been predicted.

The child's eyes through which Adorno is looking as he turns the pages of Ernst's novel is not seeing John Ruskin's pattern, his conjuring of form. This child, far from deprived, is peering into a variety of fabulous spaces. These are the spaces constructed through the nineteenth-century wood engravings used to illustrate magazines of popular science, like *La Nature*, or of commerce, like *Magazine pittoresque*, or illustrated fables, like *Amor und Psyche*, or dime novels, like *Les damnés de Paris*. Their style is unquestionably archaic, passé, outmoded, as they configure these spaces of laboratories, pampas, pool halls, train cars, war-torn streets, storm-tossed seas, cargo-laden boats . . . ; spaces that are inhabited by a variety of personages too numerous to name. But as the dust settles around their flurry of activity, the child begins to sense a recurrence, both exciting and soothing. Presented to *him* but not to *them* is an immense body, or more often a part of that body, that floats within the otherwise quotidian space.

They are oblivious to it. But there it is, like a large, welcoming pillow, strangely soft and usually whiter than its surrounds. In the fourth plate it emerges from the laboratory apparatus two scientists are manipulating: two white legs voluptuously self-entwined, ten times life-size. Ravishing, ravishing part-object.

It is recumbent, languid. An arm, a leg, a torso. Nearly always nude, it is nearly always female. Since it is never noticed by the actors in this or that scene, its place seems to be at the very front of the stage, closest to the eyes of the viewer. But since this body, this part-object, this *femme sans tête,* is experienced as recurrence, it becomes the thread on which the scenes themselves are strung. And in this sense it is more like background, the single, grand surface on which everything else is supported. A foreground, then, that is also a background, a top that is clearly a bottom.

His habit had been to show her picture . . . to his intimates, but also to people he was meeting for the first time, people to whom he was beginning to take a liking. He would indicate this by extracting his wallet and lifting a photograph from its folds, which he would proffer between the index and middle finger of his frail, aristocratically boned hands. But then his whole appearance, from the high, wide forehead and ardently sculpted nose to the elegant slouch with which he wore his clothes, was a monument to controlled languor. "This is Gala," he would say, "my wife." And in his vibrant voice that emanated carelessness one could hear an undercurrent of something else, something always, somehow, insinuating.

It would have been hard not to gasp, and wonder, even in that company priding itself on its license, on its contempt for propriety, for bourgeois manners and morals. "What is it about," some of them would ponder. "Is it simple pride? Just like that? Or is it some kind of solicitation? And for her? Or for himself?"

And the photograph of Gala Eluard, eloquently wanton in its display of her nakedness, with her high breasts, the dizzying length of her torso, and the delicate articulations of knees, ankles, and wrists, could tell them nothing. Except that she was beautiful. And carried her body like a perfectly understood weapon of seduction.

Would he have shown the photograph to Ernst, I wonder? After all, that early November day in Cologne when they finally met, after what felt like so many months of anticipation, so many postponements, so many near misses, Gala was there, along with Paul Eluard, both of them having come,

Max Ernst, *La femme 100 têtes*, 1929: "Crime or wonder; a complete man."

Or is he, too, like the souls he is calling forth on the last judgment, rising? . . . (p. 35)

Max Ernst, *La femme 100 têtes*, 1929: "Continuation."

A recurrence, both exciting and soothing . . . (p. 35)

Max Ernst, *La femme 100 têtes*, 1929: "Continuation of morning, twilight, and night games."

Presented to him *but not to* them . . . *(p. 35)*

Max Ernst, *La femme 100 têtes*, 1929: "Here is the thirst that resembles me."

*A part of that body that floats within the otherwise quotidian
space . . . (p. 35)*

expressly for this meeting, from Vienna. No need to show the copy in the presence of the original.

Given what happened next, I think he probably did show Ernst the photograph. And that the gesture carried with it all the motivations that could have been suspected: that it was pride and solicitation; for himself and for her. And that he showed him the photograph so that there would be no more near misses. But then he had always been extremely manipulative and here he could play with at least three lives, or four, or more.

The other reason to think he did was that the work Ernst made late in 1921 to commemorate the beginning of that relationship between the three of them, the onset, as he would say—through its title—of his puberty, was based on the photograph of a naked woman. Not her, to be sure. But he inscribed the work "to Gala," a work which, from the point of view of its sexual axis, can of course be read as extremely ambivalent.

Tzara had been in Paris since January 1920, spreading dada. Spreading it, among other places, in the review *Littérature*. Breton, the magazine's editor (along with Soupault and Aragon), both fascinated and repelled by dada, was biding his time. Tzara filled the year with various dada demonstrations. Readings from the newspaper accompanied by the clanging of bells. And all of that. Renting the Salle Gaveau in order to play fox-trots on the celebrated organ, performing his *Vaseline symphonique* while the audience hurled veal cutlets. And all of that. Yet somehow behind the provocation, the constant *mondainité*. There was for example the opening of Picabia's exhibition. An affair whose elegance offended Breton's sense of rigor. So, early the next year, Breton made his move, which was to write to Ernst. He had seen Ernst's work in dada reviews and had read about it in various press reports of an exhibition in Cologne. If Breton hoped for something different from Ernst, something at an angle to dada, Ernst himself was nonetheless swearing his most devoted fealty to Tzara at just that time. His letter to Tzara dated December 28, 1920, containing a picture of his wife Louise (whom he had renamed the dada Rosa Bonheur) and his son Jimmy, and asking if Tzara could arrange a show of his graphic work, of which thirty to sixty items could be sent to Paris, ends with:

W
———
3

Who greets Tzara? The Rosa Bonheur of the dadas
Who greets Tzara? Baargeld
Who greets Tzara? Job
Who greets Tzara? Jimmy
Who greets Tzara? Max Ernst
the dada Maid of Orleans is missing

But it was from Breton that the invitation Ernst was seeking came, for indeed a show had been organized for May 1921 at the bookstore Au Sans Pareil. Whatever it was Breton had bargained for, he got it.

Fifty-six collages by Ernst had been shipped to Paris. It was at Picabia's house that the unpacking of the works took place. André Breton describes the encounter with these objects as revelatory, a kind of originary moment, almost, one could say, surrealism's primal scene. For here was a group of objects through which nascent surrealism would understand something of both its identity and its destiny. Breton explains:

> In fact surrealism found what it had been looking for from the first in the 1920 collages [by Ernst], which introduced an entirely original scheme of visual structure yet at the same time corresponded exactly to the intentions of Lautréamont and Rimbaud in poetry. I well remember the day when I first set eyes on them: Tzara, Aragon, Soupault and myself all happened to be at Picabia's house at the very moment when these collages arrived from Cologne, and we were all filled immediately with unparalleled admiration. The external object had broken with its normal environment, and its component parts had, so to speak, emancipated themselves from it in such a way that they were now able to maintain entirely new relationships with other elements, escaping from the principle of reality but retaining all their importance on that plane.

Was it because Ernst had served in the German army, or because, a notorious dada, he was labeled Bolshevik by the British authorities in charge in Cologne, that they denied him a passport? In any event he missed his own explosive vernissage at the Au Sans Pareil, held in the basement with the lights out, with Breton chewing matches and Aragon meowing continuously and someone shouting insults at the guests from inside a cupboard. But lights out or no, the effect of his work was palpable. Breton was stunned. So that in September on his way to Vienna to visit Freud he went first to the Tyrol to meet Ernst. To pay him homage or to reassert his, Breton's, own authority? For bringing his volume of Lautréamont with him, Breton insisted on reading the *Chants de Maldoror* for hours at a time *at* a disconcerted Ernst.

Eluard had not been at Picabia's for the unpacking of the collages. He only saw them at the opening of Ernst's exhibition. But his excitement reached a pitch that was even higher than the others'. "Eluard was the most

Max Ernst, *La femme 100 têtes*, 1929: "And her phantom globe will track us down . . ."

A foreground, then, that is also a background . . . (p. 36)

La puberté proche n'a pas encore enlevé la grâce tenue d'
pléiades/ Le ngard de nos yeux pleins d'ombre est dirigé vers
pavé qui va tomber/ La gravitation des ondulations n'ext.

Max Ernst, *La puberté proche . . .* , 1921.

But he inscribed the work "to Gala". . . (p. 41)

affected," his biographer tells us. "He suddenly understood that a brother had just been given to him." Indeed, so strong was Eluard's experience that by summer's end he did not wait to meet Breton in Vienna as planned, but hurried to the mountains to encounter Ernst. But Ernst had, along with the Rosa Bonheur of the dadas, already returned to Cologne.

Eluard launched a series of frantic postcards at the retreating artist. And he wrote to Tzara:

> The 1st of next month we will leave for Munich where we'll spend two or three days, and from there for Cologne. I want to be sure that Ernst will be there then. Would you ask him? . . . We're only going to Cologne to see Ernst. Naturally. I haven't any answer to my cards and I'm afraid he hasn't received them. I have no reason to deny myself what gives me pleasure. Please give me his address again. I LEAVE IN 9 DAYS.

On November 4 Gala and Paul arrived in Cologne. They left the 13th. Ernst registered the fact to Tzara:

> Cher Tzara (bis)   *Cher Tzara (bis)*
> The two Eluards gone, the two Ernsts have regressed to childhood. *Who now will wear for us the flamboyant flag in her hair, which will attract the idyllic deer etc. etc.* da capocaspar. *With their departure they have left a growing sadness . . .*

Could the Rosa Bonheur of the dadas really have been sad to see them go? Is it possible that, in the excitement of their foursome's frenetic gaiety, the frolicking at amusement parks, the gyrations through dance halls, the early morning poetry readings soaked in eau de vie, *she could have missed what was so palpably there for the other three, making the air in every room seem to rustle with the sharp static of sexual excitement? Where was she when Gala, entering Max's studio late one night, placed herself squarely in the luminous beam of both men's most attenuated desire as, removing her clothes with the swift agility that marked all her movements, she took up once again the pose of the photograph? Or did Gala never do that?*

There are only imaginary documents to say she did. Ernst's achingly beautiful overpainting called La puberté proche, *dedicated to her and executed during the six weeks between the time she left and the turn of the year, is a monument to her nakedness, real or fantasized. And Eluard's poem "Max*

Ernst," written during the same period as the new work that would open his collection Répétitions, ends by "describing" that scene: "In the glow of youth/ Lamps lighted very late/ The first shows her breasts, killed by red insects." But was he remembering, or anticipating?

To make La puberté proche Ernst found himself turning to the medium he had invented two years earlier, the technique sometimes referred to by the term collage but which Ernst himself called Übermahlung, overpainting. Although a few of the works unpacked by Breton at Picabia's house that day had been conventional collages, most of them in fact were overpaintings. Which is to say that instead of collage's additive process, in which disparate elements are glued to a waiting, neutral page, the overpaintings work subtractively. They delete; they take away. In order to make them, Ernst had selected a commercially printed sheet, and with the aid of ink and gouache, he had opaqued out various elements of the original to produce a new generation of image. As the matrix or substructure of what is subsequently seen in the work, this sheet underlay what was to fascinate both Breton and Aragon. It was this that directed what they had to say about the overpaintings at the time they first encountered them. Aragon's report, written in 1923, notes that "Max Ernst borrows his elements above all from printed drawings, advertisements, dictionary images, popular images, newspaper images." And in his 1927 essay "Surrealism and Painting," Breton agreed that Ernst proceeded "from the inspiration that Apollinaire sought in catalogues." But the term that Breton had originally used for this element is the far more suggestive word "readymade," as, in his text for the 1921 exhibition at Au Sans Pareil, he notes that the collages are built on grounds constituted by "the readymade images of objects," adding parenthetically, "(as in catalogue figures)."

Now, late in 1921, for this monument to Gala, the page from an illustrated catalogue or some other kind of book did not seem to have satisfied Ernst. Instead his readymade ground had had to have been a photograph . . . of a nude woman, lying stretched out upon a couch, her arched body supported by one elbow, the other arm reaching for her head.

It had floated into his view from out of the vast commercial production of turn-of-the-century erotica. He now remade it, in order to dedicate it anew. First he attacked it with a glutinous layer of cobalt blue gouache, severing the body from the entirety of its context, detaching it from the space in which it had originally appeared, from the accoutrements of the room, from the couch, from the supporting arm, and finally, from the body's own face. Strangely headless and contextless, the naked form acquires a peculiarly streamlined look, seems, to use an almost unimaginable term for this object, *bald*.

But then he had also turned it, the photograph and hence, by the same token, the body; so that, swiveled 90 degrees, it had been made newly pendent, a weightless vertical suspended in the strangely material, velvety ether of the gouache that covers the surface of the photograph like a hardened skin. Upright and headless, the nude now appears from within this thickened field as having been transmuted into the very image of the phallus—as having become, that is, the object and subject of that unmistakably Oedipal fantasy of both having and being the sex of the mother. And in the inscription with which Ernst frames this space, the froth of pleasure is invoked by the words "la grâce tenue de nos pléiades": as the idea of the Milky Way summons up the old iconography of the body's secretions writing themselves over the page of the heavens.

If this suspended, weightless, phallic body-of-the-woman, both a part of her setting and at some kind of remove from it, was to anticipate that thread on which the images of the collage-novel *Femme 100 têtes* would, at the end of the decade, be strung together, it also must be seen as looking backward. In fact its whole import and structure was about looking backward. Which is to say that the temporal displacement of desire back to adolescence, effected through the notion of "puberty," is only one link in an implied series of temporal displacements, of an origin steadily receding under the artist's gaze. For Gala entered Ernst's imagination accompanied by the words "perturbation, my sister," the name of a collage he had made at the same time as *Puberté proche*. This was the phrase that would more and more clearly emerge as evoking the adolescent fantasies that had arisen in relation to his very young sister Loni, and which he would inscribe many times in *Femme 100 têtes*. But just as Gala is a screen for Loni, Loni is a screen for even earlier feelings. The woman-as-phallus clothes these feelings with a kind of excited radiance even as she locates them at the point of awakening to the fact of sexual difference.

And Eluard's account of this meeting. Did it also operate on the logic of regression, I wonder. For his poem "Max Ernst" is structured, of course, on the fourfold repetition of the phrase "dans un coin." First he says "In a corner nimble incest moves round the virginity of a little dress." Then it's the sky that's "dans un coin"; later it's a car loaded with greenery; and once it's himself, the focus of everyone else's gaze. Dans un coin four times adds up, you might point out, to the game called, in French, le jeu de quatre coins. *Musical chairs of course. Eluard's evocation of childhood.*

Not by playing "doctor," for example. Rather, through a play of exclusions. Everyone moves in a circle; everyone changes places; someone is always left out. Eluard is in a corner, lighted up by the brightness of being looked at. Eluard is in a corner, left out and looking.

This derivation of the sexual game of *le jeu de quatre coins* from the fourfold repetition of "dans un coin" is offered by an extremely plausible, literary-critical reading of Eluard's poem. To this analysis the critic adds another. In the poem's four "corners" there is, he says, Eluard's acknowledgment of Ernst's artistic medium as something distinct from his own, something whose pictorial condition is supported by a page not given to reading but rather to vision, a page defined by its shape, its space, its condition as quadrilateral. Which puts the finishing, modernist touch on the interpretation, you might say.

This drive always to perform a relay back to the base of the artistic medium, back to the support, back to the objective conditions of the enterprise, is a modernist obsession. Vision must never overlook this task. It must constantly reaffirm how even the physical givens of the picture support—the flatness of the sheet, the rectangularity of its frame—mirror the essential features of visuality itself: its simultaneity; its reflexiveness. There must be no giving way to transparent illusion. There must be no self-forgetting. The four corners of the sheet are more than a merely physical limit, they are a logical premise. They are the conditions of possibility. Like the four corners of the structuralists' Klein Group from the logical relations of which a whole system can be derived, they construct a frame that both generates and contains a universe.

If Eluard plots his own conditions of looking, of watching and being watched watching, as shaped not by logic but by desire, would he, do we think, imagine Ernst's vision otherwise? Would he assign it that disembodied form of mastery we associate with modernism?

When the package of Ernst's collages was unwrapped that day, early in 1921, Picabia, Breton maliciously reported, was sick with envy. This seems hard at first to imagine. Most of these objects, with their somewhat frail whimsy, their rather fragile dada charm, seem hardly capable of provoking this intensity. And particularly not from Picabia. For the overpaintings, the majority of them cast on the pages of a catalogue of elementary and high school teaching aids, often deploy their added planes of color to project a shallow, stagelike space within which the images of beakers and retorts and cathode tubes could be shaped into the kind of mechanomorphic

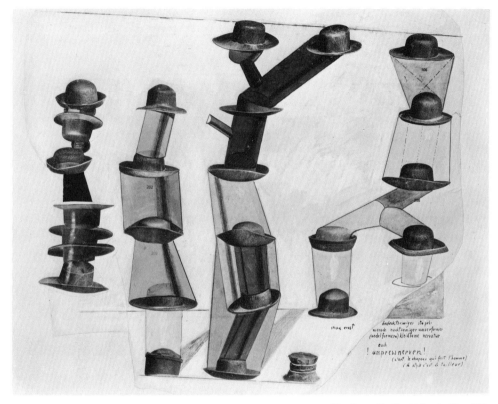

Max Ernst, *The Hat Makes the Man*, 1920.

"The readymade images of objects," adding parenthetically, "(as in catalogue figures)". . . (p. 46)

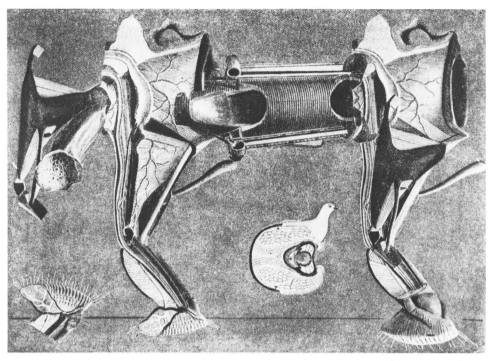

Max Ernst, *The Horse, He's Sick,* 1920.

Picabia, Breton maliciously reported, was sick with envy . . . (p. 48)

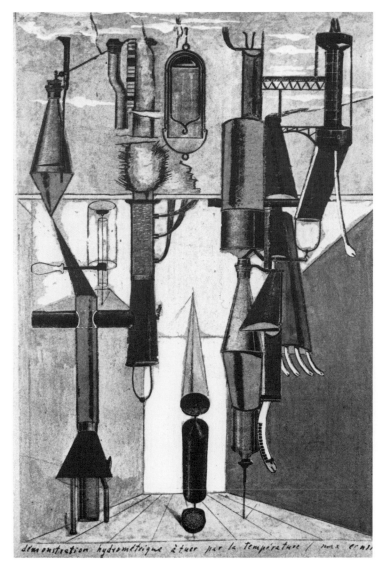

Max Ernst, *Démonstration hydrométrique à tuer par la température*, 1920.

Their somewhat frail whimsy, their rather fragile dada charm . . . (p. 48)

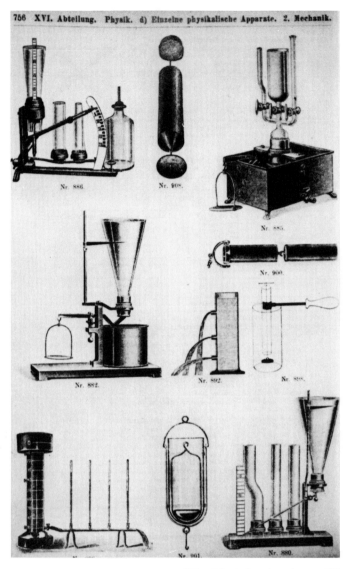

Kölner Lehrmittelanstalt catalogue, p. 756.

Cast on the pages of a catalogue of elementary and high school teaching aids . . . (p. 48)

personages that Picabia himself had for some years perfected. The commercially produced (and thus self-evidently readymade) object abounds in Picabia's work as the vehicle of portraiture, as in his *Ici, c'est ici Stieglitz* of 1915, or as the medium of a dada-based derision, as in *Infant Carburetor* (1919).

Yet certain of these images go far beyond Picabia's notion of a mechanical being that dada liked to think of as the robotic result of modern technoculture. Instead, a few of Ernst's overpaintings seem to compose the paradigm for an idea of mechanical *seeing*—a notion, unprecedented in 1920, of an automatist motor turning over within the very field of the visual. This idea, which would come to operate at the center of surrealism's critique of modernism, contests the optical model's schema of visual self-evidence and reflexive immediacy, substituting for this a model based instead on the conditions of the readymade, conditions that produce an altogether different kind of scene from that of modernism's.

The model Ernst constructs is indeed structured as a scene—contained within a proscenium frame in a way that is like the cognitive image provided by the modernists' Klein Group. But it is there that the comparison with a modernist visual model stops. Found most clearly in an overpainting called *The Master's Bedroom* (with an inscription in both French and German that adds, "It's worth spending a night there"), this paradigm generates a scene that is concerted to turn one's very conception of space inside-out, thereby picturing automatism's relation to the visual not as a strange conflation of objects, and thus the creation of new images, but as a function of the structure of vision and its ceaseless return to the already-known.

The Master's Bedroom is structured like the other overpaintings, with Ernst having summoned a cloudy film of gouache to mask out the parts of the underlying sheet that are to be suppressed and at the same time to project a new space in which the remaining objects—in this case animals and a few pieces of furniture—will take their places. As in the other cases also the gouache is somewhat skinlike, its film seeming to have congealed over the surface of the image. Unlike most of the others, however, the space projected by this film is insistently deep, organized indeed as a full-blown perspective. And the objects assembled are not the bizarre hybrids of the other collages but the unexceptional depictions of whale, bear, sheep, snake, bed, table, chest . . . , the elements left in reserve from a teaching-aid sheet on which row upon row of such animals and objects originally displayed themselves within the abstracted and gridlike circumstances of what could be called the space of inventory. From the diagrammatic, wooden nature of the poses, from the juxtaposition of the elements in rows, from their obliviousness to the demands of perspective, which would require the distant animals to be smaller than the near ones, and from the occasional bleed of the underlying parts of the inventory through the gouache skin, the flattened grid of the supporting sheet remains apparent across the newly wrought terms of the perspective. And it is this appearance that was, I would guess, decisive for the surrealists' original experience of the image as revelatory. Because what is projected here is a visual field that is not a latency, an ever renewed upsurge of the pure potentiality of the external, but instead a field that is already filled, already—to say the word—readymade.

Readymade. There is nothing readymade about the painter's blank canvas or the draftsman's white sheet, even if we could say that each of those surfaces is already organized, already structured by the lattice through which perspective will map the coordinates of external space. For the smooth white surface of each is nonetheless the index of a kind of emptiness, a fundamental blankness which is that of the visual field itself understood as a field of projection. It stands, that is, for what is assumed to be the nature of vision's spontaneous opening onto the external world as a limitless beyond, an ever retreating horizon, a reserve assumed from the outset but never filled in in advance. If in traditional perspective vanishing point and viewing point, horizon line and canvas surface, finally mirror one another in a complicitous reversibility, this is because they represent two funds of pure potentiality, two locations of the always-ever never-yet-filled: on the one hand, the horizon that vision probes, and on the other, the welling up of the glance.

That the ground of *The Master's Bedroom* is not a latency but a container already filled, so that the gaze is experienced as being saturated from the very start; that the perspective projection is not felt as a transparency opening onto a world but as a skin, fleshlike, dense, and strangely separable from the objects it fixates; these features present a visual model that is at one and the same time the complete reversal of traditional perspective and the total refusal of its modernist alternative.

How to characterize the visual model adumbrated here; how to picture something that is neither figure-against-ground nor their modernist sublimation? Would it help to think of the little apparatus that so fascinated Freud and about which he wrote his "Note on the Mystic Writing Pad"? Not to enter into anything like a game of sources. Rather because the

das schlafzimmer des meisters es lohnt sich darin eine nacht zu verbringen

la chambre à coucher de max ernst cela vaut la peine d'y passer une nuit / max ernst

Max Ernst, *The Master's Bedroom*, 1920.

The structure of vision and its ceaseless return to the already-known . . . (p. 53)

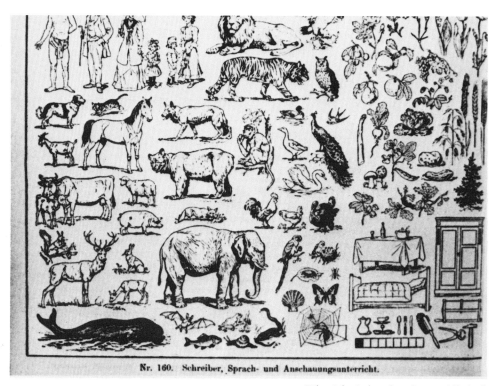

Nr. 160. Schreiber, Sprach- und Anschauungsunterricht.

Kölner Lehrmittelanstalt catalogue, p. 142, detail.

*Within the abstracted and grid-like circumstances of what could be called
the space of inventory . . . (p. 53)*

model of the Wunderblock helps to analyze the peculiar layering of experience that is here put in place.

The top sheet of the device—the one that registers the impressions etched upon it—is in Freud's model analogous to the system he calls *Pcpt.-Cs.*, that is, the part of the mental apparatus that receives stimuli (either from the outside world or from within the organism itself) as a set of impressions that are not, however, permanent within this layer of the system. In the Wunderblock this top sheet holds the visible mark only as long as it is in contact with an underlying slab of wax to which it temporarily sticks under the pressure of the stylus; once the two surfaces are detached from one another, the marks vanish and the Wunderblock presents itself as a kind of slate wiped clean. But though they are no longer available to view, the lines that have been pressed onto it are in fact retained by the waxen support, where they form a permanent network of traces. And this Freud analogizes to the mental operations of memory and thus to that part of his topological model given over to the unconscious.

In *The Master's Bedroom* the Wunderblock's waxen slab finds its analogue in the underlying sheet of the teaching-aid page, in its inventory-like concatenation of objects, the stored-up contents of unconscious memory; while the apparatus's top sheet appears as the perspectival covering of the gouache overpainting, the skinlike thickness of which seems to be an index of the way this receptor surface is detachable from its ground. This implication of detachment and reattachment relates to a further point Freud makes about the structure of the Wunderblock and its capacity to model the very nature of sensory stimulation. This stimulation, he says, is periodic in nature. It is pulsatile, "the flickering up and passing away of consciousness in the process of perception." Such a flicker or pulse, such a connection and disconnection within the perceptual field, draws from neurophysiology's theory that, as Freud says, "cathectic innervations are sent out and withdrawn in rapid periodic impulses from within into the completely pervious" perceptual system. "It is as though," he goes on, "the unconscious stretches out feelers, through the medium of the system *Pcpt.-Cs.*, towards the external world and hastily withdraws them as soon as they have sampled the excitations coming from it."

In *The Master's Bedroom* it is not that this pulsatile motion is illustrated. Indeed the scene's peculiar stillness is a striking feature of the collage. Rather, what is rendered is the sense of the gap, the detachment, the split that results from the pulse.

But the pulse, the stillness, the visual apparatus projected within the spectacle itself as a detachable covering, and the contents of vision figured forth as originating in optical space only because they are readymade, all of these elements are the structural features of the scene around which *The Master's Bedroom* is obviously organized. And it is just this through which the object was able to speak with the kind of power it did to Breton, Eluard, and Aragon in 1921. Ernst may have claimed this bedroom as his own, I find myself interjecting, but he could have done so only through a patent identification with Freud's patient, the Wolf Man, and thus by evoking the famous dream of the wolves and behind them the Wolf Man's primal scene. All of it is there, indeed: the immobility of the animals; the window opposite the bed; the raising of a curtain on the scene in the form of the window opening by itself which is the dream's figure for the onset of vision in the opening of the child's eyes; and underneath it all the element of repetition, the anxiety brought on by the uncanniness of the experience, by the fact of an already-there that is returning, returning in the form of an object that can only represent loss, an object whose identity resides precisely in the fact that it is lost. As a screen for the primal scene the dream allows that first uncanniness—the castration misperceived across the plane of the parents' love-making—to reappear. And it does so in the upsurge of a new uncanniness, in which the lost object is summoned forth through the first of that long series of substitutions—wolf, butterfly, cut finger—that repeat the mark of the lost object, not as found again, but as recurring through the very condition of absence.

Yes, it was Karl Otten who had shown him the books that day. It was in Bonn, in 1912, at the University. He could never have forgotten. He had read them voraciously, storing up the images, the examples, the analyses. Birds. Hats. Canes. Umbrellas. Stairs. Swimming pools. Flying. Falling. And always, always dreaming. Even now, he had to admit, he could recall large passages of the Interpretation *almost verbatim. And the* Joke *book. And* The Psychopathology of Everyday Life. *It was clear to him, from that moment, that the great thing would be to be a* Freudian *painter, to be able to make art out of all of that. But he also knew that he hadn't the means to do more than to make feeble and inadequate illustrations. And the books, the ideas, were too precious for that. No matter. He knew even then that he would be able to wait.*

What helped him wait had been seeing their drawings and paintings, the things they whittled or pieced together from scraps of cloth and buttons, the images they confabulated in wild profusions of miscellaneous detail, heads made up of hundreds of tiny heads put together, bodies composed

Max Ernst, *Dada in usum delphini*, 1920.

Confronted by the priapic outrageousness of the vacuum tube . . . (p. 63)

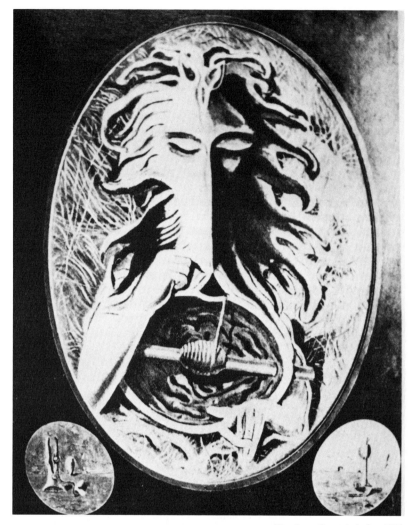

Max Ernst, *Souvenir de dieu*, 1923.

His father simultaneously as all-powerful and in the guise of a wolf . . . (p. 63)

Max Ernst, *The Virgin Chastising the Infant Jesus in Front of Three Witnesses: A. B., P. E., and the Artist*, 1926.

Ernst's projection of himself into the Leonardo story . . . (p. 65)

Oskar Pfister, *Picture Puzzle*, 1919.

The shadow of a bird cast onto the garments of the Virgin . . . (p. 65)

of hundreds and hundreds of spasmodically rendered curlicues. He thought he might write a book on this strange, delusionary production, the affluvia of these mental wards, where his studies in psychology had taken him.

Later, after he had come to know de Chirico's work and had seen that it would indeed be possible to build that kind of affect into an image, he had begun to weave all the themes he'd thought about for so long into his work. In 1920 he gave the collage of the child seated at the little schoolroom desk, confronted by the priapic outrageousness of the vacuum tube, the title Dada in usum delphini, *remembering how Freud had announced in his* Introductory Lectures *that he would not refer to the genitals in* usum delphini, *as one would speak to children, but would call them instead by their names. In 1922 he based a collage for* Les malheurs des immortels, *his book jointly written with Eluard, on the contraptions Judge Schreber's father had devised for children's exercises and published as* Kallipädie. *The sheer extravagance of Schreber's madness excited him and so he went on to make* Of This Men Shall Know Nothing *and* Revolution by Night. *But the Wolf Man's case had pushed him even further. It was not just that he made* Souvenir de Dieu *to show his father simultaneously as all-powerful and in the guise of a wolf. The Wolf Man, he began to realize, would be the armature for his own surrealist text, the obligatory oneiric production that had to be submitted to the magazine for one to earn, so to speak, one's stripes in the revolution.*

In 1969 Robert Lebel interviewed Ernst about the appearance, so many years before, of what I am calling his Wolf Man text. Lebel wonders:

> In October 1927, you published the "Trois visions de demi-sommeil" in nos. 9–10 of *La Révolution Surréaliste*, which carried your first explanation of the concept of automatism as well as of the mechanisms of collage and of frottage. How was this exceptionally interesting communication, where you affirmed your priorness and your supremacy in this area, received by the surrealist group and notably by Breton? Had you already spoken about it to Breton or was he reacting to a complete revelation?
> *Max Ernst:* I never mentioned it to him before deciding on its publication but André Breton, with whom my relations were at that time quite cordial (with certain interruptions), was spontaneously interested in it. He even helped me correct certain misusages of the French language.

Robert Lebel: Wasn't it curious that, in a group so intensely preoccupied with dreams, you had never made allusion to these?
Max Ernst: Yes, I agree, that could seem strange. . . .

How strange it might seem is, of course, a function of Ernst's participation in that whole range of experiments—with drugs, with hypnosis, with automatic writing—that went on in 1923, as Breton, during the period known as the *époque des sommeils,* tried to invent this new system that he was to call surrealism. Jacques Baron remembers:

> The first sessions took place at Breton's, rue Fontaine. In as faithful a way as possible, the participants there were, Crevel—at the beginning as master of ceremonies—Breton and Simone, of course, Aragon, Eluard, Peret, Desnos, Morise, Vitrac (very seldom), Fraenkel probably, Limbour, once or twice. Pardon me if I forget some names. Jacques-André Boiffard must have been one . . . Soupault, I don't remember . . . And Man Ray? And Max Ernst? Certainly. Gala Eluard accompanied Paul. Janine not yet. Queneau was there and Denise soon Naville, and still others.

Question: It's Ernst who gives you his hand. Do you know him?
Desnos (in a hypnotic trance): Who?
Question: Max Ernst.
Desnos: Yes.
Question: Will he live a long time?
Desnos: Fifty-one years.
Question: What will he do?
Desnos: He will play with lunatics.
Question: Will he be happy with lunatics?
Desnos: Ask the blue lady.

His "Wolf Man dream," written for La Révolution Surréaliste. *He composed it around his memory of the headboard of his little bed in Bruhl, a wooden panel, elaborately grained, into which before going to sleep as a child he would project imaginary rocks and far-off mountains, visualizing tiny horsemen making their way from one promontory to another. It was this panel that he remembered after he realized the immense possibilities of frottage. And so it is in front of this panel that he would place his father and have him make "obscene gestures" with a "fat crayon" he pulls out of his trousers before, according to the logic of the dream work, turning his whole body into a vase, a top, a frantic whirling thing whose name could only be that absent presence of fantasy, the phallus. The connection to the Wolf Man would be made through this reference to his father making love, overseen by "little Max" and reexperienced via the screen of the dream. The screen within the screen-memory. That would be it.*

Yet the most specific and far-reaching example of Ernst's identification with Freud's case histories does not involve the Wolf Man per se. It is, rather, Ernst's projection of himself into the Leonardo story. For example, in the 1926 picture *The Virgin Chastising the Infant Jesus before Three Witnesses (A.B., P.E., and the Artist)*, this connection is dropped in as a kind of private witticism, in the shadow of a bird cast onto the garments of the Virgin. Formed in the profile of the innumerable doves Ernst was to paint in the late 1920s, the appearance of this phantom mimes the Oskar Pfister diagram of the hidden vulture in *The Virgin and Saint Anne*, which accompanied the 1919 edition of Freud's Leonardo essay. But Ernst's identification with Leonardo was to be far more systemic than that. In his assumption of Loplop, "Bird-Superior," as his own alter ego, calling this creature, the subject of innumerable pictures, "my private phantom, attached to my person," it would achieve the resonance of a totem. At another, iconographic level, it would control Ernst's relation to the realm of natural history, whether in the early collages or in the cycle of frottage drawings that assimilate themselves to the character of Leonardo's sketchbook projects in both facture and scope. But in this matter of *The Master's Bedroom* and the "Three Dreams of Half-Sleep," Ernst's connection to the Leonardo case turns on the very function of screen memory as the central element of Freud's analysis: screen memory, that is, not as a supplier of content but as a condition of how something is structured. For it is not the bird itself but the bird as fundamental absence that plays so important a role in the operation Freud will put in place.

Leonardo's supposed recollection of a bird's having visited him in his cradle and having beaten its tail between his lips is interpreted by Freud as a screen, a blind onto which the remembered remnants of infant arousal caused by an overaffectionate mother are projected in disguised form. Too young for these feelings to be understood, the infant retains this inchoate experience as a memory whose meaning lies dormant, awaiting the interpretation that will only be given to it later, a meaning that is thus a function of what Freud calls deferred action. That what should finally be produced as the perceptual content of this memory would be a bird Freud explains in a way that is parallel to the Wolf Man's wolf, or indeed to the various objects presented in the screen memories of so many of his patients.

These elements are provided to the subject readymade, Freud states; they are what the child picks up from the scraps of overheard conversation, from images happened upon in books, from the behavior of animals both seen and recounted. They are the data uncovered in the research the child's own sexual curiosity is constantly driving him or her to perform, the data that, once discovered, are retrojected onto the formless past in the guise of "memory." They are the completely factitious referents that come, after the fact, to attach themselves to the floating signifiers of what Freud had come to think of not even as the primal scene, but as the primal fantasy.

In Freud's reconstruction of Leonardo's case, the bird derives from an old wives' tale, the mother's repeated story of an omen of her child's future greatness, and it is then reinforced as the specific memory object, Freud hypothesizes, by the information that vultures have no mates and are instead inseminated by the wind. The screen memory is, then, an apparatus by means of which vision is retrojected, projected after-the-fact onto the fully saturated ground of the readymade.

The Leonardo of the screen memory is different, we should notice, from the Leonardo of the projective screen, the famous spotted wall or burning embers within which he instructed young painters to let their imaginations wander. And it's the second screen, the one conceived as the setting for a free play of imagery, a latency that permits the welling up of associations within the creative process, that has always been summoned in relation to Ernst. For it's only the second, the art historian reasons, that is properly surrealist. Even Ernst seems to agree.

In his treatise *Beyond Painting* Ernst obligingly quotes Breton's explanation of "Leonardo's lesson, setting his students to copy in their pictures that which they saw taking shape in the spots on an old wall (each according to his own lights)." And this Ernst juxtaposes with his own account of his discovery of frottage, which begins, "On the 10th of August, 1925, an insupportable visual obsession caused me to discover the technical means which have brought a clear realization of this lesson of Leonardo," a story that tells how a sudden fixation on the groves in the floorboards of his bedroom at a seaside inn led him to invent his own projective procedure. The reference to Leonardo's projective screen is clearly intended here to give frottage a pedigree of unparalleled luster.

But in this account Ernst then goes on to make a claim that is inexplicable as long as the projective screen is thought of as a latency that, like the blank page of conventional painting, can be analogized to the ground of vision as traditionally conceived. That claim is that frottage and collage (or collage as Ernst practiced it, saying "ce n'est pas la colle qui fait le collage") are indistinguishable as procedures, making it no surprise that the circumstances that suggested each of them to him should have been nearly identical. "The similarity of the two is such," he writes, "that I can, without changing many words, use the terms employed earlier for the one, to relate how I made the discovery of the other." And then his account for collage begins: "One rainy day in 1919, finding myself in a village on the Rhine, I was struck by the obsession which held under my gaze the pages of an illustrated catalogue showing objects designed for anthropologic, microscopic, psychologic, mineralogic, and paleontologic demonstration."

For the twinning of these two inventions to be possible, Ernst must have conflated the two screens—Leonardo's spotted wall and Freud's account of the vulture memory—understanding the vision configured in the one as structured by the mnemonic retroactivity of the other. And in this conflation it is the unconscious that is understood to be at work, with the two processes made to occupy the same perceptual stage due to what Freud describes as common to both dreams and hallucinations, namely a regression toward the visual. Thus the parent space for both collage and frottage, the single plane from which both were launched, is explained in *Beyond Painting* as the screen of Ernst's own rather carefully fabricated screen memory, the burled mahogany panel of his bedstead which he casts in the drama of a twilight-state dream he claimed for himself in early childhood. This is the panel he imagines his father to be copulating with and on which is produced an inventory of images: "menacing eye, long nose, great head of a bird with thick black hair, etc."

When they moved—the four of them, Paul, Gala, Max, and the six-year-old Cécile—from Saint-Brice to another suburban villa, this time in Eaubonne, Max had the idea of decorating the child's room with wonderful, fanciful paintings. But somehow, as it always did, the focus got shifted to Gala. And it would now be the walls of the entire apartment that he would cover with a profusion of images. The very idea of such a cycle reminded him of Pompeian houses and from this he made a connection to Gradiva and Freud's Delusion and Dream, *its analysis of a story set after all among those ruins. The Pompeian girl of antiquity—Gradiva—as a screen for the living girl Zoë, the delusional image in the present of a live Gradiva through*

67

two

which the adolescent sexual stirrings, lying dormant in memory, are finally given their interpretation. Gradiva as a screen.

The hand that would play "Gradiva" in this outsized mural was a found image. He had seen it in the magazine La Nature *as the illustration for a little essay on sensory illusions. It was a hand with its index and middle fingers crossed one over the other, the tips of each stroking either side of the little ball or pellet positioned between them. The hand, indescribably languid, was wholly suggestive, its crossed fingers turning the tender web of flesh at the fingers' base into a beautifully folded crotch, the feminized source of what could now be read as two voluptuously dangling legs. But it wasn't just the transformation of hand into "woman" that caught his attention. The ball, you see, pushed things farther than that. The verticality of the fingers with the ball at their tips rephallicized the image, causing a meaning to rise upward, to flood back over the lineaments of the baffling genital secret; in it he could see the woman's body beckoning with all the pleasure and terror of the dawning excitement of the experience of sexual difference. And this made the hand, in its verticality, in its sense of weightless suspension, in its Oedipal overtones, another avatar of* La puberté proche.

But this time the hand, as it reaches from behind the depicted, Pompeian wall to perform its gesture of seduction against the terra cotta surface, beckons to him, Max Ernst, from in front of a screen. Behind the screen is the fantasy of Gala in La puberté proche *and behind that the photograph of her in Eluard's wallet. And behind that the long chain of images that had lain dormant for so long, the siren images with "Max" on their lips as they murmured to him the truth of his childish desire.*

In what Freud calls vision's "other scene"—the one toward which the unconscious regresses in the conditions of dreaming, fantasizing, hallucinating, or screen memory—the operation of dormancy is at work. This deferred action or *Nachträglichkeit,* or *après-coup,* is importantly a function of the readymade, which, lying at hand, becomes the vehicle for a past experience—one that had made no sense at the time it occurred—to rise up on the horizon of the subject's vision as an originary, unified perception. Freud describes this, for example, in relation to secondary revision, that process of the dream work that comes, *après-coup,* to construct a facade for the dream—the one we seem to remember upon waking, the one that gathers the chaos of the dream representations together, creating the relative coherence of a narrative. This facade, Freud says, is a readymade—a narrative lying in wait to be affixed to the dream material,

Max Ernst, *At the First Clear Word*, 1923.

The hand, as it reaches from behind the depicted, Pompeian wall to perform its gesture of seduction . . . (p. 68)

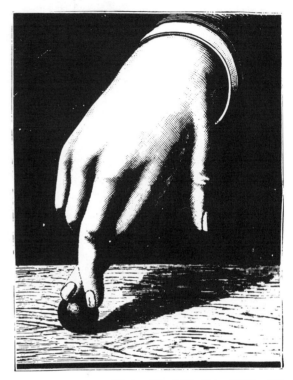

"Illusion of Touch," *La Nature* (1881), p. 584.

But it wasn't just the transformation of hand into "woman" that caught his attention . . . (p. 68)

its readymade condition making its attachment possible in the very split second of waking. Offering many examples of the way this works, Freud asks of one of them, "Is it so highly improbable that [this] dream represents a phantasy which had been stored up ready-made in [the dreamer's] memory for many years and which was aroused—or I would rather say 'alluded to'—at the moment at which he became aware of the stimulus which woke him?" Secondary revision, however, is not the affixing of just any prefabricated plot line to the surface of the dream. The relation between the narrative facade that secondary revision erects and the desire that functions at the dream's core is that these two in fact mirror one another. And further, that inner kernel is itself readymade, a function of daydreams elaborated in infancy or puberty that "form within the nexus of the dream thoughts." And as we know, in that infinite regress in which the referent is constantly displaced from its supposed causal connection to the fantasy's origin, those daydreams will also be described by Freud as readymade for the subject, lying in wait for him in the scraps he picks up from his parents and grandparents, the legends the family tells about itself and him, its favorite sayings, the myths about itself that it weaves out of the prefabricated material of social chitchat and cultural aspirations, the romances in short that he takes from others and assumes as his own.

Now, if the daydreamer is able to produce these secondhand scraps of excitement as his own, if they appear to him on the screen of his memory as his personal experience, this is due to that particular structure of visual perception that Lacan has termed the "*belong to me* aspect of representations." It is this phenomenological experience of something's being both outside himself and *his* that turns this bric-a-brac into the deictic markers of the subject's own being, the evidentiary signposts that appear to him the indices of his own history, his own identity, the touchstones of his most intimate connections to the real. Which is all the more astonishing in that the readymades he will come to identify as "his" are the markers erected after the fact to commemorate an event that never happened, an encounter whose traumatic effect on him arises from the very fact that he missed it. The sexuality of the child, Freud says, will always be traumatic, because it will always be a missed encounter, one for which he was always either too early or too late.

The traumatic event, the missed encounter, what Lacan comes to call the *tuchē,* produces not excitement but loss, or rather excitement *as* loss, as a self-mutilation, as something fallen from the body. The repetition automatism set in motion by this trauma will work thereafter to restore that unknown and unknowable thing, attempting to find it, that is, on the other side of the gap the trauma opened up in the field of the missed encounter. The structure of the trauma, then, is not just that it initiates a compulsion to repeat but that it institutes the gap of the trauma itself—the missed encounter—as the always-already occupied meaning of that opening onto a spatial beyond that we think of as the determining character of vision. For it is from the other side of the perceptual divide that the signifier will come, the object capable of standing for what the subject has lost. It is this object that the child sets out to find, supplying itself with an endless series of substitutes that present themselves to it, in the world beyond the gap.

To the reservoir or inventory of this series of stand-ins Lacan gives the name automaton to indicate the quality of uncanniness that surrounds the finding of each of these objects, the sense not only of anxiety the encounter produces but also its aura of happenstance, an encounter one was not prepared for, a meeting that always, one insists, takes place by chance. But the term *automaton* also underscores the inexorability and order that rule this series, that create the logic of the substitutions that will take place within it. The automaton inaugurated on the site of that gap of the missed encounter will both mark that spot and attempt to fill it, to produce from its grab bag of readymades the stopgaps presumed by the subject to be made to the measure of his own desire.

In the question period following Lacan's session on "Tuchē and Automaton" he is asked why, in describing the formation of intelligence up to the age of three or four, he seems to have abandoned the notion of developmental stages—first oral, then anal, then Oedipal—and to have organized everything around the fear of castration. Lacan's answer is: "The fear of castration is like a thread that perforates all the stages of development. It orientates the relations that are anterior to its actual appearance—weaning, toilet training, etc. It crystallizes each of these moments in a dialectic that has as its center a bad encounter. If the stages are consistent, it is in accordance with their possible registration in terms of bad encounters."

In another, earlier seminar on the notion of "object relations" as viewed from within a Freudian structure, he had spoken of the castrative status of weaning. "What happens," he asks, "when the mother no longer responds to the solicitation of desire, when she responds according to her own will? She becomes real, she becomes powerful. All at once access to objects is modified: until then objects which were pure and simply objects of satisfaction, are now transformed into gifts coming from this source of power. We witness, in short, a reversal of position. From being symbolic the mother becomes real, and objects from being real, become symbolic."

Suppose we were to try to graph this relation. We might start by characterizing the primal appearance of the object within the infant subject's perceptual field as the advent of something that separates itself out from a hitherto undifferentiated ground to become distinct as figure. *That object, which is the mother's breast—and by extension the mother—becomes a figure, of course, by dint of its withdrawal from the contiguous field of the infant, by virtue of setting him up no longer as the amorphous and all-inclusive subject of satisfaction but now as the subject of frustration and longing, the subject that is, of desire. The very moment that produces the visibility of the object brackets it, then, as an object submitted to the terms of absence. As such, this "figure" is conditioned by its own contradiction, which is that of not-figure. But the figure, as image, is also mirrored back to the infant perceiver, who understands it as the representation of not just any object but that object which is uniquely his, which was invented for his satisfaction and pleasure, which in being his marks him as a unique being, and in this character of "belonging to him" both points to him deictically—"this," "here," "you"—and reproduces itself deixically—one term mirroring another, implying another—as part of his own identity. As in the Klein Group's diagonally opposing terms, as in the L Schema's a = a', so here the "figure" of the image equals the "not-ground" of his self-differentiation as ego. Rewritten in this way:*

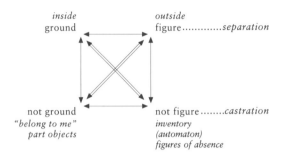

the appearance of the object as the psychoanalytically construed function of separation begins to suggest a schema with which we are familiar.

If modernism's logic of vision can be constructed with the Klein Group as its basis, that same structuralist model is also the support for the L Schema. This schema, as we know, sets the subject of the unconscious in contrast to its objects, which Lacan comes to term *objets a* (or objects of desire). From that initial contrast two derivations then occur, as the *objets a* are first doubled along the mirroring relationship of the deixic axis to structure the field of the subject's ego and then configured in terms of an absence that projects them into the unconscious field, also to be termed the Symbolic and the locus of the Other.

Like the Klein Group, like the modernist visual graph, the L Schema is set up to acknowledge structuralism's drive toward logical clarity. To this end it shares in the synchrony and cognitive immediacy that are the features of structure. But this the L Schema does only to challenge the very transparency announced by the structuralist diagram itself. For the terms of logic that rule within the diagram—making possible the mirror relation of the axis of visuality—set up a reversibility between *a* and *a'* that is the basis not of lucidity but of what Lacan will label "misrecognition." Permanent and opaque, this obstacle is installed within the very heart of a diagrammatic clarity that is now a model both of vision's claims and of vision's failure.

If transparency is one feature of structure, synchrony is the other. For it is the synchronous display of relations that, by gathering the elements of a system into the field of a single picture, allows for the thought of cognitive mastery. It is synchrony, therefore, that becomes the other term upon which the L Schema declares its own logical war. Constructed as a circuit rather than a diagram or table, the L Schema plots the effects set in motion by the trauma's production of the compulsion to repeat. Mapping this circularity onto the stability of the structure, the L Schema implies that it is only that sequentiality and time taken up into the heart of the system that give it its character as homeostatic and its appearance as atemporal.

Would it be possible to modify the L Schema as the basis for mapping a visuality that both subtends and subverts the field of modernist vision in the same way that Lacan's psychoanalytic circuitry erodes the structuralist relations from within? For if the mirror relation as it is graphed in the L Schema divides the subject from the unconscious, by driving a wedge of opacity through the diagonal center of the graph, it is nonetheless true that the subject is the effect of the unconscious, or what needs now to be called a "subject-effect."

In a similar way the graph of an automatist visuality would show how the vaunted cognitive transparency of the "visual as such" is not an act of consciousness but the effect of what is repressed: the effect, that is, of seriality, repetition, the automaton. Which is to say, it is a function of a caesura in vision, a gap:

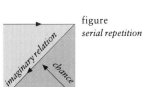

ground   figure
field of synchrony   *serial repetition*
"visual as such"

imaginary relation   *chance*

not ground   *missed encounter*   automaton
(part objects)   *(figures of absence)*
"belong to me"

The figure, constituted by separation, is deixically redoubled as not-ground: *as those parts of the subject's own body that are identified with the external object. But since that external object is given through its very condition as retreating or separating, those part-objects belonging to the subject are similarly parts lost to the subject, and for that reason they are written along the axis of castration. At the pole at the far end of that axis, the pole of the* not-figure, *the inventory of all those substitutes for the lost object pile up in a potentially endless series. The appearance of each of these figures, as it rises from behind the barrier of the missed encounter, out of the field of the unconscious and into that of perception, will strike the subject with surprise, will seem to him the result of chance.*

Max Ernst, *La femme 100 têtes*, 1929:
"Truth will remain simple, and gigantic wheels will ride the bitter waves."

The stormy landscapes, the urban squares, the desk-lined schoolrooms . . . (p. 81)

Max Ernst, *La femme 100 têtes*, 1929: "The might-have-been Immaculate Conception."

Their obvious allusion to the part-object: the breast, the eye, the belly, the womb . . . (p. 81)

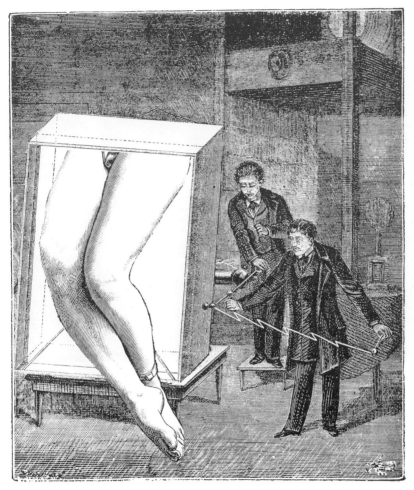

Max Ernst, *La femme 100 têtes*, 1929: ". . . and the third time missed."

In their posture, in their function, in their affect, the legs reconvene an image we recognize . . . (p. 82)

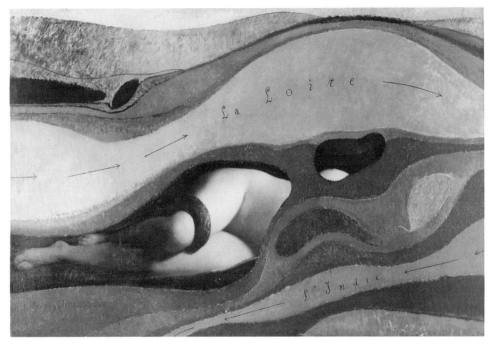

Max Ernst, *The Garden of France*, 1962.

Its final avatar, perhaps, the clutched knees and crossed ankles of the nude . . . (p. 82)

For the gambler's passion is nothing but that question asked of the signifier, figured by the automaton *of chance.*

"What are you, figure of the die I turn over in your encounter (tychē) *with my fortune? Nothing, if not that presence of death which makes of human life a reprieve obtained from morning to morning in the name of meanings whose sign is your crook. . . ."*

—Lacan, Seminar on "The Purloined Letter"

In the summer of 1929 Max Ernst was spending a long vacation on a farm in the Ardèche. There, as he claimed to one of his biographers, he was confined to bed for several weeks. Whether or not this bed had a headboard and if so whether of burled mahogany, or whether this confinement even occurred, is probably not important. Ernst was reconfiguring what can easily be spotted as his "collage conditions": that formula of the twilight-state dream, of the master's bedroom, of the perspective space effortlessly unrolling toward its readymade horizon. The feverish production of those few weeks was the collage novel *Femme 100 têtes.*

The stormy landscapes, the urban squares, the desk-lined schoolrooms, the corridor of railroad dining car—in the world of the novel each prospect is transected by an apparition that both occupies a part of the space and blocks its backward recession. The apparition is most frequently a ghostly white profile, the classically drawn figure of a woman, sometimes nude, sometimes draped, inserted within the cross fire of light and shadow that tells of the banal solidity of the surrounding space. Sometimes the apparition is accompanied, or even substituted for, by a wheel-like form suggesting a turning disc, a circle that in the second plate of the novel resembles Duchamp's optical machines, or his rotoreliefs, with their obvious allusion to the part-object: the breast, the eye, the belly, the womb. In the fourth plate of the book, the one that tells of the immaculate conception's missing or failing for the third time, that uncanny gap we have come to expect opens within the visual continuum. Here it is manifested by the silhouette of two huge, white legs, knees pressed together, ankles crossed, emerging from the boxlike apparatus two scientists are manipulating from within the shadowy interior of their laboratory. These legs, truncated just above the thigh, end at the upper face of the box, a tiny observable ripple of cloth gesturing toward the joint between them. In their posture, in their function, in their affect, the legs reconvene an image we recognize. We've seen it before in *La puberté proche;* we've seen it in the "Gradiva" mural at Eaubonne; and, we might suspect, we will see it again: its final avatar, perhaps, the clutched knees and crossed ankles of the nude that Ernst will lift from Cabanal's *Birth of Venus* and bury just below the screenlike surface of his own *Garden of France.*

And as with the bird, whether Ernst's or Leonardo's, it is not the perceptual content of the figure that counts so much as it is the way it structures the field. Emerging from the box, just like the hand dangling through the opening in the wall at Eaubonne, the figure enters the field of vision as radically disembodied. This effect of a truncated body part—eyes, headless torso, most often hands—emerging into the field of vision is a leitmotif of Ernst's production: the hand poking through the window in *Oedipus Rex;* the two hands suspending the eyeball between them for the cover of *Répétitions;* the hands that would gesture toward the viewer in the many versions of *Loplop Presents.* These hands, which seem to gesture, seem to point, seem to teach, always appear to beckon, thereby establishing an intimate, even personal order of connection between the space of the image and that of the viewer. It is therefore important to note that this gesture of showing, of pointing, of welcoming, is the gesture in Ernst's work that is most demonstrably readymade. Over and over he lifts it from the pages of *La Nature* where the hands that reach into the image from a point just beyond its frame are busily engaged in demonstrating simple principles of physics, or performing magic tricks, or showing the operations of scientific instruments. And this gesture with which Ernst seems to identify with all his might is a gesture that holds up a frame around an absence. For what the hand is proffering, toward its viewer, toward Ernst, is always a kind of hole in vision, since it is always made the space of substitution, is always a screen, a field within which there enters the automaton.

The hand is Ernst's *objet a;* as such it introduces the screen, the rupture, the blind spot.

The hand that gestures toward the infant establishes a bond that the child can only read as unique, a gesture meant utterly and undividedly for itself. This pointing gesture is deictic, it says "you." But far beyond that it says "you are," or "you exist." It is the dumb, preverbal, presymbolic pointing to which Barthes refers in the opening of his *Camera Lucida,* a pointing that he likens to the Buddhist *tathata* (the fact of being this) or to the

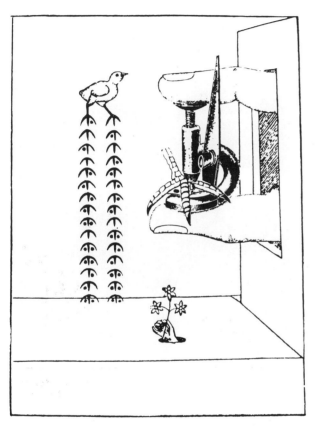

Max Ernst, *The Invention*, 1922.

Hands—emerging into the field of vision . . . (p. 82)

"Electrical Experiment, Carried Out on a Walnut,"
La Nature (1891), p. 272.

Over and over he lifts it from the pages of La Nature . . . (p. 82)

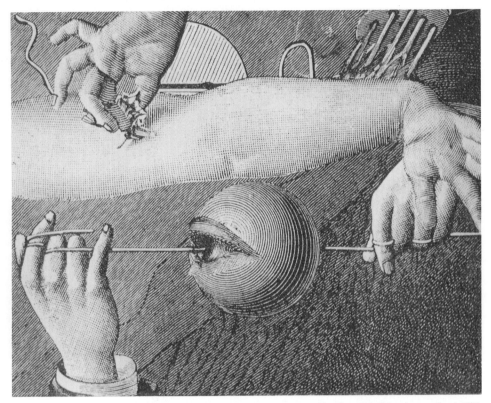

Max Ernst, *Répétitions* (cover collage), 1922.

This gesture of showing, of pointing, of welcoming . . . (p. 82)

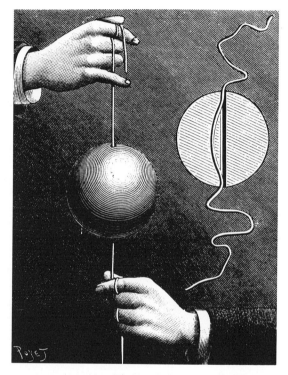

"The Magic Ball," *La Nature* (1887), p. 144.

. . . is the gesture in Ernst's work that is most demonstrably readymade . . . (p. 82)

child's jubilant discovery: *Ta, Da, Ca!* This deictic marker, this index of pure individuality, is a function, for the infant, of the part-object: the mother's gaze, her breast, her hand.

But almost immediately it becomes a function of the *tuchē*—"the real as encounter—the encounter in so far as it may be missed, in so far as it is essentially the missed encounter." In calling the encounter with the real "the *tychic . . .* from the word *tuchē*," Lacan adds that since this is an encounter essentially missed the phenomenon one is dealing with here is "*dustuchia*," or the split. It is the break in the field of vision or the break within the flow of language for which we could use the term distich, the split between the two lines of a poem that both divides them and couples them. Deictic and distich. They almost rhyme.

Lacan's discussion of vision in *The Four Fundamental Concepts of Psycho-Analysis* is centered on a scopic drive structured by the distich, the rupture, the schiz. He calls the opening chapter "The Split between the Eye and the Gaze." But the whole of his account is called "The Gaze as *objet a*," or the gaze as part-object, the object that, because it marks the subject with the individuation of his existence, is most fundamentally the object of desire. Lacan wants to show the dialectic between deictic and distich, between pointing and screen, between this! and absence.

The space of pointing, or of deixis, is the space that Lacan terms "geo-metral," namely the space of perspective, a space that as Diderot shows in his *Letter on the Blind* is actually a *tactile* space, a space mastered by the subject as though he were reaching out to grasp it, to palp it, running fingers over its front and sides, manipulating it.

In contrast to this tactile "visuality" is the space of light, which Lacan calls "dazzling, pulsatile": an atmospheric surround that illuminates the viewer from both back and front, so that from the start there is no question of mastery. And in the context of this space of the luminous, the viewer is not the surveyor—standing at a point just outside the pyramid of vision—but, caught within the onrush of light, he is what blocks the light, what interrupts its flow. In this interruption the "viewer" invisible to himself enters the "picture" created by this light as a "stain" or blind spot, as the shadow cast by the light, its trace, its deictic mark. And from this place the subject, in all his exposure to view, can neither see himself nor see the source of the light. His position is one of dependence on an illumination that both marks him (the deictic) and escapes his grasp (the distich). This illumination Lacan calls the "gaze." It is a part-object operating within the instinctual field of vision, forever unlocatable, out of focus, in metamor-phosis, pulsing. "It is always that gleam of light," Lacan declares, "which holds me, at each point, as a screen, and therefore makes the light appear as an iridescence that overflows it. In short, the point of gaze always participates in the ambiguity of the jewel."

I enter the picture as a cast shadow, cast because, dumbly, I get in the way of the light. And because I get in the way of it, I cannot see it. The point where it would be, if I could see it, is held for me by a marker, a placeholder, a structural substitute. This is the automaton, the readymade, the thing the gap both produces and hides behind. This is what marks the point in the optical system where what is thought to be visible will never appear.

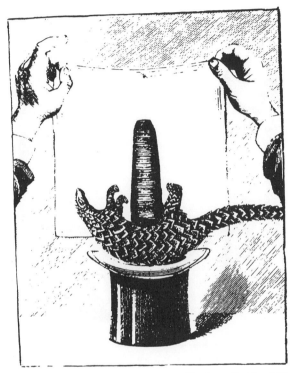

Max Ernst, *Magician,* 1921.

The hand is Ernst's objet a . . . *(p. 82)*

"The Multiplication of Eggs, the Magician Alber's Trick,"
La Nature (1881).

A gesture that holds up a frame around an absence . . . (p. 82)

Adorno's text is "Looking Back at Surrealism" (in *The Idea of the Modern in Literature and the Arts,* ed. Irving Howe [New York: Horizon, 1967], p. 222).

Werner Spies, the leading Ernst scholar, discusses the collage novels at length in his *Max Ernst: Les collages, inventaire et contradictions* (Paris: Gallimard, 1984). Curiously Spies claims that Ernst's collage novels were never addressed either by Benjamin or Adorno; this, even though Spies also quotes a letter from Benjamin to Adorno dating from after the publication of *Une semaine de bonté:* "I would like to meet Max Ernst. If you could organize something, you could be certain of my willingness" (p. 177). Among the other wealth of material, Spies's study contains an important documentary group of images displaying the various visual sources on which Ernst drew for his collages (pp. 415–455), as well as a group of unpublished letters from Ernst to Tristan Tzara (pp. 480–483) and a detailed description of the scene of unpacking the collages at Tzara's house (p. 81).

Charlotte V. Stokes, in "*La Femme 100 têtes* by Max Ernst" (Ph.D. dissertation, University of Washington, 1977), p. 3, reads *Femme 100 têtes* as a *Bildungsroman;* Gerd Bauer, in "Max Ernsts Collagenroman 'Une Semaine de Bonté,'" *Wallraf Richartz Jahrbuch* 39 (1977), patterns *Une semaine de bonté* on earlier works of literature; M. E. Warlich ("Max Ernst's Alchemical Novel: *Une semaine de bonté,*" *Art Journal,* 46 [Spring 1987]) decodes it through alchemy; Werner Spies (*Max Ernst: Les collages,* p. 197) refers to Rimbaud. See also Evan Maurer, "Images of Dream and Desire: The Prints and Collage Novels of Max Ernst" (*Max Ernst, Beyond Surrealism,* ed. Robert Rainwater [New York: New York Public Library and Oxford University Press, 1986]): "*Histoire naturelle* is essentially a surreal poetic vision describing the birth of the world and the evolution of life, and its theme and imagery reflect Ernst's continuing interest in the illustrated books and magazines of natural science that he had begun to use as sources of illustrations for his collages in the early 1920s" (p. 59). Maurer relates the water chapter of *Une semaine de bonté* to Freud's Dora case history.

André Breton remembers unpacking the Ernst collages in his "Artistic Genesis and Perspective of Surrealism" (1941; reprinted in *Surrealism and Painting* [New York: Harper and Row, 1972], p. 64); his reference to catalogue figures as "readymades" is from his essay "Max Ernst," 1920 (in Max Ernst, *Beyond Painting* [New York: Wittenborn, Schultz], p. 177). Aragon's reference to advertisements is from "Max Ernst, peintre des illusions," 1923 (in Louis Aragon, *Les collages* [Paris: Hermann, 1965], p. 29). The actual source for the overpaintings from 1920 was the 1914 *Katalog der Kölner Lehrmittelanstalt,* discussed by Dirk Teuber, "Max Ernsts Lehrmittel," *Max Ernst in Köln* (Cologne: Kölnischer Kunstverein, 1980), pp. 206–240.

Accounts of Eluard's relation to Ernst are found in: Robert Jouanny, "L'amitié magique de Paul Eluard et Max Ernst," *Motifs et figures* (Paris: PUF, 1974); Charles Whiting, "Eluard's Poems for Gala," *The French Review* (February 1968); Luc Decaunes, *Paul Eluard,* (Paris: Balland, 1982); Elaine Formentelli, "Max Ernst–Paul Eluard, ou l'impatience du désir," *Revue des Sciences Humaines,* no. 164 (1976), pp. 487–504. André Thirion, *Révolutionnaires sans révolution* (Paris: Robert Laffont, 1972), describes Eluard's showing Gala's photograph: "La photographie de Gala nue ne quittait pas son portefeuille et il la montrait volontiers: on y voyait un corps admirable qu'Eluard n'était pas peu fier d'avoir mis dans son lit" (p. 200); Patrick Waldberg (*Max Ernst* [Paris: Jean-Jacques Pauvert, 1958]) speaks of Eluard's sensing Ernst as his brother, of the ménage à trois in Saint-Brice and Eaubonne. It is Jean-Charles Gateau (*Paul Eluard et la peinture surréaliste* [Paris: Droz, 1982]) who sees Eluard's poem "Max Ernst" as the memory of a real scene that occurred in the Cologne studio; his analysis of the poem connects the fourfold "dans un coin" to the game of *quatre coins* (p. 54). The first section of "Max Ernst" reads:

> Dans un coin l'inceste agile
> Tourne autour de la virginité d'une petite robe.
> Dans un coin le ciel délivré
> Aux pointes des anges laisse des boules blanches.
>
> Dans un coin plus clair de tous les yeux
> On attend les poissons d'angoisse.
> Dans un coin la voiture de verdure de l'été
> Immobile, glorieuse et pour toujours.
>
> A la lueur de la jeunesse
> Des lampes allumées très tard
> La première montre ses seins que tuent des insectes rouges.

When Gateau turns from the literary to the visual reading, however, and invokes a modernist notion of the four-cornered, flat page of Ernst's medium as another way of interpreting Eluard's use of "dans un coin," this seems to operate against the grain of both Eluard's and Ernst's pictorial sensibilities at this time. Ernst's own sense of the corners of an image are themselves indebted to de Chirico, to the revelation he received when he saw how the Italian painter could so warp the classical proscenium of central-point perspective's stagelike cavity that looking into and entering the deep space of the picture continually led to one's feeling of being thrown back to the surface again, as though trying to enter a centrifuge. De Chirico had not embraced the modernist solution of breaking down the opposition between figure and ground, of having the one—ground, say—rise up to become the canvas's "figure." Rather, he had developed a certain kind of tension between the two; more like anamorphosis. Ernst's *Fiat Modes* capitalized on this perception, as did the overpaintings he sent to Breton for the exhibition at Au Sans Pareil.

Sigmund Freud, "A Note upon the 'Mystic Writing-Pad'" (1924), in *The Standard Edition of the Complete Psychological Works,* ed. James Strachey (London: Hogarth Press and the Institute for Psycho-Analysis), vol. 19, p. 231.

For the background of Ernst's connection to psychoanalysis, see Werner Spies, *The Return of La Belle Jardinière, Max Ernst 1950–1979* (New York: Abrams, 1971), p. 38; and Elisabeth Legge, *Max Ernst: The Psychoanalytic Sources* (Ann Arbor: UMI Research Press, 1989).

Ernst's own texts, reprinted in *Beyond Painting* (New York: Wittenborn, 1948), construct a psychobiography: a "primal scene"; a paranoid attachment to his father; an erotic attachment to his sister, who comes consistently to be referred to in his work (*Femmes 100 têtes,* and elsewhere) as "perturbation my sister." He himself connects the painting *Souvenir de dieu* to the representation of his father as a wolf (p. 28), suggesting a direct relation to the Wolf Man, as in Freud's case "From the History of an Infantile Neurosis" (1918), *Standard Edition.,* vol. 17, pp. 3–122. For an analysis of Ernst's relation to the Schreber case, see Geoffrey Hinton, "Max Ernst: 'Les Hommes n'en Sauront Rien,'" *Burlington Magazine,* 117 (May 1975), pp. 292–297; and Malcolm Gee, "Max Ernst, God, and the Revolution by Night," *Arts,* 55 (March 1981), pp. 85–91.

Hal Foster has analyzed Ernst's early work both in relation to primal fantasies and the social setting out of which Ernst's preoccupation with this arose: "Armor Fou," *October,* no. 56 (Spring 1991), and "Convulsive Identity," *October,* no. 57 (Summer 1991).

Ernst's discussion of his "Trois visions de demi-sommeil" is from "Max Ernst parle avec Robert Lebel," *L'Oeil*, nos. 176–177 (August 1969); his appearance at the early "époque des sommeils" seances is recounted in Jacques Baron, *L'an 1 du surréalisme* (Paris: Denoël, 1969), p. 67; his participation is quoted from Robert Desnos, *Écrits sur les peintres* (Paris: Flammarion, 1984)—"the blue lady" is generally understood to refer to Gala Eluard.

Werner Spies (*Max Ernst, Loplop: The Artist in the Third Person* [New York: George Braziller, 1983], pp. 103ff.) makes the connection between the Oskar Pfister diagram and Ernst's *Infant Jesus Being Chastised;* he quotes Ernst from a 1934 text, writing of "Leonardo's celebrated vulture, coaxed out of hiding centuries later by a student of Freud" (p. 105). Spies also discusses Ernst's identification with Leonardo in terms of his adoption of the bird as alter ego and his embrace of the crumbling wall as a projective screen. He does not, however, consider the other meaning of "screen image" that emerges from Freud's analysis of Leonardo (Sigmund Freud, "Leonardo da Vinci and a Memory of His Childhood" [1910], *Standard Edition*, vol. 11, pp. 59–137). The speculation that the bird fantasy was projected retrospectively onto a story, told to him by his mother, about a bird visiting him in his cradle was added in a footnote in 1919 (chap. 2). Freud presented the idea and function of the screen memory in 1899 ("Screen Memories," *Standard Edition*, vol. 3, pp. 301–322).

Ernst speaks of the bird as his totem in *Beyond Painting*, pp. 9–10; he quotes Breton on Leonardo's lesson, p. 11; and relates this to the invention of frottage, p. 14.

Freud's *Delusion and Dream,* his analysis of Jenson's "Gradiva," was written in 1906 (*Standard Edition*, vol. 9, pp. 3–93). Elisabeth Legge points out that the Gradiva story is already present in one of the poems in *Les malheurs* (see Legge, *Max Ernst*, p. 107). Werner Spies analyzes the relation between *On the First Clear Word* and *Delusion and Dream* in "Une poétique du collage" (in *Paul Eluard et ses amis peintres* [Paris: Centre Georges Pompidou, 1982], pp. 66–67).

For the analysis of secondary revision, see Sigmund Freud, *The Interpretation of Dreams,* trans. James Strachey (New York: Avon Library, 1965), chap. 6, where he speaks of the "readymade fantasy" (pp. 533–534) and the readymade nexus of dream thoughts (p. 530).

Jean LaPlanche and J.-B. Pontalis, "Fantasy and the Origins of Sexuality," *The International Journal of Psycho-Analysis*, 49 (1968), pp. 10–11.

Jacques Lacan, *The Four Fundamental Concepts of Psycho-Analysis,* trans. Alan Sheridan (New York: Norton, 1977), where he points out the belong-to-me aspect of perception (p. 81); speaks of the early encounter with the sexual as a "missed encounter," either too early or too late (p. 69); refers to the *objet a* as something fallen from the body (p. 62); stresses the chance nature of the encounter (p. 58); analyzes the automaton and its substitutions (p. 67); and answers questions about castration invading all the stages of development (p. 64). He again speaks of weaning and object relations in "La relation d'objet et les structures freudiennes," *Bulletin de Psychologie* 10, no. 7 (April 1, 1957), 429.

John Russell, *Max Ernst: Life and Work* (New York: Abrams, 1967), p. 189, tells of the circumstances of making the collages for *Femme 100 têtes.* Spies ("Une poétique de collage") reproduces various examples of Ernst's use of hands doing magic or science demonstrations, drawn from *La Nature:* see, for example, Ernst's *Le magicien* (1921) and the "multiplication of eggs" demonstration from *La Nature* (pp. 54–55). In *Loplop: The Artist in the Third Person,* Spies relates the importance of hands for Ernst to the fact that Ernst's father taught deaf and dumb children and was therefore expert in signage.

Vanessa sat silent and did something mysterious with her needle or her scissors. I talked egotistically, excitedly, about my own affairs no doubt. Suddenly the door opened and the long and sinister figure of Mr. Lytton Strachey stood on the threshold. He pointed his finger at a stain on Vanessa's white dress. "Semen?" he said.

Can one really say it? I thought and we burst out laughing.

—Virginia Woolf

three

Sometimes we tell each other Duchamp stories, which might surprise you since, you would reasonably point out, there is practically nothing about old Marcel that hasn't been told, already, to death. Yet if God is in the details, the endlessly ironic touches in Duchamp's narrative are also, even in their apparent irrelevance, the source of a strange exhilaration and brilliance.

Molly's favorite touch was to be found in the childhood memorabilia that Teeny had shown her, among them his grade-school primers with their hideously banal exercises, to be carried out in a kind of deadpan mechanical drawing, meant to teach the depiction of a range of utterly ordinary objects. Suddenly there opened before her a vista of these forced elaborations of the obvious: snow shovels, coffee grinders, French windows. And if so, she thought, why not combs, bird cages, urinals?

The story I told Molly was of an older, more devious Marcel, one who had already given up painting and had, since the early '20s, carried a business card identifying himself as "precision oculist." Now, fifteen years into this new profession, he found himself manning a tiny booth at the Porte de Versailles where the Inventors' Fair, called the Concours Lépine, was holding its annual, monthlong exhibition. His own invention, which he was trying to sell to that crowd streaming through the aisles of the hall, consisted of optical phonograph records. They came in sets of six, each cardboard disk printed with spiral designs on both sides, for a total of twelve different patterns. Mounted on a record player's turntable, the disks revolved soundlessly, the product of their turning a series of optical illusions, the most gripping of which was that rotation transformed their two-dimensionality into an illusory volumetric fullness that appeared to burgeon outward, toward the viewer.

A few of the disks had an anodyne, childlike quality. This was true of the one with the constantly rising Montgolfier balloon or the one with a goldfish set inside a series of eccentrically placed circles which, when turning, appeared to cup the little swimmer within an ephemeral, transparent bowl.

Others, the "Corolla" or the "Chinese Lantern," for example, had a more deceptive kind of jollity. Anyone who waited long enough to watch one of these whirl must have been somewhat startled. Because their turning produced an unstable kind of volume, appearing at certain moments to project forward but at others to recede, setting up the feeling of a thrusting motion. And further, the seemingly nonobjective pattern they bore, their quality of being a sort of decorative machine part—abstracted from gears or flywheels—was constantly dissolving into the experience of animate objects, or more precisely, part-objects. For the "Chinese Lantern" suggests a breast with slightly trembling nipple; the "Corolla" an eye staring outward. And both, in their reverse condition as concave rather than convex, produce a fairly explicit sexual reading. This is not merely my own projection. Others, other scholars in fact, have concurred.

The effect of the turning through space, one of them says, is "an oscillating action of systole and diastole, screwing and unscrewing itself in an obsessional pulsation that could be associated to copulatory movements." And a second writer agrees that "the indication of the central cavity through the volutes of the spirals clearly evokes vaginal penetration. The fact that the eye by means of optical illusion perceives an in-and-out motion, establishes at an abstract level a literal allusion to the sexual act." This transformation from inanimate and mechanical to animate and sexual is provoked by the perception that an eye is staring back at one. It is an eye that yet a third reporter has said "is animated by a rotary movement, a sort of gigantesque cyclops whose pupil serves as the screen for suggestive metamorphoses."

It's true, of course, that such comments raise the question of just what was on sale in this little booth, under the guise of optical pleasure. For the sexual promise of the illusions brings up the possibility that this "precision oculist" might have been pandering to the crowd. In fact, in the account of this episode given by his friend the novelist Henri-Pierre Roché, this issue of making a connection with the public had been one of the things on Duchamp's mind. "Several years later, in Paris," Roché remembers, "he wanted to attempt a 'direct contact' with the people. He had produced a dozen Rotoreliefs in a large edition. . . . He rented a tiny stand at the Inventions du Concours Lépine, and waited for the crowd. I went to see him there. The disks were all turning at the same time, some horizontally, others vertically, all around Duchamp, who looked like a smiling salesgirl."

"It was incredibly festive," Roché goes on, "but one would have said that the little stand was shrouded in invisibility. Not a single one of those visitors chasing after practical inventions stopped. A quick glance was all they needed to see that, between the machine to compress and burn garbage, on the left, and the instant vegetable cutter, on the right, this thing wasn't practical. I approached. Duchamp smiled and said, 'One hundred percent error. At least, it's clear.'"

And Roché cannot resist this parting dig at the crowd: "Those disks are now in demand by collectors," he says, "not by the people. But all the same the people can see them on Sundays if they go to the museum."

She has been silent through all of this. So now I ask her, because for me the story has a moral—From where we stand, in the present, as we watch the ever deepening commodification of the work of art, can we in fact recite those lines without the sneer freezing on our faces? Don't we have to focus on the impeccable Marcel Duchamp, standing there surrounded by his visual phonograph records and "smiling like a salesgirl," enacting the complete commodification of both art and artist?

But surely creating for each of us—Molly says—the most explicit of dialectical images. For how can we not be struck by both the sensuousness and strangeness of the spectacle, by the way that in the midst of the fair's automation of selling and buying there is one thing that redeems the machine by making it both a vehicle of pleasure and a medium of the look, one thing that offers to this unseeing crowd a moment of "secular illumination" by being the one thing that, silently, returns one's glance?

And were we to ask Clement Greenberg about his own description of "the look," the look that art solicits, the look that is the medium of the transaction between viewer and work? The time of that look is important, he claims, because it must be time annihilated. "With many paintings and pieces of sculpture," he has insisted, "it is as if you had to catch them by surprise in order to grasp them as wholes—their maximum being packed into the instantaneous shock of sight. Whereas if you plant yourself too firmly before looking at a picture and then gaze at it too long you are likely to end by having it merely gaze blankly back at you."

To understand works of art—"to grasp them as wholes"—is the function of a revelation whose very essence is that its all-at-onceness simply suspends the temporal dimension. And when time has not been thus suspended, reconfigured in this way into its own negation, then the trajectory of the gaze that runs between viewer and painting begins to track the dimensions of real time and real space. The viewer discovers that he or she has a body that supports this gaze, a body with feet that hurt or a back that aches, and that the picture, also embodied, is poorly lit so that its frame casts a distracting shadow over its surface now perceived as glassy with too much varnish. What Clem refers to as "the 'full meaning' of a picture—i.e., its aesthetic fact" drains out of this situation, relocated as it is in the all too real. And the result is that instead of generating an "aesthetic fact," the picture, now reified, simply returns the look, merely gazing "blankly" back at you.

It is this collapse into the dumbly physical that must be avoided. "The process of looking at a picture," therefore, "cannot be analyzed into discrete, sequential moments but only, if at all, into logical moments (though logic as such has very little to do with the experience of art)."

And what does it look like, the work of art's reach toward the "logical moment"?

Your suggestion, strange as it might seem, is drawn from the world of intellectual kitsch. You point to the pictorial diagram, to those weird attempts to chart the inner dynamic of a work, as in that peculiar book by Earle Loran called Cézanne's Compositions.

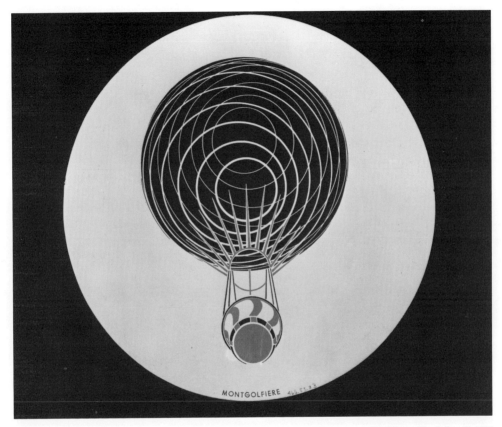

Marcel Duchamp, *Rotorelief* ("Montgolfier Balloon"), 1935.

A few of the disks had an anodyne, childlike quality . . . (p. 96)

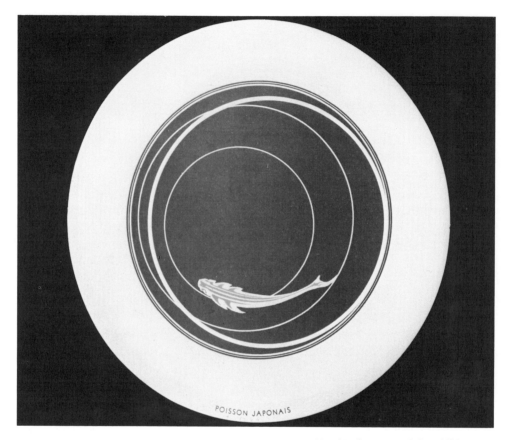

POISSON JAPONAIS

Marcel Duchamp, *Rotorelief* ("Goldfish"), 1935.

*When turning, appeared to cup the little swimmer within an ephemeral,
transparent bowl . . . (p. 96)*

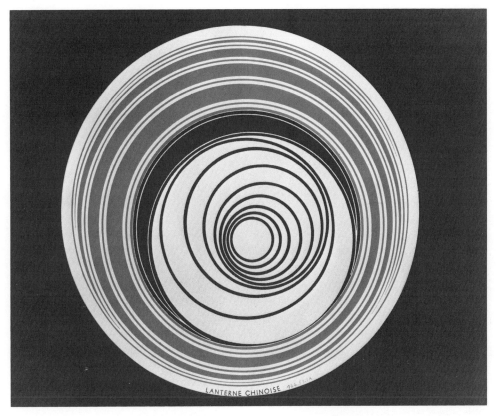

Marcel Duchamp, *Rotorelief* ("Chinese Lantern"), 1935.

A breast with slightly trembling nipple . . . (p. 96)

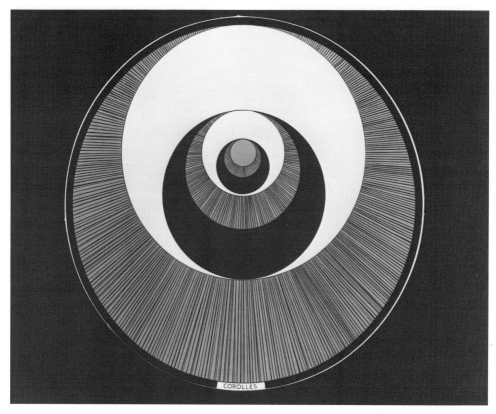

Marcel Duchamp, *Rotorelief* ("Corolles"), 1935.

"A sort of gigantesque cyclops whose pupil serves as the screen for suggestive metamorphoses". . . (p. 97)

Nothing would seem to be further from the intellectual tastes of Clement Greenberg than the pedagogical simplifications of the painter-turned-educator who set out to capture the logic of Cézanne's art through a reductive set of diagrams. We all remember them as something of a joke, the ultimate send-up of art appreciation at its most deadly earnest. The thesis of significant form had spread into the art schools and whether it was Hoffmann's "push and pull" or Berenson's "tactile values," painting was understood as having a problem to solve: how to produce the vibrancy and tension of an illusioned three-dimensional volume without violating the two-dimensional integrity (the word was unfailingly used) of the picture plane? For without that tension, so the problem ran, the painting would be nothing but linear arabesques, the flat patterns of a lifeless and meaningless decorative frieze. That tension, however, implied always running the danger of rupturing the fragile membrane of the picture surface, of puncturing it with the holes produced by a too imperious flight into distance. By the time the formal questions posed by Bloomsbury had found their way to California, 1940s art education was busy rendering the answers formulaic. And so there were Loran's bizarre graphs of Cézanne's pictures, the bodies of Madame Cézanne or of the gardener sitting with folded arms, drained of everything but a set of their now brutishly definitive silhouettes, traced for them by Loran's own hand, each element notched in turn into the overall diagram of the picture plotted by means of the same myopic contour. The whole of this pictorial map was then vectored by a series of lines and arrows intended to reveal the hidden secrets of Cézanne's construction, the logic of a drawing that could create the experience of pyramid or cone while never dropping the ball in the smooth juggling act of maintaining the continuity of the surface planes.

The bluntness of the demonstration, its presentation of the work stripped bare, its bloodlessness: none of this seemed, in 1945, to bother Greenberg, for whom, instead, these diagrams constituted simply a series of images of the logical moment, that instance of coalescence—which happens in no time at all—of a separate set of facts into a virtual unity.

So the logical moment is, then, a cognitive event, one within which this unity is produced. And although we may find Loran's diagrams arid, reductive, Greenberg seems to have found them satisfying. This love of the diagrammatic, this pleasure taken in an image of the general principle swooping down on the powerless, aimless, feckless particular and gathering it up into the stark clarity of a demonstration of the inner workings of the law, this is the frisson that reflection on the cognitive event produced in the first half of this century.

And to each his own diagram. The structuralists were in love with the Klein Group. Are in love. Who can fail to be charmed by its little motor of double negatives producing all the relations that—within its universe of possibility—are? Saussure himself, however, took the game of chess as his favorite model. It was his "image" of language's structure cut free from the real time of its evolutionary history; it was his machine for producing the logical moment. "A game of chess," he explains, "is like an artificial realization of what language offers in a natural form."

There on the grid of the chessboard each piece has a value that is not intrinsic (a knight or a rook can come in any form, any material, can be substituted for, even, by another piece if necessary). Instead its value derives from a system of oppositions between its position and that of all other pieces on the board. These values are further vested in the pieces by an absolutely invariable convention, "the set of rules that exists before a game begins and persists after each move." Since each move changes the relations between all the pieces, creating a new utterance by producing a new set of oppositions, at any moment in the game a new synchrony reigns. But each synchronous state—displayed on the board as a distinct "picture"—is utterly dissociated from the game's history, folded into the embrace of meaning only because the law resonates through its present set of relations. Listen to Saussure:

> In a game of chess any particular position has the unique characteristic of being freed from all antecedent positions; the route used in arriving there makes absolutely no difference; one who has followed the entire match has no advantage over the curious party who comes up at a critical moment to inspect the state of the game; to describe this arrangement, it is perfectly useless to recall what had just happened ten seconds previously.

And to tie this back into the linguistic reality Saussure intends it to demonstrate, he adds, "All this is equally applicable to language and sharpens the radical distinction between diachrony and synchrony. Speaking operates only on a language-state, and the changes that intervene between states have no place in either state."

The chessboard, the chess pieces, the pattern, all participate in a logic. They are, as it were, transparent to that logic, cognitively galvanized by it. They do not stare back at you "blankly," the inert, reified objects of a merely physical gaze. They are wholly "for" the subject, a subject who is

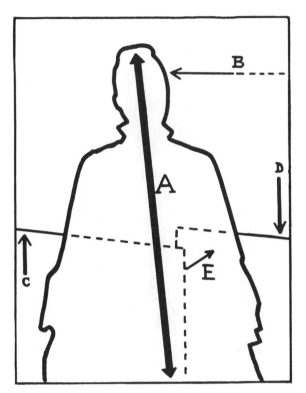

Earle Loran, diagram from *Cézanne's Compositions*.

Your suggestion, strange as it might seem, is drawn from the world of intellectual kitsch . . . (p. 98)

Earle Loran, diagram from *Cézanne's Compositions.*

The overall diagram of the picture plotted by means of the same myopic contour . . . (p. 103)

swept up into his relation to an intention to mean, who is the function of a gaze that grasps this meaning in no time at all, a gaze that in this logical moment has completely transcended the subject's body. For this gaze is "punctual," time and space reduced to the tiniest of points.

Duchamp, too, was a fanatic of chess. Yet can it be said of him that he was, like Clem, a champion of the disembodied look?

> *Fais dodo*
> *'Colas mon petit frère;*
> *Fais dodo*
> *T'auras du lolo;*
> *Maman est en haut,*
> *Qui fait du gateau;*
> *Papa est en bas,*
> *Qui fait du chocolat*
>
> —French lullaby

Mommy, as this little song from the nursery puts it, is upstairs, baking a cake; and Daddy is downstairs making some cocoa. It is a two-part arrangement that would have amused Duchamp had he known it, mapping as it does the distribution of his own *Large Glass:* Bride above and Bachelors—grinding their chocolate—below. And indeed, there is no reason he would not have known it, being, as it is, the most popular of children's lullabies in France.

No one is invoking a source here, however, another key to add to that long succession of iconographic systems that are now invoked in order to unlock the meaning of the *Glass.* Duchamp scholars are fond of images taken from alchemy or Neoplatonism, ones in which the Bride is also to be found upstairs and the Bachelors down. These images are drawn from systems of thought that will allow a higher order of meaning to come, as it were, to redeem the *Glass,* to purge it of its merely carnal connections, to raise it to a loftier, more conceptual order. If the Bride is stripped by the Bachelors, it is in order to be ritually cleansed, transfigured, sublated.

It's not, of course, that the lullaby, in displaying the program of that domestic machine laboring toward the baby's happiness, portrays a world any less systematic than that of the various metaphysical orders so often brought to bear. It's just that the signifiers through which the song operates to generate its particular meaning—doubled phonemes like *dodo* for "bed" and *lolo* for "milk"—are much closer to the object world of the body from which they sprang: like *caca,* for example. Caca, of course, does not appear in the song, except by implication. And this is because the lullaby, in its very act of projecting this milk and cake and chocolate into the rhythms of sleep, seems to stumble over its own meter and, tripping, to perform a break in the tune's order through which the body can reclaim and rescatter these objects. For its final line, by disturbing the five-syllable rhythm with the addition of a sixth, suggests—at the edge of consciousness—a substitute rendering that would restore the song's metric evenness and thereby reconstitute the slow regularity of the breath of sleep. "Qui fait du chocolat" is too long and must be hurried past by singer as well as listener; "qui fait du caca" is both rather more like it and rather more to the point.

More to the point for a Duchamp who, enamored of the body's secretions, produced work after work in their honor. He imagined a transformer, for example, that would make use of little bits of wasted energy such as "the fall of urine and excrement," or "the spill of tears," or again "the ordinary spitting of mucus or blood."

Of course it must be admitted that this Duchamp, the Duchamp of *Fountain,* and *Objet d'ard,* and *Prière de toucher,* has always been carefully segregated from the detachedly cerebral Duchamp, the one who "gave up painting for chess," the one who read seventeenth-century treatises on perspective at the Ste. Geneviève library and wrinkled his nose at abstract art because it appealed merely to the retina and not to the "gray matter." In interview after interview Duchamp made statements underscoring this opposition.

To Pierre Cabanne, for example, he characterized his attitude as "antiretinal" and therefore opposed to a preoccupation with "visual language," open instead to matters that are "conceptual." In talking to others this distinction between retinal and conceptual, or the world of material sensation and the world of ideas, would again be described as an opposition between the retina and the gray matter. He compared himself in this respect to artists of the Renaissance, saying that along with them he felt that "pure painting is not interesting in itself as an end. For me," he said, "the goal is something else, it is a combination, or at least an expression that only the gray matter can succeed in rendering."

The gray matter is what is most forcibly at stake in the game of chess, a purely conceptual interaction, shorn of visual "incident." And Duchamp's passion for chess is therefore seen as all of a piece with his stated predilection for the conceptual.

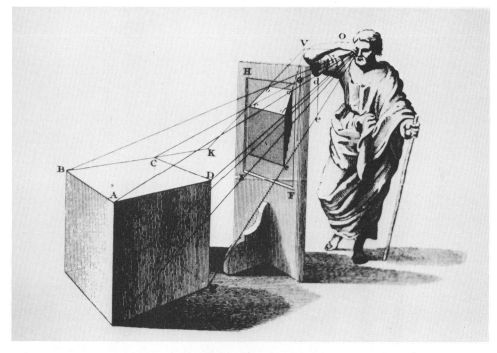

The visual cone, from B. Taylor, *New Principles of Linear Perspective* (1715).

*The theoretical identity between viewing point and vanishing point, an
identity written into the geometrical underpinnings of the system . . . (p. 113)*

Marcel Duchamp, *Etant donnés: 1° la chute d'eau, 2° le gaz d'éclairage*, 1945–1966, exterior view.

A kind of optical machine through which it is impossible not *to see . . . (p. 112)*

Gray matter is also behind the mathematical operations that undergird what the Renaissance referred to as the "legitimate construction" and we call perspective projection: that perfectly rationalized lattice of logarithmically ever more closely spaced lines that spin the two-dimensional surface into a web of virtual three-dimensionality. Duchamp's repeated references to gray matter have therefore ballasted a tradition of interpretation in which visuality on Duchamp's terms is understood as a condition of intellect, of the diagrammatic mastery of a reality disincarnated into what has been called the "purely ideal" status of the perspective image. And indeed perspective is thought to be at one and the same time the vehicle through which painting is remade into a *cosa mentale* and the historical medium that links Duchamp to both past and future. It ties him, that is, to "a family that extends from Leonardo to Seurat by way of Vermeer," even while it opens him onto the future of that completely ideational space known as the fourth dimension.

Yet for all those viewers of Duchamp's work who have ever focused on its courting of the conditions of obscenity, on its obvious connecting of the mental to the carnal—as in his notorious remark "I want to grasp things with the mind the way the penis is grasped by the vagina"—on its constant recycling of the bodily fluids by means of an infantilized corporeal machinery, on its lodging the moment of visuality right at that fold between body and world where each seems to occlude the other—as when he describes the *Bottlerack* as something that one doesn't even look at, "that one looks at *en tournant la tête*"—for this part of Duchamp's audience the destiny of vision as *idea* seems peculiar indeed. For, one would have to object, doesn't this interpretive notion of classical perspective or of the *cosa mentale* act to short-circuit that connection—forged again and again in Duchamp's world—by which vision is demonstrably hooked up to the mechanisms of desire?

And Duchamp put all of this extremely clearly in the specifications he left in 1966 for assembling *Etant donnés*, his elaborate posthumous work. For throughout those pages of instructions for how to set up and light the little diorama on which he had worked from 1946 to the time of his death, he consistently refers to the beholder who will be positioned at the viewing point of the spectacle—the peepholes drilled into the assemblage's rustic door—by a very explicit term. Voyeur, he says. Not viewer. Voyeur.

It is Sartre's chapter on "The Look" that, inadvertently of course, tells us quite a lot about Duchamp's "voyeur." For here is the passage where

Sartre, arrested in front of a door just like Duchamp's participant in the *Etant donnés*, depicts himself poised at a keyhole that has become nothing but transparent vehicle for his gaze to penetrate, a keyhole that as he says "is given as 'to be looked through close by and a little to one side.'" And if, in this position, hunched and peering, Sartre is no longer "for" himself, it is because his consciousness leaps out beyond him toward the still unseen spectacle taking place behind the as yet unbreached opacity of the door. Yet in this scenario, as we know, what comes next is not the capture of the spectacle but the interruption of the act. For the sound of footsteps announces that the gaze of someone else has taken him both by surprise and from behind.

It is as this pinioned object, this body bent over the keyhole, this carnal being trapped in the searchlight of the Other's gaze, that Sartre thickens into an object, and thus an outsider to his own eyes. For in this position he is no longer pure, transparent intentionality beamed at what is on the door's far side, but rather, simply as body caught on *this* side, he has become a self that exists on the level of all other objects of the world, a self that has suddenly become opaque to his own consciousness, a self that he therefore cannot *know* but only *be,* a self that for that reason is nothing but a pure reference to the Other. And it is a self that is defined by shame. "It is shame," Sartre writes, "which reveals to me the Other's look and myself at the end of that look. It is the shame . . . which makes me *live,* not *know* the situation of being looked at."

To be discovered at the keyhole is, thus, to be discovered as a body; it is to thicken the situation given to consciousness to include the hither space of the door, and to make the viewing body an object for consciousness. As to what kind of object, Sartre defines this only in relation to the Other— the consciousness of the one who discovers him, and in whose look he ceases totally to master his world. As for himself, this thickened, carnal object produces as the content of *his* consciousness the carnation of shame.

The voyeur that Duchamp began, in 1946, to prepare for us is both the same and different. He (or she) too is positioned at the peephole, penetrating the door of the assemblage *Etant donnés,* all attention focused through this funneling of the gaze toward the waiting display. But nothing, in this case, breaks the circuit of the gaze's connection to its object or interrupts the satisfaction of its desire. Having sought the peephole of *Etant donnés,* Duchamp's viewer has in fact entered a kind of optical machine through which it is impossible *not* to see.

Examining that optical machine, Jean-François Lyotard shows us how at one and the same time it is based on the system of classical perspective and is maliciously at work to lay bare that system's hidden assumptions. For in the *Etant donnés,* all the elements of perspective are in place, but in a strangely literal way. The role of the picture surface that slices through the visual pyramid of classical perspective is played, for example, by a brick wall, with the possibility of seeing-through that is normally a function of pictorial illusion now a matter of literally breaking down the barrier to produce a ragged opening. And the viewing and vanishing points whose normal status as antimatter derives from their condition as geometric limits, these points are similarly incarnated. For the vanishing point, or goal of vision, is manifested by the dark interior of a bodily orifice, the optically impenetrable cavity of the spread-eagled "bride," a physical rather than a geometrical limit to the reach of vision. And the viewing point is likewise a hole: thick, inelegant, material.

"The *dispositif* will be specular," Lyotard writes, referring by this to the way perspective is constructed around the theoretical identity between viewing point and vanishing point, an identity written into the geometrical underpinnings of the system in order to secure the image on the retina as a mirror of the image propagated off the object by the rays of light. "The plane of the breach," Lyotard continues, "will be that of a picture that will intersect the focal pyramids having for their summits the viewing- or peepholes. In this type of organization, the viewpoint and the vanishing point are symmetrical. Thus if it is true that the latter is the vulva, this is the specular image of the peeping eyes; such that: when these think they're seeing the vulva, they see themselves. *Con celui qui voit,*" Lyotard concludes, "He who sees is a cunt."

It could not be clearer how this viewer, caught up in a cat's cradle of identification with what he sees, is specified by Duchamp as essentially carnal. But it should be obvious as well that Duchamp's "voyeur" is also—like Sartre at his keyhole—a prey to the intervention of the Other. For Duchamp, leaving nothing up to his old buddy Chance, willed that the scene of *Etant donnés* be set within a museum, which is to say, within an unavoidably public space. And this means that the scenario of the voyeur caught by another in the very midst of taking his pleasure is never far from consciousness as one plies the peepholes of Duchamp's construction, doubly become a body aware that its rearguard is down.

When Kant displaced the space of beauty from the empirical realm to the wholly subjective one, declaring taste a function of a judgment stripped of concepts, he nonetheless preserved the public dimension of this subjectivity by decreeing that such judgments are necessarily, categorically universal. Their very logic is that they are communicable, sharable, a function of what could only be called the "universal voice." Aesthetic experience's pleasure, diverted from the exercise of desire, is channeled precisely into a reflection on the possibility of universal communicability. It is only this, Kant says in the Second Moment of the Analytic of the Beautiful, "that is to be acknowledged in the judgment of taste about the representation of the object." Doubly paradoxical, then, such experiences of the beautiful are conceived as pleasure disincarnated because without desire, and as pure individuality that can only act by assuming the assent of others.

This space of cognitive access to the universality of the language of art describes, of course, not just a theory of aesthetic judgment, but its institutional setting in the great museums that are part of the development of nineteenth- and twentieth-century culture. The museum as we know it was indeed constructed around the shared space of a sense of the visual grounded in the possibility of individual subjects forming a community. Yet it is this system of the museum that *Etant donnés* enters only to disrupt by "making it strange." For, threatened by discovery on the part of a fellow viewer, the purely cognitive subject of Kant's aesthetic experience is redefined in this setting as the subject of desire, and subjectivity itself is taken from the faculty of cognition and reinscribed in the carnal body.

Twice over, the vision of this viewer is hooked up to that glandular system that has nothing to do with the pineal connection, and everything to do with the secretions of sex and of fear. Descartes's notion of the bridge between the physical and the mental carefully preserved the autonomy of the intellect. The optic chiasma that Duchamp suggests, however, is unthinkable apart from a vision that is carnal through and through. *Con,* as they say, *celui qui voit.*

Why, she had sometimes wondered, were there so very many photographs of him playing chess? There he would be, his extraordinary profile bracketed by the dark background of the shrubbery, leaning over this or that garden table, his brow furrowed, facing off against an adversary who, like himself, could be seen looming over the little portable chess set. But then chess was part of what one remembered about him, his insistence on talking about it so that at parties for example you suddenly found yourself standing next to the fireplace deep in a conversation with him, about chess. Here is Clive Bell recounting a typical day during a visit by him to Charleston, as he contemplates the rhythms of Roger Fry's seemingly inexhaustible en-

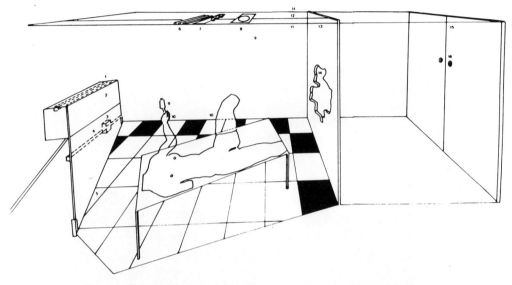

Diagram of Duchamp's *Etant donnés,* from Jean-François Lyotard, *Les TRANSformateurs DUchamp.*

"The dispositif will be specular". . . *(p. 113)*

Marcel Duchamp, *Etant donnés,* view through the door.

"Con celui qui voit". . . *(p. 113)*

ergy: ". . . back in time for an early tea so that he can drag Vanessa and Duncan to Wilmington to paint landscape; after dinner just runs through a few of Mallarmé's poems, which he is translating word for word into what he is pleased to consider blank verse; bedtime—'Oh just time for a game of chess, Julian.'"

And her Aunt Virginia had also made a considerable place for chess in her biography of Fry, remembering how he had transmitted his notion of the all-important Form to those young people of her, Angelica's, own generation by means of Mallarmé on the one hand and chess on the other. "He would make them help to translate Mallarmé," she wrote, "he would argue for hours on end with 'terrific Quaker scrupulosity and intellectual honesty'; and he would play chess, and through playing chess bring them to understand his views on aesthetics." The aesthetic views that were the very linchpin of Bloomsbury.

Which is why the idea that he cheated at chess, she thought, is so fantastic. Bunny had often spoken of how the two of them played, with Roger of course much the stronger, so that "he usually beat me fairly easily. But if I made an unexpectedly good move which put him in difficulties Roger would always try to find a way of altering the course of the game. He would pick up one of my pieces, start an exposition of what I might have done, and put the piece back on the wrong square." And to underscore how bizarre it seemed, he would wonder, "I was never quite sure how far he was aware that he cheated at chess."

With me it was a bit different, she thought, but not much, as she remembered those rare times when an inspired move of hers would put the outcome momentarily in doubt. "Oh, I don't think it was wise to move your bishop," Fry would say. "Better go there with your knight." And that, she smiled ruefully as she thought of the disarray that inevitably followed, would do the trick.

That he cheated at chess was all the more peculiar in that it was through their sense of the utter honesty of his account of his experience, his refusal to report on what he did not feel, that he held his huge audiences in the Queen's Hall so completely rapt. No matter that the work on the screen might be apparently unengaging, or that the black-and-white slide was upside-down. They were watching the greatest art critic of his or any age in the act of reacting, of allowing to well up within him in that very moment the wave of aesthetic emotion. "He added on the spur of the moment," says Virginia Woolf, "what he had just seen as if for the first time. That, perhaps, was the secret of his hold over his audience. They could see the sensation strike and form; he could lay bare the very moment of perception. So with pauses and spurts the world of spiritual reality emerged in slide after slide—in Poussin, in Chardin, in Rembrandt, in Cézanne—in its uplands and its lowlands, all connected, all somehow made whole and entire, upon the great screen in the Queen's Hall."

But at some juncture the long pointer—"trembling like the antenna of some miraculously sensitive insect," as it settled in the painting before him on this or that "rhythmical phrase"—would become rigid, still. And he would, faced with a late Cézanne landscape, speak of his bafflement, confessing that it went beyond any analysis he could make. So suddenly the lecture would, simply, stop. And as the audience that had just spent two hours looking at pictures left the hall, the most vivid picture that would remain in many minds would be "one of which the lecturer himself was unconscious—the outline of the man against the screen, an ascetic figure in evening dress who paused and pondered, and then raised his stick and pointed. That was a picture," Virginia Woolf muses, "that would remain in memory together with the rest, a rough sketch that would serve many of the audience in years to come as the portrait of a great critic, a man of profound sensibility but of exacting honesty, who, when reason could penetrate no further, broke off; but was convinced, and convinced others, that what he saw was there."

And what he saw there was a pattern, he was to explain, a pattern forged by the creative "look" that artists possess as they scan the chaotic rubble of ordinary appearances and, through an extraordinary act of selective seeing, manage to extract a series of intervals, of harmonic relationships between darks and lights, an intuition of that organic intermeshing to which could be affixed the term unity. What this look entails is, at one and the same time, utter detachment from the objects themselves—their meaning, their worth, their moral value (so much for Mr. Ruskin!)—and complete passion about the implications of form. "Almost any turn of the kaleidoscope of nature may set up in the artist this detached and impassioned vision," Fry later wrote, "and, as he contemplates the particular field of vision, the (aesthetically) chaotic and accidental conjunction of forms and colors begins to crystallize into a harmony; and as this harmony becomes clear to the artist, his actual vision becomes distorted by the emphasis of the rhythm which had been set up within him. Certain relations of directions of line become for him full of meaning; he apprehends them no longer casually or merely curiously, but passionately, and these lines *begin to be so stressed and stand out so clearly from the rest that he sees them far more distinctly than he did at first."*

This is what he wanted chess to model, she thought, the utterly disinterested, disincarnated passion of "the artist's vision."

When Lyotard speaks of the cuntishness of Duchamp's model of vision, he is sticking it of course to all those idealists who want to turn Duchamp's work into metaphysics. Among them the art historians, with their conceptual schemas built on the ideogrammatic foundation of central-point perspective. They point to the transparency of the *Large Glass:* as transparent—they declare—as a thought to the consciousness that thinks it. And they point to the insistence of the classical perspective through which the *Glass*'s objects are projected.

Balls, says Lyotard, quoting Duchamp.

The visuality Duchamp proposes, he says, is carnal, not conceptual. It views the body as a psychophysiological system. Using as proof Duchamp's statement that the *Glass* is intended to "isolate the sign of accordance between a state of rest" and a series of possible facts, Lyotard says, "Now, the *Glass* is indeed this isolated sign, this immobile sensitive surface (the retina) onto which the diverse facts of the account come to be inscribed according to the possibilities scrupulously chosen by Duchamp and such that the viewer will literally have nothing to see if he disregards them." And, going even further than this, Lyotard characterizes the *Glass* as a display, not of the facts of the event but of the physiological surfaces onto which they are registered. Not only retina but also cortex. "What the viewer sees on the *Glass*," he concludes, "is the eye and even the brain in the process of forming its objects; he sees the images of these imprinting the retina and the cortex according to the laws of (de)formation that are inherent to each and that organize the screen of glass. . . . The *Large Glass,* being the film, makes visible the conditions of impression that reign at the interior of the optical chamber."

And, indeed, there is no want of evidence on the *Glass* itself that it must be seen as a surface of impression. For many of the signs it bears are organized as traces, deposited there like footprints left in sand, or the rings that icy glasses leave on tables. They are imprints rather than images, striking a receptive surface—like that of nervous tissue: the Sieves with their residues of dust, the Oculist Witnesses with their ribbons of mirror, the Draft Pistons with their indexically deformed contours.

Lyotard would, in fact, be amused by all those features of the *Glass* one could show him that allude to the neurophysiology of the optic track. The sieves, for example, through which the illuminating gas is processed are referred to in Duchamp's writing as "cones," and he is explicit that it is in the labyrinthine passage through these cones that a transformation of the gas takes place. For what he calls the "spangles of the illuminating gas"—which might be interpreted here as light in its form as a pulsion from the visible band of the electromagnetic spectrum hitting the retinal field—these spangles get "straightened out" as they move through the sieves; and due to this straightening, "they lose their sense of up and down." It was this very fact—that the image on the retina is inverted with respect to reality, top and bottom, right and left—that stood for the larger problem facing late nineteenth-century optics, namely, how information gets from eye to brain. At the heart of this inquiry into vision was the problem of just how the (geometrical) optical display, focused by the lens of the eye onto the retina, is transformed to an entirely different order of signal. For it is not a "picture" that goes to the higher neurological centers. It is another form of information through which the body's real orientation to the world is synthesized. Duchamp's words place both illuminating gas and sieves (or what he calls the "*labyrinth of the 3 directions*") within the field of this problem. "The spangles dazed by this progressive turning," he writes, "imperceptibly lose . . . their *designation* of left, right, up, down, etc., lose their awareness of position." But in relation to this loss, Duchamp adds the qualification "*provisionally*" for, as he reminds himself, "they will find it again later," that later being suggestive of the level of cortical synthesis.

Other terms of the neuro-optical system can also be set in relation to the *Glass*. Electricity, the form of the body's nerve signals, is continually invoked by the notes describing the Bachelor Apparatus. But even more explicitly, in the late drawing *Cols alités* where Duchamp returns to the *Glass*, we are shown a telegraph pole on the right, hooked up to the apparatus itself, telegraphy having served as a useful analogy in nineteenth-century discussions of nerve transmission, as in Helmholtz's remark: "The nerve fibers have been often compared with telegraphic wires traversing a country, and the comparison is well fitted to illustrate this striking and important peculiarity of their mode of action."

Lyotard is clear, however, about the fruitlessness of using physiological optics as a "key" to unlock the mysteries of the *Glass*, the work's transcendental signified uncovered at last. We could, he imagines, go on multiplying the symptoms through which the *Large Glass* shares in

Marcel Duchamp, *La Mariée mise à nu par ses célibataires, même*
(Le grand verre), 1915–1923.

"The Large Glass, *being the film, makes visible the conditions of impression*
that reign at the interior of the optical chamber". . . *(p. 119)*

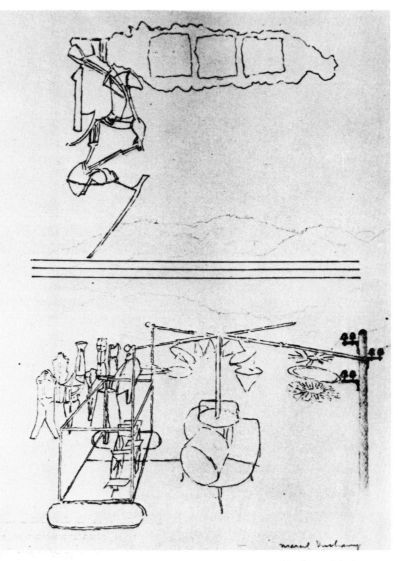

Marcel Duchamp, *Cols alités*, 1959.

"The nerve fibers have been often compared with telegraphic wires traversing a country". . . (p. 120)

physiological optics' understanding of embodied vision. But to substitute the laws of neurophysiology for any of those other master codes—such as the practices of alchemy, or the rituals of courtly love, or the incestuous secrets of a possible psychobiography, or the rules of *n*-dimensional geometry—codes that have been proposed as a hermeneutic for Duchamp's work, is not his game. To the contrary. It's the physics of vision he wants to stress, not its metaphysics. This is why the persistence of physiological optics at work within Duchamp's thinking would not surprise him.

Lyotard is right, of course. The whole of Precision Optics that Duchamp went on to embrace—the Rotoreliefs *and the* Rotary Demisphere *but also stereoscopy and anaglyphy as well as the pure exercise in simultaneous contrast of* Coeur volant—*all of this reaches back into the experimental and theoretical situation of the psychophysiology of vision. But here is where the art historians will try to take their revenge.*

Balls, indeed—they will answer, quoting Duchamp. Their man Duchamp has always vehemently rejected the "retinal," heaping invective on "retinal painting." And what could retinal painting be if not the specific turn that painting took in the 1870s in the grip of the discoveries of Helmholtz and Chevreul, the discoveries promulgated by Charles Blanc and Ogden Rood?

Indeed, Duchamp had always been clear that he had impressionism in mind as a premier example of the retinal. "Since the advent of impressionism," he explained, "visual productions stop at the retina. Impressionism, fauvism, cubism, abstraction, it's always a matter of retinal painting. Their physical preoccupations: the reactions of colors, etc., put the reactions of the gray matter in the background. This doesn't apply to all the protagonists of these movements. Certain of them have passed beyond the retina. The great merit of surrealism is to have tried to rid itself of retinal satisfaction, of the 'arrest at the retina.' I don't want to imply that it is necessary to reintroduce anecdote into painting," Duchamp then cautions. "Some men like Seurat or like Mondrian were not retinalists, even in wholly seeming to be so."

Duchamp's attack on the whole system of the visual as that is put into place by mainstream modernism—the line that moves from impressionism to abstraction by way of cubism—has its exceptions, then, "like Seurat or like Mondrian." For him they are "not retinalists," even though Seurat's is the most flagrant case of the application of the principles of modern optics to paintings. So Duchamp's rejection was not simply a wholesale condemnation of all those aspects of science that modernism had thought

123

three

to appropriate. Rather, what he objects to is the "arrêt à la rétine," the stopping of the analytic process at the retina, the making of the interactions between the nerve endings—their coordinated stimulation and innervation—a kind of self-sufficient or autonomous realm of activity. Within the development of modernist painting, the consequence of this analysis was the reification of the retinal surface and the conviction that by knowing the laws of its interactive relationships, one possessed the algorithm of sight. The mapping of the retinal field onto the modernist pictorial plane, with the positivist expectation that the laws of the one would legislate and underwrite the autonomy of the operations of the other, is typical of the form in which high modernism established and then fetishized an autonomous realm of the visual.

This is the logic we hear, for example, in Delaunay's assertions that the laws of simultaneous contrast within the eye and the laws of painting are one and the same. "Color," he frequently declared, "colors with their laws, their contrasts, their slow vibrations in relation to the fast or extra-fast colors, their interval. All these relations form the foundation of a painting that is no longer imitative, but creative through the technique itself." What makes this possible, he would reiterate, is a scientifically wrought understanding of "simultaneous contrast, [of the] creation of profundity by means of complementary and dissonant colors, which give volume direction. . . . To create," he insists, "is to produce new unities with the help of new laws."

It was the idea of the self-sufficiency and the closed logic of this newly conceived retino-pictorial surface that gave a program to early abstract painting such as Delaunay's and a coherence to much of modernist theory. It is this logic that refuses to "go beyond" the retina to the gray matter, and it is to this refusal that Duchamp objects.

But the gray matter—and here Lyotard really has to insist—though it undoubtedly refers to the cerebral cortex, does not thereby invoke a disembodied faculty of cognition or reflection, does not propose the transcendental ego's relation to its sensory field. The cerebral cortex is not above the body in an ideal or ideated remove; it is, instead, *of* the body, such that the reflex arc of which it is part connects it to a whole field of stimuli between which it cannot distinguish. These stimuli may come from outside the body, as in the case of normal perception, but they may also erupt internally, giving rise, for example, to what Goethe celebrated as "physiological colors," or those sensations of vision that are generated entirely by the viewer's body. The production of sensory stimulation from within the body's own field, the optical system's porousness to the operations of its internal organs, this fact forever undermines the idea of vision's transparency to itself. Instead of that transparency there now arises the density and opacity of the viewing subject as the very precondition of his access to sight.

Duchamp's view of the gray matter—that part that exists beyond the retina—cannot be separated from other kinds of organic activity within the physical body. For to do so would leave one, for example, with no way of interpreting the visual activity projected within the domain of the Bride in the upper half of the *Large Glass*. Duchamp describes the Bride's blossoming—which is to say the orgasmic event toward which the whole mechanism of the *Glass* is laboring—as an ellipse with two foci, an ellipse through which the circuitry of the Bachelor Machine connects to that of the Bride. In so doing he seems to be describing what neurophysiology calls reflex arcs, by which the stimulation of sensory receptors is transferred to the brain. The first of the foci, which he designates as the stripping by the Bachelors, seems to relate to the perceptual part of the arc he is mapping: the Bride is what the Bachelors see. But the second focus, the Bride's "voluntarily imagined blossoming," as she fantasizes the Bachelors' look, connects the reflex arc of this ellipse to a source of the impulse to be found in the organs of the Bride, an organ that Duchamp says "is activated by the love gasoline, a secretion of the Bride's sexual glands and by the electric sparks of the stripping."

If the mechanism of the *Large Glass* obeys Duchamp's dictum of "going beyond" the retina, it does so not to achieve the condition of vision's transparency to itself—which is suggested by the model of classical perspective when applied to the *Glass*—but rather, quite obviously, to arrive at the threshold of desire-in-vision, which is to say to construct vision itself within the opacity of the organs and the invisibility of the unconscious.

I make it a point never to stay in a room with a Christian.
—James Strachey

The lines in Bloomsbury were clearly drawn, Stephen Spender explained. "Not to regard the French Impressionist and Post-Impressionist painters as sacrosanct, not to be an agnostic and in politics a Liberal with Socialist leanings, was to put oneself outside Bloomsbury."

But Keynes makes it clear, in his own accounts of Bloomsbury, that agnostic or not, what gripped them all with inexplicable intensity was nonetheless a kind of religion. The religion was acknowledged as Moorism, by those undergraduates at Cambridge for whom the appearance of G. E. Moore's Principia Ethica *in 1903 struck with the force of revelation. Keynes gives its outlines:*

> Nothing mattered except states of mind, our own and other people's of course, but chiefly our own. These states of mind were not associated with action or achievement or with consequences. They consisted in timeless, passionate states of contemplation and communion, largely unattached to 'before' and 'after'. Their value depended, in accordance with the principle of organic unity, on the state of affairs as a whole which could not be usefully analyzed into parts.

And what sorts of subjects were appropriate to this passionate contemplation and communion? There were, he says, three: first, a beloved person; second, beauty; third, truth. "One's prime objects in life," he writes, "were love, the creation and enjoyment of aesthetic experience and the pursuit of knowledge."

Roger Fry, the Bloomsburian who had not gone to Cambridge, was always vocal in attacking Moorism. But this, Leonard Woolf insists, only showed he was obsessed with it. Underneath it all, Fry too was a Moorist. And indeed, how could it be otherwise? The certainty about the aesthetic state as one of man's highest achievements. The insistence that it "is unconditioned by considerations of space or time." The continually renewed visits to Europe's great museums to insure that the experience would occur in a perpetual present, a communion with the work undimmed by the deadening intervention of memory. As he writes to Virginia: "I spent the afternoon in the Louvre. I tried to forget all my ideas and theories and to look at everything as though I'd never seen it before. . . . It's only so that one can make discoveries. . . . Each work must be a new and a nameless experience."

The fervor of that "must," of that search for purity. The insistence that nothing frivolous or irrelevant should intervene. Frances Partridge tells of her youthful adoration of Roger Fry: "I remember how in the train he explained to us"—she is traveling with Julia Strachey—"in his beautiful deep voice why it was wicked to like peacock blue."

But the idea that there was anything religious about their ardor would have been furiously rejected by them at the time, by Fry as well as the other members of Bloomsbury. They thought of their contemplation as entirely rational, scientific, the separation of experience into logical moments. "Like any other branch of science," Keynes points out, "it was nothing more than the application of logic and rational analysis to the material presented as sense-data. Our apprehension of good was exactly the same as our apprehension of green." But their method of analyzing experience he calls "extravagantly scholastic." He gives a sample of the discussions:

> If A was in love with B and believed that B reciprocated his feelings, whereas in fact B did not, but was in love with C, the state of affairs was certainly not so good as it would have been if A had been right, but was it worse or better than it would become if A discovered his mistake? If A was in love with B under a misapprehension as to B's qualities, was this better or worse than A's not being in love at all? If A was in love with B because A's spectacles were not strong enough to see B's complexion, did this altogether, or partly, destroy the value of A's state of mind?

Keynes is continually struck by the gait of Moore's reflection, of its utter obliviousness to the character of the life of action. "He was existing in a timeless ecstasy," Keynes says. "His way of translating his own particular emotions of the moment into the language of generalized abstraction is a charming and beautiful comedy. Do you remember the passage in which he discusses whether, granting that it is mental qualities which one should chiefly love, it is important that the beloved person should also be good-looking?—'It is, indeed, very difficult to imagine,'" Keynes quotes Moore, "'what the cognition of mental qualities alone, unaccompanied by any corporeal expression, would be like; and, in so far as we succeed in making this abstraction, the whole considered certainly appears to have less value. I therefore conclude that the importance of an admiration of admirable mental qualities lies chiefly in the immense superiority of a whole, in which it forms a part, to one in which it is absent, and not in any high degree of intrinsic value which it possesses by itself.'

"The New Testament," Keynes smiles, "is a handbook for politicians compared with the unworldliness of Moore's chapter on 'The Ideal.'"

Combined with this unworldliness there was also a refusal of pleasure, or rather, a denial—religious indeed—that pleasure could be serious. "In our prime, pleasure was nowhere. It was the general view that pleasure had nothing to do with the case and, on the whole, a pleasant state of mind lay under grave suspicion of lacking intensity and passion."

Intensity. Passion. Seriousness. It was all in the service of these completely Puritanical emotions.

—Of these completely adolescent emotions.

And like every other form of faith, "knowing that . . ." in Bloomsbury came down to a matter of direct inspection of one's own experience; it was a question of unanalyzable intuition that would admit of no argument. It could only be voiced with appropriate conviction. This alone would silence one's interlocutor. Conviction rang out in tones of complete absence of doubt and total assumption of infallibility. "Moore at this time was a master of this method—greeting one's remarks with a gasp of incredulity— Do you *really* think *that, and expression of face as if to hear such a thing said reduced him to a state of wonder verging on imbecility."*

The eye that surveys the inner space of experience, analyzing it into its rationally differentiated parts, is an eye born of seventeenth-century epistemology and the particular apparatus that was frequently used as its model: the camera obscura. Beaming light through a pinhole into a darkened room and focusing that light on the wall opposite, the camera obscura allowed the observer—whether it was Newton for his *Optics* or Descartes for his *Dioptrique*—to view that plane as something independent of his own powers of synthesis, something that he, as a detached subject, could therefore observe. It was due to this structural disconnection between plane of focus and observing subject that the camera obscura came to function as a model for the "classical" subject of knowledge. Richard Rorty, for example, characterizes both Descartes's and Locke's use of this model in terms of "the conception of the human mind as an inner space in which both pains and clear and distinct ideas passed in review before an Inner Eye. . . . The novelty was the notion of a single inner space in which bodily and perceptual sensations . . . were objects of quasi-observation."

Insofar as this epistemic subject is the observer of a projection that occurs within a field conceived as being exterior to "himself," he is a knowing subject independent of a body. The unified space of order he surveys is never thought of as something that could be affected by his own sensory apparatus, never seen as dependent on his bodily subjectivity. With the close of the eighteenth century, however, the camera obscura ceased to function as a pertinent model of vision. For if in his *Farbenlehre* (1810) Goethe reassembles the elements of the darkened room, the ray of light, and the plane of focus, it is only to direct the subject immediately to close off the opening so that the phenomenon of the afterimage might appear.

Marcel Duchamp, *Rotary Demisphere (Precision Optics)*, 1925.

As if this, perhaps the most widely disseminated manual on optical color, had already presented blueprints . . . (p. 135)

Wheatstone stereoscope, 1830.

"The relation of observer to image is no longer to an object quantified in relation to a position in space, but rather to two dissimilar images whose position simulates the anatomical structure of the observer's body"... (p. 134)

Marcel Duchamp, *Handmade Stereopticon Slide*, 1918–1919.

The effect of viewing the figure through a stereoscope and the uncannily dramatic illusion of the result . . . (p. 134)

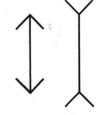

The Müller-Lyer illusion.

When it had to confront its own peculiar laboratory rat: the optical
illusion . . . (p. 137)

With this severing of the dark room's relation to the perceptual field, Goethe initiates the study of a physiology—and no longer an optics—of vision, a physiology that now understands the body of the viewer as the active producer of optical experience. Color, which can simply be produced by electrical stimulation of the optic nerve, is henceforth disjoined from a specifically spatial referent. Color, the form of the body's registration of light, is thus conceived as always potentially "atopic" so that the natural sign's necessary connection to the visual field can no longer be maintained. And now, fully embedded within the nervous weft of the body's tissues, color comes to be understood as well as something subject to the temporality of the nervous system itself, to its access to fatigue, to its necessary rhythm of innervation, to that which causes color to ebb and flow within experience in an infinitely mutable evanescence.

In taking over from the camera obscura as conveyor of the image, the body, solid and dense, becomes instead producer of that image, a producer that must forge a perception of the real from a field of scattered signs. "None of our sensations," Helmholtz explained in 1867, "give us anything more than 'signs' for external objects and movements," so that what we call seeing is really a matter of learning "how to interpret these signs by means of experience and practice." With regard to the signs provided by retinal excitation, he added, "It is not at all necessary to suppose any kind of correspondence between these local signs and the actual differences of locality [in the empirical field] which they signify."

Typically, in this lecture presenting "The Recent Progress of the Theory of Vision," Helmholtz would bring these facts home by the example of the stereoscope's capacity to use two flat pictures to simulate, with uncanny convincingness, the depth perception of normal binocular vision. What the stereoscope demonstrates, Helmholtz says, is that "two distinct sensations are transmitted from the two eyes, and reach the consciousness at the same time and without coalescing; that accordingly the combination of these two sensations into the single picture of the external world of which we are conscious in ordinary vision is not produced by any anatomical mechanism of sensation, but by a mental act."

The specific stereoscopic instrument to which Helmholtz refers his audience could not make his point more graphically. For the Wheatstone stereoscope, a product of physiological research in the 1830s, was constructed to produce its experience of depth in a way that proved to be much more powerful than later devices such as the Holmes or Brewster stereoscopes, a way, indeed, that Duchamp would later capture by coining the term "mirrorique." In the Wheatstone apparatus the viewer would actually look—each with one eye—at two mirrors set at a 90-degree angle to one another onto which would be reflected the two slightly divergent images, these held in slots at the sides of the device such that they were actually parallel to his line of sight and totally out of his field of vision. In this way the powerful impression of the three-dimensional array opening up "before" him would in fact be a function of two flat images that, like a strange pair of earmuffs, actually flanked his head.

Nothing could more effectively shatter the idea projected by the camera obscura model, in which the relationship between viewer and world is pictured as fundamentally scenic, than this literal dispersal of the stimulus field. "The stereoscopic spectator," Jonathan Crary writes,

> sees neither the identity of a copy nor the coherence guaranteed by the frame of a window. Rather, what appears is the technical reconstitution of an already reproduced world fragmented into *two* nonidentical models, models that precede any experience of their subsequent experience as unified or tangible. It is a radical repositioning of the observer's relation to visual representation. . . . The stereoscope signals an eradication of "the point of view" around which, for several centuries, meanings had been assigned reciprocally to an observer and the object of his or her vision. There is no longer the possibility of perspective under such a technique of beholding. The relation of observer to image is no longer to an object quantified in relation to a position in space, but rather to two dissimilar images whose position simulates the anatomical structure of the observer's body.

Lyotard picks up Duchamp's *Handmade Stereopticon Slide*. The art historians who want to construct a conceptualist Duchamp, a Duchamp of the *cosa mentale,* a Duchamp descended from Leonardo by way of Vermeer—from Renaissance perspective, that is, by way of the camera obscura—fasten on the two prisms penciled in against the photographic background of sea and sky. They imagine the effect of viewing the figure through a stereoscope and the uncannily dramatic illusion of the result. The resulting sense of volume—they say—which will endow this rickety figure with the formal majesty of a Platonic solid, will not be a product of the painter's art; it will happen in the viewer's brain, a function of the gray matter. It will short-circuit the physical site of mere phenomena to

134
three

exfoliate within the domain of Mind. But Lyotard sees the *Slide* as just one more symptom of Duchamp's mounting concern with the physiology of seeing, a concern that would lead to the fifteen-year production of Precision Optics.

Indeed the devices Duchamp fashioned to pursue this interest look uncannily like illustrations from a book on psychophysiological research. O. N. Rood's *Modern Chromatics* shows pedestals on which to mount the Maxwell's disks whose turning would produce the all-important optical mixing and subjective color. It is as if this, perhaps the most widely disseminated manual on optical color, had already presented blueprints for the *Rotary Demisphere* or the *Disks Bearing Spirals*. Duchamp himself underscores this. The illusion of three-dimensionality projected by his disks will be achieved, he says, "not with a complicated machine and a complex technology, but in the eyes of the spectator, by a psychophysiological process."

In the laboratory of the physiologist the spinning disks will not, however, flower into an erotics of three-dimensional illusion. The optical mixture that simulates the luminous impact of perceived color will not erupt into those disturbingly organlike figures of Duchamp's Precision Optics, figures whose pulsing appearance and disappearance underscores the way in which they are the events of a *false* perception. For unlike Maxwell's turning disks, Duchamp's are intent on addressing vision's relation to desire. And thus illusion will be used by him as a lever on the operations of the unconscious in vision.

That the erotic theater of Duchamp's Precision Optics in all its various forms is staged within the space of optical illusion places this enterprise at a kind of threshold or bridge moment between a nineteenth-century psychophysiological theory of vision and a later, psychoanalytic one. For the phenomenon of the optical illusion was an important, because troubling, issue within the associationist explanatory model to which physiological optics had recourse. Helmholtz's famous positing of "unconscious inference" as the psychological ground of all perception—unconscious inference being a process of subconscious, inductive reasoning from the basis of past experience—was continually brought up short by the obvious exception of the optical illusions. "An objection to the Empirical Theory of Vision," he admitted, "might be found in the fact that illusions of the senses are possible; for if we have learnt the meaning of our sensations from experience, they ought always to agree with experience." The possibility of false inductions rendered by these "unconscious judgments" urgently needed to be accounted for if the theory were to be viable.

Attempts to provide purely physiological explanations having failed, Helmholtz had recourse to an associationist psychological one. "The explanation of the possibility of illusions," he maintained, "lies in the fact that we transfer the notions of external objects, which would be correct under normal conditions, to cases in which unusual circumstances have altered the retinal pictures." Specifically, in the case of those famous optical illusions spawned by physiological research's attempts to solve the perceptual puzzle—the Müller-Lyer illusion, the Ponzo illusion, the Zöllner or Hering illusions—unconscious inference reasons from the inappropriate application of perspective cues. Memory is seen as three-dimensionally contextualizing these figures so that in the acute-arrow part of the Müller-Lyer pair, for example, what is supplied through association is the past experience of retinal images obtained when the vertical line is the closest part of a three-dimensional figure, such as the edge of a building nearest the observer; while for the obtuse-arrow half, the context provided refers to images projected when the vertical line is the most distant part, such as the far corner of a room in which the viewer stands. The Ponzo figure, sometimes called the railroad track illusion, is similarly referred to the mistaken inference of perspective convergence and the resultant miscuing of the viewer with regard to relative size.

The fact that the physiologist Helmholtz breathed the word "unconscious" into the discourse of empirical science raised a storm of protest that would dog him all his life. But for Sartre, later assessing the theoretical grounds of the associationist psychology Helmholtz was advocating, it was obvious that such an explanatory model would be utterly incoherent did it not posit (no matter how covertly) an unconscious. The memory image sitting in the brain below the threshold of consciousness, a sensory content waiting to be revived and newly animated by thought, was, Sartre maintained, not only the very picture of the unconscious, but as such it was theoretically untenable. Sartre's famous rejection of the concept of the unconscious applied not only to the Freudian version but to the associationist one as well. Whereas, he held, there can be only two types of things: the in-itself of objects or the for-itself of consciousness; the idea of the unconscious posits the ontologically impossible condition of an in-and-for-itself. There can be nothing *in* consciousness that is unavailable to it, nothing, that is, that is not already in the *form* of thought. Once thought is "hypostatized and hardened into the notion of an unconscious," Sartre argued, "such thought is no longer accessible to itself."

Although Sartre insisted that there was no distinction to be drawn between the unconscious of perceptual psychology and that of psychoanalysis (and indeed the former's "laws of association" had already put in place the relations of metaphor and metonymy, of condensation and displacement, long before Freud availed himself of these terms), associationism obviously veers off from psychoanalysis in that it posits no mechanism of repression. The unconscious on which Helmholtz's theory of vision relies is, like that of associationism in general, a store of memory, and thus a reserve of consciousness. It was psychoanalysis that would view the unconscious as divisive, as the turbulent source of a conflict with consciousness. The only point of recognition within associationist theory that consciousness might be shot through by unconscious conflict, and this at the very heart of perception, was when it had to confront its own peculiar laboratory rat: the optical illusion. And there it found itself staring at something like an "optical unconscious."

It is in that languidly unreeling pulsation, that hypnotically erotic, visual throb of Duchamp's Precision Optics, that one encounters the *body* of physiological optics' seeing fully enmeshed in the temporal dimension of nervous life, as it is also fully awash in optical illusion's "false induction." But it is here, as well, that one connects to this body as the site of libidinal pressure on the visual organ, so that the pulse of desire is simultaneously felt as the beat of repression.

The rhythm of the turning disks is the rhythm of substitution as, at an iconic level, various organs replace one another in an utterly circular associative chain. First there is the disk as eye; then it appears as breast; this then gives way to the fictive presence of a uterine cavity and the implication of sexual penetration. And within this pulse, as it carries one from part-object to part-object, advancing and receding through the illusion of this three-dimensional space, there is also a hint of the persecutory threat that the object poses for the viewer, a threat carried by the very metamorphic rhythm itself, as its constant thrusting of the form into a state of dissolve brings on the experience of formlessness, seeming to overwhelm the once-bounded object with the condition of the *informe*.

There was a dish of spring onions on the table. Julia [Strachey] said suddenly: "What are those little long things some people have got?" [Dora] Carrington: "Those mean they are males, dear."
　　　　—Frances Partridge, 1927

Angelica Garnett is remembering Roger Fry standing alone before the crowd that fills the Queen's Hall. It is a London winter and the great room

*seems filled with a greenish mist. People snuffle and cough in the cold.
And there is nothing to entertain them, as her Aunt Virginia says, "but a
gentleman in evening dress with a long stick in his hand in front of a
cadaverous sheet."*

*This is not, as we know, a lecture in medicine. The sheet will not be
removed to reveal a corpse into the hidden, formless depths of which the
demonstration will probe. The cadaverous sheet, white, amorphous, will
serve instead as the background for a projected image. It is to this image,
floating above the sheet, that the stick will point, as it releases the outlines
of figure against the formlessness of ground. Probing the image with this
vision that does not serve the body—indeed, "blasphemes" against it—the
eye of which this stick is the prolongation is searching for the purest
manifestation of form. "He had only to point to a passage in a picture,"
a friend tells of these evenings, "and to murmur the word 'plasticity' and
a magical atmosphere was created."*

*Or was it a religious atmosphere? Virginia Woolf understood Fry as "prais-
ing a new kind of saint—the artist who leads his laborious life indifferent
to the world's praise or blame," a saint whose punishment for pride would
be to find himself outcast, "cut off from the chief source of his inspiration."
Grace, indeed. No revelation without faith. Fry came from Quaker stock.
A fact to which she refers when she remarks, "No Fry among all the
generations of Frys could have spoken with greater fervor of the claims of
the spirit, or invoked doom with more severity. But then, 'Slide, please,'
he said. And there was the picture . . ."*

*There was the picture. With Fry's vision mastering it, releasing form from
the ground of the white sheet, revealing its outlines with his long stick.*

*And what had she said about the figure Fry himself made standing in front
of the sheet? She had said that for his audience this was perhaps the most
impressive outline of all, adding that it was, however, a figure of which
Fry himself was unconscious.*

*This eye placed in front of the projected image is attached to a body.
Indeed it is this body that blocks the light. But Fry, an absence in his own
field of vision, was oblivious of his body. It was an obliviousness that was
part of his ethos, issuing in such symptomatic behavior as his mode of
dress, described by a pained Clive Bell. The classically tailored suits worn
with outlandish ties and hunting shoes. The peculiar hats. Virginia Woolf
is struck by this void in the center of Fry's visual field. "Only one subject
seemed to escape his insatiable curiosity," she says, "and that was himself.*

*Analysis seemed to stop short there." The eye probes the background,
finding form; but there persists "this lack of interest in the central figure."*

*Fry places himself in front of the projection screen as he places himself
before the chessboard. An eye without a body. Pure giver of form. Pure
operation of the law. Pure phallus.*

*Sartre places himself in front of the door with the keyhole and understands
himself as figure against ground, figure, that is, in the eyes of the other
who observes him, who catches him in the act. And in this moment, as
Sartre fails to coalesce into figure* for *himself, he watches in dismay as
he becomes merely ground. Ground against ground. The amorphe. The
non-form.*

*He reaches for the term that will capture this sense of himself as embodied
watcher, as voyeur who is now leaching away from this* for *himself into a
nonarticulated surround. The term he uses is "hemorrhaging." He is bleed-
ing away from "himself." And thus, quite inadvertently, he gives to this
formlessness if not a shape, for that is impossible, at least a gender. In this
surrender of mastery he is celui qui voit qui est con.*

Writing about "psychogenic visual disturbance" in 1910, Freud speaks of
the various bodily organs' accessibility to both the sexual and the ego
instincts: "Sexual pleasure is not connected only with the function of the
genitals; the mouth serves for kissing as well as for eating and speaking,
the eyes perceive not only those modifications in the external world which
are of import for the preservation of life, but also the attributes of objects
by means of which these may be exalted as objects of erotic selection."
The problem for the organ can arise when there is a struggle between these
two instincts and "a repression is set up on the part of the ego against the
sexual component-instinct in question." Applying this to the eye and the
faculty of vision, Freud continues, "If the sexual component-instinct which
makes use of sight—the sexual 'lust of the eye'—has drawn down upon
itself, through its exorbitant demands, some retaliatory measure from the
side of the ego-instincts, so that the ideas which represent the content of
its strivings are subject to repression and withheld from consciousness, the
general relation of the eye and the faculty of vision to the ego and to
consciousness is radically disturbed." The result of repression is then, on
the one hand, the creation of substitute formations at the level of the libido
and, on the other, the onset of reaction formation within the operations
of the ego.

The sequence of substitutions within Precision Optics and the sense of perceptual undecidability projected through the object's condition as a state of perpetual disappearance, all this rehearses the Freudian scenario of the unavailability of what is repressed and the structural insatiability of desire. For desire-in-vision is formed not through the unified moment of visual simultaneity of the camera obscura's optical display, but through the temporal arc of the body's fibers. It is an effect of the two-step through which the object is eroticized. Freud's theory of this erotic investment of the object (or anaclisis), as set forth by Jean Laplanche, accounts among other things for the scopophilic impulse. It is a theory of the two-step.

According to the anaclitic model, all sexual instincts lean on the self-preservative or ego instincts, but they only come to do so at a second moment, always a beat after the self-preservative impulse. Thus the baby sucks out of a need for sustenance, and in the course of gratifying that need receives pleasure as well. And desire occurs at this second moment, as the longing to repeat the first one understood not as milk but as pleasure, understood, that is, *as* the satisfaction of desire. Thus it searches for an object of original satisfaction where there is none. There is only milk, which can satisfy the need, but cannot satisfy the desire, since it has become something that the little hiccup of substitution will always produce as insufficient. What this model clarifies is the way the need can be satisfied, while the desire cannot.

To relate this psychoanalytic model of desire's longing for a lost origin and a structurally irretrievable object to the experience of Precision Optics is to try to capture the effect of this projection of desire into the field of vision. It is also to hold onto that field as something that is both carnally constituted and, through the activity of the unconscious, is the permanent domain of a kind of opacity, or of a visibility invisible to itself. That oscillation between the transparent and the opaque, an oscillation that seems to operate in Duchamp's work at all the levels of his practice, is revealed here, I would say, as the very precondition of any visual activity at all.

There is no way to concentrate on the threshold of vision, to capture something *en tournant la tête,* without siting vision in the body and positioning that body, in turn, within the grip of desire. Vision is then caught up within the meshes of projection and identification, within the specularity of substitution that is also a search for an origin lost. *Con,* as they say, *celui qui voit.*

Fry's vision was never, for one moment, stilled, she told them. He was always looking, in the secure knowledge that his look, exactly because it was so temporally detached, would redeem what it saw. "Everything was drawn in, assimilated, investigated," she said. The intelligence, the formalism of his vision, Virginia Woolf explained, "reached out and laid hold of every trifle—a new stitch, a zip-fastener, a shadow on the ceiling. Each must be investigated, each must be examined, as if by rescuing such trifles from mystery he could grasp life tighter and make it yield one more drop of rational and civilized enjoyment."

—A new stitch, a zip-fastener, a shadow on the ceiling. Fry? But why not Duchamp? Who more than he had reached out for the zip-fastener, the shadow on the ceiling, and declared them art?

The hierarchy of Fry's vision, of Bloomsbury's vision, of Formalism's vision, works this way. The body exerts its demands. For nurture; for comfort. The eye accommodates those demands by routinizing vision, by achieving a glance that can determine in an instant the purpose to which each object can be put. It's not a look that "sees," it's a look that sorts. "In actual life," Fry says, "the normal person really only reads the labels as it were on the objects around him and troubles no further." In modern society the commodity is precisely what is the recipient of this instrumental look. "The subtlest differences of appearance that have a utility value" are what it scans, leaving out all matters of form, or what Fry calls the "important visual characters." Nothing can fool this glance in its task of categorizing the visual field according to the body's needs: nothing will "prevent the ordinary eye from seizing on the minute visual characteristics that distinguish margarine from butter. Some of use can tell Canadian cheddar at a glance, and no one was ever taken in by sham suede gloves."

Because art, a function of Fry's "creative vision," releases the gaze from this ceaseless functionalism, "biologically speaking, art is a blasphemy." The creative gaze soars above the body, arrested by the gratuitous satisfaction of what Fry always referred to as "plastic form" but we will translate into the pleasures released by the "logical moment." Indeed Virginia Woolf has supplied the transition when she pictures Fry wanting to "rescue such trifles" so that he can make "life yield one more drop of rational and civilized enjoyment."

The commodity, then, even though it was for Fry a zero point in the field of form—nothing, visually speaking, but a cipher operating within a system of exchange: more valuable/less valuable? real/fake?—the commodity could be visually redeemed. It could be raised to the level of form. Prized loose from the level of the body, it could be sublimated.

What Clem detests in Duchamp's art is its pressure toward desublimation. "Leveling" he calls it. The attempt to erase distinctions between art and not-art, between the absolute gratuitousness of form and the commodity. The strategy, in short, of the readymade.

Duchamp is not interested in redeeming the commodity for plastic values, for form, *for "the artist's vision," for the logical moment. Because the commodity has always already been swept up into* form, *has already, by its very condition as an item of exchange, been rationalized. Its nature and the formalizing look that would "redeem" it are nothing but two aspects of the same thing.*

The Rotoreliefs *are spinning, vertically, horizontally, all around Duchamp. He is among them, smiling like a salesgirl. The gaily colored helixes—red, green, blue—are busily enacting the images of industry: the flywheels, the turnscrews, the propellers. But the experience of an archaic, infantilized desire irrupts inexorably in their midst, creating, if ever so fleetingly, a space of resistance to rationalization. Temporal, carnal, it is the space of what I am projecting as Duchamp's version of the optical unconscious.*

I first developed the material on Duchamp's Precision Optics for a conference paper, published as "Where's Poppa?" in *The Definitively Unfinished Marcel Duchamp*, ed. Thierry De Duve (Cambridge: MIT Press, 1992), pp. 433–462.

Molly Nesbit, my interlocutor, has published her work on French nineteenth-century instruction in drawing and its relation to Marcel Duchamp in her "Ready-Made Originals," *October*, no. 37 (Summer 1986); and "The Language of Industry," in *The Definitively Unfinished Marcel Duchamp*, pp. 351–384.

The French lullaby could be translated, approximately, as follows:

> *Go beddy-bye, my little brother Nick.*
> *Go beddy-bye, you will have some milk.*
> *Mommy is upstairs, baking a cake.*
> *Daddy is downstairs, making some chocolate.*

Duchamp's writings have been anthologized in *Duchamp du signe: Ecrits*, ed. Michel Sanouillet (Paris: Flammarion, 1975), hereafter referred to as *DDS*; and *Salt Seller: The Writings of Marcel Duchamp (Marchand du Sel)*, ed. Michel Sanouillet and Elmer Peterson (New York: Oxford University Press, 1973) hereafter referred to as *SS*. Duchamp's business card is reproduced in *DDS* (p. 153) and *SS* (p. 105); Roché wrote two different accounts of Duchamp hawking the *Rotoreliefs* at the Concours Lépine: the one "MARCELDUCHAMPSOPTICALDISCS" (*Phases*, no. 1 [January 1954], and *SS*, p. 191), from which come the phrase "smiling like a salesgirl" and the final statement about the crowd's being able to see the *Rotoreliefs* at the museum; the other "Souvenirs de Marcel Duchamp" (in Robert Lebel, *Sur Marcel Duchamp* [Paris: Editions Trianon, 1959], p. 79), from which the major part of the description here is drawn. Duchamp's note on the transformers that would operate on bodily waste is in *DDS*, p. 272, and *SS*, p. 191; "Balls"—written as "PODE BAL"—was sent to Duchamp's brother-in-law Jean Crotti, in answer to an invitation to participate in the 1921 Salon Dada (*DDS*, p. 261, and *SS*, p. 180); on the illuminating gas, *DDS*, pp. 73–74, and *SS*, p. 49; on the Bride's imagination activated by "the love gasoline, a secretion of the bride's sexual glands," *DDS*, pp. 64–65, and *SS*, pp. 42–43.

Duchamp's statement about grasping things by the mind "the way the penis is grasped by the vagina" is from Lawrence Steefel ("The Position of *La Mariée mise à nu par ses célibataires, même* (1915–1923) in the Stylistic and Iconographic Development of the Art of Marcel Duchamp" [Ph.D. dissertation, Princeton University, 1960], p. 312; his saying that one looks "in turning away" is from Alain Jouffroy, *Une révolution du regard* (Paris: Gallimard, 1964), p. 119; his note on the Sieves as "cones" is from a 1914 sketch for the Bachelor Machine (in Arturo Schwarz, *La Mariée mise à nu chez Marcel Duchamp, même* [Paris: Editions Georges Fall, 1974], p. 160); his description of the illusion produced by his optical disks as a "psychophysiological process" is from an account by Hans Richter (*Dada: Art and Anti-Art* [London: Thames and Hudson, 1965], p. 99).

Duchamp specifies the viewer as *voyeur* in *Manual of Instructions for "Etant Donnés"* (Philadelphia: Philadelphia Museum of Art, 1987), in the note for the 5eme Op. ("La Porte"), n.p.

Duchamp's "anti-retinal" statements come from Pierre Cabanne, *Dialogues with Marcel Duchamp,* trans. Ron Padgett (New York: Viking Press, 1971), p. 43, and Jouffroy, *Une révolution du regard,* p. 115; his remarks against impressionism are from Jouffroy, p. 110.

The *Rotoreliefs* have received very little attention in the mountainous literature on Duchamp. Lawrence Steefel ("The Position of *La Mariée mise à nu,*" p. 56) associates their "obsessional pulsation" to "copulatory movements"; Toby Mussman ("Anémic Cinéma," *Art and Artists,* no. 1 [July 1966], p. 51) speaks of "vaginal penetration"; while the cyclops is spoken of by Robert Lebel, *Sur Marcel Duchamp,* p. 52.

The ideas of the dialectical image and of the importance of returning the gaze are of course Walter Benjamin's; see "On Some Motifs in Baudelaire," *Illuminations,* trans. Harry Zohn (New York: Shocken Books, 1969), p. 188: "Experience of the aura rests on the transposition of a response common in human relationships to the relationship between the inanimate or natural object and man. The person we look at, or who feels he is being looked at, looks at us in turn. To perceive the aura of an object we look at means to invest it with the ability to look at us in return"; and "Surrealism," *Reflections,* trans. Edmund Jephcott (New York: Harcourt Brace Jovanovich, 1978), p. 190: "We penetrate the mystery only to the degree that we recognize it in the everyday world, by virtue of a dialectical optic that perceives the everyday as impenetrable, the impenetrable as everyday." His account of the dialectical image as set out in his *Passagen-Werk* is discussed by Susan Buck-Morss in "The Flaneur, the Sandwichman and the Whore," *New German Critique,* no. 39 (Fall 1986), pp. 99–141; and throughout her *The Dialectics of Seeing: Walter Benjamin and the Arcades Project* (Cambridge: MIT Press, 1989). See also Miriam Hansen, "Benjamin, Cinema and Experience," *New German Critique,* no. 40 (Winter 1987), on Benjamin's concept of returning the gaze, pp. 187–188 and 203; on dialectical optics, p. 199; and on Benjamin's notion of the optical unconscious, pp. 207–211, 219–221. For a critique of Benjamin's concept of "secular illumination," see Jürgen Habermas, "Consciousness-Raising or Redemptive Criticism," *New German Critique,* no. 17 (Spring 1979), p. 47.

Greenberg's discussion of the "logical moment" is from "On Looking at Pictures," *The Nation* (September 8, 1945), and his review of *Cézanne's Compositions* is from *The Nation* (December 29, 1945), both anthologized in *Clement Greenberg: The Collected Essays and Criticism,* vol. 2, ed. John O'Brian (Chicago: University of Chicago Press, 1986), pp. 34 and 46–49. His attacks on Duchamp have been peppered throughout his writing of the late 1960s and after; see, for example, his "Necessity of 'Formalism'," *New Literary History,* vol. 3 (1971–1972), pp. 171–175.

Saussure's references to chess are from his *Course in General Linguistics,* trans. Wade Baskin (New York: McGraw-Hill, 1966), pp. 88–89, 110. Hubert Damisch has discussed Duchamp's work, and his chess game, in relation both to Saussure and to the history of chess, in "The Duchamp Defense," *October,* no. 10 (Fall 1979).

The alchemical reading of the *Glass* has most elaborately been given by Arturo Schwarz, "The Alchemist Stripped Bare in the Bachelor, Even," in *Marcel Duchamp,* ed. Anne d'Harnoncourt and Kynaston McShine (New York: Museum of Modern Art; Philadelphia: Philadelphia Museum of Art, 1973), pp. 81–98; the Neoplatonic one by Octavio Paz, *Marcel Duchamp: Appearance Stripped Bare* (New York: Viking, 1978). Claims for the centrality of Duchamp's relation to perspective are in the work of Jean Clair, "Marcel Duchamp et la tradition des perspecteurs," *Marcel Duchamp: Abécédaire* (Paris: Musée National d'Art Moderne, 1977). The importance of the fourth dimension as a key to Duchamp's work is argued both by Clair (*Marcel Duchamp ou le grand fictif* [Paris: Galilée, 1975] and *Duchamp et la photographie* [Paris: Chêne, 1977]) and by Craig Adcock, *Marcel Duchamp's Notes from the "Large Glass": An n-Dimensional Analysis* (Ann Arbor: UMI Research Press, 1981).

Sartre's chapter on "The Look" is in *Being and Nothingness,* trans. Hazel E. Barnes (New York: Washington Square Press, 1966). The citations here are from pp. 348, 352.

Jean-François Lyotard's analysis of *Etant donnés* is *Les TRANSformateurs DUchamp* (Paris: Galilée, 1977), pp. 137–138. He connects the *Large Glass* to the surface of the retina and to the cortex, pp. 133–134. For an analysis of the *Glass* as an indexical field of impressions see my "Notes on the Index," *The Originality of the Avant-Garde and Other Modernist Myths* (Cambridge: MIT Press, 1986).

The accounts of Roger Fry come from: Virginia Woolf, *Roger Fry: A Biography* (1940), as cited in *The Bloomsbury Group,* ed. S. P. Rosenbaum (Toronto: University of Toronto Press, 1975), pp. 129–132, 136–138; Angelica Garnett, *Deceived with Kindness* (London: Chatto & Windus, 1984), pp. 81, 90–104; Frances Partridge, *Love in Bloomsbury* (Boston: Little, Brown, 1981), p. 37; David Garnett, on Fry cheating at chess, *The Flowers of the Forest* (London: Chatto & Windus, 1955), p. 158; Clive Bell on Fry and chess, Rosenbaum, *The Bloomsbury Group,* p. 154. Accounts of Bloomsbury and Moorism: John Maynard Keynes, *Two Memoirs,* 1949, as cited by Rosenbaum, pp. 52–59; and Desmond MacCarthy, *Portraits I,* 1931, in Rosenbaum, p. 31.

Roger Fry discusses the difference between ordinary, utilitarian vision and aesthetic vision in "The Artist's Vision," *Vision and Design* (New York: Brentano's, n.d.), pp. 31–33. See Molly Nesbit's analysis of this essay in her *Atget's Seven Albums* (New Haven: Yale University Press, 1992).

Robert Delaunay theorizes color in relation to optics in his *The New Art of Color,* ed. Arthur Cohen (New York: Viking Press, 1978), pp. 35, 41, 63. Thierry de Duve has situated Duchamp's "nominalist" relation to color and his conception of the readymade within the history of abstract painting's reception of nineteenth-century optical and color theory. His argument describes two separate theoretical traditions, Goethe's *Farbenlehre* which fuels a symbolist/expressionist practice and Chevreul's *De la loi du contrast simultané* which founds a more objective and ultimately structuralist one; de Duve emphasizes the need on the part of modernist artists to legitimate abstraction, to defend it from the arbitrariness of "mere" decoration. See Thierry de Duve, *Nominalisme pictural* (Paris: Editions de Minuit, 1984), pp. 211–227.

Jonathan Crary's *Techniques of the Observer: On Vision and Modernity in the Nineteenth Century* (Cambridge: MIT Press, 1990) is a radical revision of art-historical understanding of the significance of physiological research and of the relationship between the camera obscura model of vision and that of later optical mechanisms such as the photographic camera and the stereographic apparatus. Crary cites Richard Rorty's analysis of the camera obscura as an epistemic model (Rorty, *Philosophy and the Mirror of Nature* [Princeton: Princeton University Press, 1979]) and compares this with the model onto which Goethe's *Farbenlehre* opens (Crary, pp. 43 and 67–69, respectively). Crary's discussion of the stereoscope (pp. 116ff.) describes its attack on the "scenic model" and the basis of that model in perspective (p. 128). For a discussion of Goethe's relation to the notion of the transience of vision, see Elaine Escoubas, "L'oeil (du) teinturier," *Critique,* no. 37 (March 1982), pp. 233–234.

Helmholtz compares the nervous system to telegraph wires in *Helmholtz on Perception,* ed. Richard Warren and Roslyn Warren (New York: John Wiley & Sons, 1968), p. 83; he speaks of our sensations as giving us nothing but signs (p. 110); he describes the problems that optical illusions pose for an empirical theory of vision (p. 129). Helmholtz's attempt to use associationist reasoning to explain optical illusions is analyzed by Richard Gregory (*Eye and Brain* [New York: World University Library, 1978], pp. 142–143).

Sartre's discussion of the issue of the unconscious in both associationist psychology and psychoanalytical theory is from his *Imagination, a Psychological Critique,* trans. Forrest

Williams (Ann Arbor: University of Michigan Press, 1962), p. 71. For an important discussion of Sartre's relation to associationism and to Charcot, see Joan Copjec, "Favit et Dissipati Sunt," *October*, no. 18 (Fall 1981), pp. 21–40.

Freud speaks of a scopic drive in "Psychogenic Visual Disturbance According to Psychoanalytical Conceptions" (1910), *Standard Edition*, vol. 11, pp. 211–218; the passages cited in the text are from pp. 215–216. Jean Laplanche's discussion of this drive and of anaclisis in from his *Life and Death in Psychoanalysis*, trans. Jeffrey Mehlman (Baltimore: The Johns Hopkins University Press, 1976), chapters 1 and 5.

A dictionary begins when it no longer gives the meanings of words, but their jobs.

—Georges Bataille

four

1 *Anamorph.* And how does Dalí describe it, the thing that so captivates him, transfixing him with its glamour, its seemingly endless powers of seduction? He wants to place his listener in front of a "psycho-atmospheric-ana-morphic object," although how, given the peculiar status of the thing, one can even occupy this place is far from clear. One is before it only by mistaking it for something else; it is seen in that sense through the modality of misrecognition. So he imagines a man staring at a tiny point of light that he takes to be a star but is in fact the glowing tip of a cigarette, the only visible part of the object in question.

One way to described the psycho-atmospheric-anamorphic object is that it is the avoidance of *form*. Dalí recalls to his listener how, in general, it is made. Everything goes on in total darkness: the selection of an object to be simulated; the dropping of this simulation from a great height; the photographing of the resultant mass; the compacting of the photograph within a molten metal cube. The aspect of invisibility that marked the initial process is retained in the final product. But it is an invisibility deeper than a mere falling away of the illumination necessary to see the object. It is a new order of the unseeable. Dalí characterizes it as *informe*.

We return to the tiny point of smoldering light and Dalí tells us the history of the object it signals. He manages to persuade us that among the other elements buried within it are "two authentic skulls—those of Richard Wagner and of Ludwig II of Bavaria" that, "softened up by a special process," are now the fodder the cigarette is slowly consuming. "The tip of this cigarette," Dalí exults, "cannot but burn with a brilliance more lyrical in human eyes than the airy twinkle of the clearest and most distant star."

The stars present us with infinity under the sign of concept, under the sign, that is, of form. The psycho-atmospheric-anamorphic object displays an altogether different version of infinity, that of deliquescence, of entropifaction, of a resistance to form.

2 *Base Materialism, and Gnosticism.* Bataille tells the story of the heteromorph, of the panmorph, of the acephalic god that burgeons into relief under the impress of the Gnostic seals. There is the god of the sun, a human figure whose body climaxes in a ruff of multiple necks that constitute a kind of altar on which is placed the double head of an ass. The photograph that reproduces this image organizes the burgeoning convexities and etched contours of the figure into splendid sharpness. And yet however near the photograph draws to this tiny residue of a suppressed society, the image of the thing itself refuses to come into focus.

How can we think the heteromorph, we for whom the very notion of form is to shape matter into that which is single, unified, and identical to itself? What would it mean to worship not that which is self-same but that which is self-different?

To our way of thought, derived as it is from a tradition of monism, matter cannot be conceived as distinct from form, because matter has already been caught up in a "systematic abstraction." It has been constructed within a relationship between two verbal entities; "abstract God (or, simply, Idea) and abstract matter, the prison keeper and the prison walls." Matter, thought through this "metaphysical scaffolding," is never base. Base materialism, says Bataille, begins with the heterological thought of nonidentity.

3 *Caves.* In many of the caves, but particularly those at Gargas, the paleolithic paintings include palm prints that were made, twenty millennia ago, by placing an outstretched hand against the wall and blowing pigment onto the exposed surface to create the image in negative. The image as a residue of its maker. No matter how simply, I leave my trace. Kilroy was here.

Displaced from a Golden Age Greece to the dawn of humanity, the birth of art never seemed, therefore, to require a break with the myth of Narcissus. If the mimetic urge led to the depiction of mammoth and horse and bison, it even more surely required the reflection of the artist himself.

At Gargas where these prints proliferate, many of the hands are curiously missing one or several finger joints, from one or several fingers. Abbé Breuil, the first great theoretician of the art of the caves, had a theory for this disfigurement as well. It was, he said, the result of initiation rites in which certain digits of the young hunter would be, as it were, circumcised. Nothing is changed in the theory of art-as-imitation. It is simply that certain of the models were "flawed."

The structuralist in Leroi-Gourhan bridles at this theory that has stubbornly hung on from the late nineteenth century into the middle of the twentieth. That is repeated even now, if you go to Gargas. He knows that the caves are not a case of imitation but of representation and that they therefore work like Saussure's chess game with each "piece" having a value relative only to every other. He knows that representation occurs within a combinatory universe. A universe like the one pictured by the Klein Group. A universe of male versus female. Of bison versus mammoth. Of arrow versus lattice. Of open hand versus truncated palm. Images are signs, he says. And the caves will use these to tell a story. A story of fecundation. By means of a mythogram. No hunter would mutilate the fingers of a young male initiate, he rolls his eyes. If the digits are "missing" at Gargas it is because what is represented there is, as always, the mythogram, the signification: male/female. And these very signs, enacted through the pure difference between the erectile finger and the squat, digitless palm, already existed as units in a code before their memorialization on the walls of Gargas. Hunters speak to each other through a language of signs. Two fingers raised, three fingers down. Thumb and little finger outstretched, index and middle fingers retracted. And so forth. A silent language. So as not to alert the animals.

If Bataille would have disagreed with Leroi-Gourhan and in fact found himself siding, here, with Abbé Breuil, it is not through any desire to embrace the theory of imitation. It is the notion of mutilation that arrests him. For, writing in *Documents* in 1930, he has quite a different theory of cave painting and the birth of art.

In the first place, he says, our own little primitives—our children—are not "creative." If they doodle it is not to *make* something; it is, instead, to despoil a surface. Their instincts are purely sadistic. They like to drag their dirty fingers along the walls. Because they like to deface them. Kilroy was here. If the "primitive" is to be understood on the model of the child, the birth of art is, as well, an act of defacement, of self-mutilation, of the digit removed. Not to produce the forms of language: male/female; but to produce the absence of difference: *informe*. This will toward self-deface-ment, this antinarcissism, is borne out by the hideousness of the represen-tations of humanity within the caves. On the same wall as noble bison and mighty mammoth one finds humans only as grotesques. The will is not to representation, he says, but to *alteration*.

It is because of its wonderful ambivalence that Bataille likes the word *alteration*. Its Latin root, *alter*, opens equally onto a change of state and a change (or advancement) of time, therefore containing the divergent sig-nifications of *devolution* and *evolution*. Bataille illustrates this by saying that alteration describes the decomposition of cadavers as well as "the passage to a perfectly heterogeneous state corresponding to . . . the *tout autre*, that is, the sacred, realized for example by a ghost." Using *alteration*, the primal impulse of man's self-representation is defined by Bataille as double-headed, leading simultaneously downward and upward. In this way the primordial, the originary, the source, is maintained as irresolvably diffuse—fractured by a doubleness at the root of things that was, in his closeness to Nietzsche's thought, dear to Bataille.

4 *Double*. "Beauty," said Breton, "will be convulsive, or will not be." Was he thinking of those photographs from the Salpêtrière to which Charcot had affixed the title "Passionate Attitudes"? Those images of the famous hysterics—the lovely "Augustine" in their lead—convulsed in myriad ges-tures of ecstasy. Pleading. Submitting. Writhing. A simulated ecstasy, it must be said. The body producing signs of a phantom exchange.

There are those who are sure this must have been the case. Breton thinks of nothing, they say, that does not have woman as its object. Woman, in fact, *as* object. The *con* in convulsive.

But in *L'amour fou* where this convulsive aesthetic is broached, the ex-amples are from an altogether lower level of the natural order. Breton

Jacques-André Boiffard, *Gnostic Seal*, photograph from
Documents, 2, no. 1 (1930).

A ruff of multiple necks . . . (p. 150)

Salvador Dalí, *Phenomenon of Ecstasy*, 1933.

Women falling, falling from the vertical into the horizontal . . . (p. 156)

speaks of a cave wall's perfect modeling of the ripples and falls of satin drapery, or of the Great Barrier Reef's production of the twists and turns of desert cacti. Breton's interest in simulation is an interest in nature's doubling over on itself to produce itself as always already in the grip of representation. As non-self-identical, because the double it generates within itself restructures it as sign. It is thus matter that is revealed as never wholly in-itself but always already signifying and thus always already shaped by the desires of its viewer. Unconscious desires that it, as sign, now makes manifest. The *con* in unconscious.

Bataille doesn't believe a word of this. And certainly not the notion—for Breton—of the *con* in unconscious. Breton's unconscious, riddled with signs, is busy producing *form*. His materialism isn't *base* at all, Bataille says, as he classes Breton with the eagles, soaring in the imperium of an idealist aesthetic. "Old Mole," he muses, "and the prefix *sur* as in *Sur-homme* and *Surrealism*."

It was up to the group that formed around Bataille and his magazine *Documents* to conceive of a doubling that would not be the generator of form. For example, Roger Caillois on animal mimicry. The insect becomes the double of its background. The moth's wings imitate shriveled leaves. The caterpillar's body is indistinguishable from arching twigs. The praying mantis fashions itself as so many emerald blades of grass. Entomological wisdom calls this phenomenon protective coloration. The prey is in hiding, having acted in relation to its predator. If it has passed from figure against ground to ground on ground, it is in order, by outsmarting its tracker, to hold itself intact.

Caillois does not agree. The animal's camouflage does not serve its life, he says, because it occurs in the realm of vision, whereas animal hunting takes place in the medium of smell. Mimicry is not adaptive behavior; instead, it is a peculiarly psychotic yielding to the call of "space." It is a failure to maintain the boundaries between inside and outside, between, that is, figure and ground. A slackening of the contours of its own integrity, of its self-possession, it is, as Denis Hollier calls it, a case of "subjective detumescence." The body collapses, deliquesces, doubles the space around it in order to be possessed by its own surrounds. It is this possession that produces a double that is in effect an effacement of the figure. Ground on ground.

Caillois compares this to the experience of schizophrenics. "Space seems for these dispossessed souls to be a devouring force," he says. "It ends by

155

four

replacing them. The body then desolidifies with his thoughts, the individual breaks the boundary of his skin and occupies the other side of his senses. He tries to look at himself from any point whatever of space. He feels himself becoming space. . . . He is alike, not like something but simply *like*. And he invents spaces of which he is 'the convulsive possession.'"

There, Bataille might have said, there you really have the *con* in convulsive.

5 *Ecstasy.* To represent ecstasy, Dalí finds, it is enough to rotate the head 180 degrees, to disorient the human axis from its vertical alignment—eyes, then nose, then mouth—to a horizontal in which, curiously, the mouth is now uppermost. His *Phenomenon of Ecstasy* is a photographic collection of such heads, which, like the Salpêtrière hysterics, are for the most part women. They are women falling, falling from the vertical into the horizontal. How is it that with that simple implication of falling, ecstasy is produced as image?

The scenario, as it were, for this collage had been published in 1930 by Georges Bataille in the "Dictionary" project ongoing in *Documents*. It came as the "definition" for "Mouth." For animals, Bataille writes, the mouth is a "prow." It is the foremost projection of that sleek horizontal that, like the ship's silhouette on the sea, comprises the animal's natural geometry. Mouth/anus. A straight line. The formal relations of the alimentary drive. Which every other animal knows how to read. By standing up, the human being has abandoned that simple, direct geometry and assumed, in his verticality, a more confusing form. For the top of his head, his "prow," is an inertly nonsignifying element of his body. We have to descend the facial facade to the level of the eyes to arrive at the evocative element in the human architecture. And the eyes have driven the mouth into obscurity.

Yet this architecture of the human will be transformed in moments of greatest pain or greatest pleasure. Then, the subject will grip his or her neck and, throwing the head fully back, will reassume that position in which it is the mouth that is at the end of the vertebral column. And from this newly projecting, newly expressive member there will issue the cry.

l. Rotating the head to produce the mouth as the human "prow" is not an elevation of the mouth but a lowering of the human structure, which has, by assuming the animal "geometry," fallen into the horizontal.

2. To attain the formal coherence of the animal's structure is nonetheless to descend into a condition of *informe*. For it is to blur the distinctions

between human and animal and thus to produce a formal rupture that goes deeper than any apparent form. Shapeless matter, like spittle or a crushed worm, says Bataille in his little "Dictionary" piece on *informe*, are instances of formlessness. But far more importantly, the *informe* is a conceptual matter, the shattering of signifying boundaries, the undoing of categories. In order to knock meaning off its pedestal, to bring it down in the world, to deliver to it a low blow.

So many falling bodies. So many mouths brought uppermost. Brassaï's *Nudes,* Man Ray's *Anatomy* or his *Facile,* Ubac's *Affichez Vos Images.* Surrealist photographers learned from this simplest of all formal notions. Rotate the image of body and you produce a different geography. A geography that undoes the *form* of the human form.

6   *Foundation.* The palm print gracing the cover of Amédée Ozenfant's *Foundations of Modern Art* has all its fingers intact. It is, for that matter, in Ozenfant's mind, the very image of the intact, of the coming into being of the silhouette that will bound a shape, separating inside from outside, light from darkness, figure from ground. Though it is not a simple geometric figure, like a circle or triangle or square, it is nonetheless an instance of the first, primitive urge to shape the inchoate through the bounding of form. And it is in that sense the very emblem of the formal, its "foundation." Ozenfant writes from Les Eysies de Tayac:

> At Cabrerets a cave has just been discovered which some fall of earth has blocked for 15,000 years: deeply moving are the pictures that were found in it. Man in his entirety is revealed in them. Ah those HANDS! those silhouettes of hands, spread out and stencilled on an ocher ground! Go and see them. I promise you the most intense emotion you have ever experienced. Eternal Man awaits you.

If eternal man not only awaits you but is capable of moving you so, it is because visuality is a channel through which formal constants are able to act directly on sensory perception. No accessory information is needed. The address to the eye is immediate. "The fact that works from a prehistoric era grip us without any explanation being necessary as to their origins or the reasons that motivated them or even the subjects they represent" Ozenfant gives as proof of the absoluteness of vision. Of the fact, as he claims, that the eye responds to optical phenomena invariantly, so that nothing changes in this experience from the dawn of man to the present moment.

Vision, the foundational condition of the visual arts, is itself founded on a set of formal "constants" that are on the one hand revealed to vision through light, but are just as actively sought out by vision as if in fulfillment of deep "psycho-biological" needs for form. The search for the good gestalt. Although Ozenfant doesn't use this term.

In sketching these conditions of the visual in their full primordiality, Ozenfant constructs an image that is curiously like Caillois's mimetic insect yielding to the seduction of space. "I suggest that it is possible," he writes, "that forms are the consequence of a sort of call from space! Matter, by which I mean the densest waves, would appear to infiltrate itself, as into a mould, into such space as offers the least resistance to it: it then becomes perceptible to us." The difference, however, between the Purist parable and that of the mimeticist is that Ozenfant's primal spatiality is itself always already formed. Its "mould" is the grid of an abstract geometry such that when matter leaches into it, it flows into the meshes of *form*. Thus the visual and the formal are the same, and it is the revelation of this similitude that is the genius of art: "When the artist succeeds in creating some such miracle, it may be he is unveiling the abscissa and coordinates of the perceptible universe: or alternatively, those of our deepest depths: which comes to the *same* thing."

When Ozenfant invokes the idea of foundations he is reaching toward a condition of possibility for vision itself. This he finds in the notion that even before the separation of figure from ground, the ground has always already been figure.

7 *Game.* Without speaking of the vertigo of disgust in Breton when he first saw Dalí's *Lugubrious Game* and noticed that the breeches of the one unambiguously recognizable figure in it were unmistakably besmirched with shit; without imagining the exaltation felt by Bataille as he prepared the analysis of the painting for *Documents;* without mentioning his dismay when Breton struck against his old enemy by asking Dalí to withhold permission to reproduce the work, or Dalí's motives for complying, or Bataille's decision to strike back by publishing it in any case, this by means of a schematic drawing; let us consider Bataille's reading of Dalí's game.

Like so many others, this game, he demonstrates, unfolds on a gridded field, here a quadrilateral in which the subject can be represented four times, in its character as a function of relations. It is an emasculated subject, Bataille says, the subject of castration. He plots this subject as/at (A). But as a subject it is the complex function of an interplay between its need to

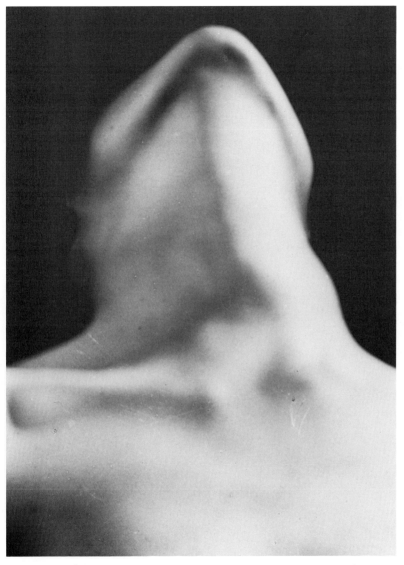

Man Ray, *Anatomies*, c. 1930.

For animals, Bataille writes, the mouth is a "prow"... (p. 156)

Diagram of Salvador Dalí's *Lugubrious Game* (1929),
as published in *Documents*, 1, no. 7 (1929).

*Or Bataille's decision to strike back by publishing it in any
case . . . (p. 158)*

provoke punishment through the outrageousness of its fantasized desires (B); its regressive attempts to evade that punishment by soiling itself, an act that both imitates castration and outwits it in an ejaculatory extravagance (C); and its voluptuous yielding to the very law of punishment by allying itself with its register, i.e., language (D).

The quadrilateral has two axes then, along which the subject can be both distributed and plotted. The subject, its objects, its ego, its unconscious. Long before Lacan had ever laid out his L Schema, Bataille is sketching what he calls the "Psychoanalytic schema of the contradictory figurations of the subject":

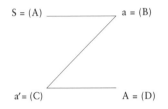

It is in the very geometry of the game, in its axis of relations, that the subject, in being played upon, does not succeed in becoming identical to himself. Spread out over the board of the game, he is a subject in *alteration*.

8 *Geometry.* Le Corbusier and Ozenfant picture the city dweller's excited response to that urban marketplace where "geometry lends all its force of attraction to commerce." Far from being cold or distancing, geometry tempts. Geometry seduces. Back in the countryside, they point out, the meat in the village butcher stalls lay in a heap, disgusting, redolent of the slaughterhouse. In the city's markets, however, lambs and chickens are made into elegant friezes and fruit is mounded into precise pyramids. It is this order that whets our appetites, they remark, that "causes jubilation to stir in us." But then modernity is a machine for the multiplication of the geometric. "These constant incitements of the brain, provoked by spectacles resulting from geometry, are already determined," they write, "by the very presence of the city whose street plan—the houses in an almost uniform grid of windows, the neat stripes of the sidewalks, the alignment of trees with their identical circular grills, the regular punctuation of street lamps, the gleaming ribbons of tramway lines, the impeccable mosaic of paving stones—always and forever encloses us within geometry." Not even the sky escapes the grip of geometry. For the sky is now organized by the

urban frame through which it is seen as mere interstice, as cutout. It is what throws the urban geometry itself into relief, giving us "in a precise contour the tracing of the urban geometry, counterproof imposed on nature."

But if the machine has constructed a "modern optic," it has done nothing more than connect modern man to his beginnings, his "subsoil," his primal need for the geometric, his cognitive apparatus:

> Man is a geometrical animal
> Man's mind is geometrical.
> Man's senses, his eyes, are drawn more than ever to
> geometrical clarities.
> We are in possession now of a refined, alert,
> penetrating eye.
> And of an exacting mind.

9 *Hat.* The hats winging their way upward in Dalí's *Lugubrious Game* represent, says Bataille, female organs as fantasized by the desiring subject. No problem in that. The hat is gendered female in the standard lexicon on the sexual symbolism of dreams. But by the time Tristan Tzara publishes his "Automatism of Taste" this assertion of gender with regard to the hat has undergone a considerable complication.

Like Dalí's, Tzara's hats are of felt, with their softly sloping crowns creased along their summits to produce the parallel lips of the fashionable fedora. A labial crease. A genital smile. But why is it, Tzara asks, that this vaginal image is used to place the finishing touches, as it were, on a quintessentially male garment? And then, even more curious, why in this year of 1933 is it the height of fashion for *women* to don this most mannish of hats? And to underscore the transvestite nature of this mode-for-women by decorating the fedora with the symbols of strictly male apparel—garters, bow ties, etc.? Man Ray gives this spiral of cross-identifications yet one more spin in the photographs he makes to illustrate Tzara's essay for its publication in *Minotaure*. The fedora, pulled firmly down on the head of the model, is photographed from above, the mannequin's face obscured by its brim. Firmly rounded, aggressive, the crown of the hat rises up toward its viewer like the tip of the male organ, swelling with so much phallic presence.

A click of the shutter and Man Ray enacts the institution of the fetish: the "glance" that refuses what it sees and in this resistance turns black into white, or rather, insists that black *is* white. In the logic of the fetish the

Man Ray, *Hat*, 1933.

A labial crease. A genital smile . . . (p. 162)

Alberto Giacometti, *Suspended Ball*, 1930–1931.

Every alternation produces an alteration . . . (p. 166)

paradigm male/female collapses in an adamant refusal to admit distinction, to accept the facts of sexual difference. The fetish is not the replacement of the female genitals with a surrogate, coded /female/; it is a substitute that will allow a perverse continuation in a belief that they are male, that the woman (mother) is—beyond all apparent evidence—phallic.

The evidence in question is visual. In Freud's scenario the fetish develops around a point of view within which the child sees but refuses what he sees, falls into a ritual of denial that his mother has been "castrated." Freud speaks of this point of view: "When the fetish comes to life, some process has been suddenly interrupted . . . what is possibly the last impression received before the uncanny traumatic one is preserved as a fetish . . . the last moment in which the woman could still be regarded as phallic." The impressions into which the trauma falls are visual impressions, points of view within which the evidence arrives only to be denied through a sleight-of-vision that will produce the sexually indeterminate substitute of the fetish. Freud pulls an example from one of his case histories, a patient whose fetish object is *a shine on the nose.* Lacan will later speak of such a "shine" in relation to a tin can he once saw bobbing on the seas of Brittany. He calls it the "jewel," the "screen," the "gaze." Freud had already marked this shine as the acknowledgment of a fissure that has opened within the field of vision: *ein Glanz auf die Nase,* says the patient, naming his fetish. This patient's first language, it seems, was not German, however, but English, the mother tongue of his nanny. So the "shine" of *Glanz* was really "glance" and the "last impression" before the fatal interruption was in fact "a glance at the nose." Perfectly bilingual, *Glanz(ce)* now allows the fusion of looking at and looked at, subject and object, seer and seen, a fusion that reenacts the defense that the fetish itself will stage as the misperceived blurring of male and female organs.

Man Ray's image captures the hat within a radically oblique point of view, one that hangs suspended over the top of the head, so that the split crown of the fedora seems to yield to the upsurge of the skull below it, both expressing and denying its aggressive contour: a shine on the nose.

10 *Informe.* Leaving aside the fact that Giacometti's first critical acclaim was registered in *Documents,* which is to say, within that part of the avant-garde to which André Masson had introduced him, the part that was excoriated by Breton in his "Second Manifesto" of 1929, and that nonetheless the sight, in 1930, of Giacometti's sculpture *Suspended Ball* triggered Breton's most earnest enthusiasm, opening a place for the sculptor

within the official wing of surrealism, *Suspended Ball* is a textbook case of the *informe* as that was developed by Bataille. And this all the more so in that its elements are clearly formed.

We know what it looks like, this assemblage first elaborated in plaster, and then later in beautifully finished wood, of open cage, flat platform, and two opposing objects, the one reposing on the cage's bottom, the other swinging from a wire affixed to a strut at its top. The gisant form is a wedge, prismatic, crescent-shaped. The pendular one is a sphere, perfectly convex except for the deep gash that threatens to cleave the underside of the ball into two half-moons. The mechanical relationship between the two is precise; the ball passes rhythmically over the ridge of the wedge. Swish forward. Swish back. But the erotic relationship between the two is a problem. For it is less precise. "Everyone who saw this object functioning," Maurice Nadeau reports, "experienced a strong but indefinable sexual emotion related to unconscious desires. This emotion was in no sense one of satisfaction, but one of disturbance, like that imparted by the irritating awareness of failure."

Disturbance occurs here in the modality of *alteration,* of ambivalence, of the splitting of every "identity" from itself into that which it is not. Of the dissolution, then, of form. For it is not clear, will never be clear, whether the gesture is a caress or a cut; it is not clear, will never be clear, whether the wedge is passively receiving stimulation from the sphere or, sadistic, aggressive, is violating the surface of the ball, like the razor slicing the eye in Dalí's *Un chien andalou* or the bull's horn in Bataille's *Histoire de l'oeil* that kills the matador by tearing out his eye. As the instrument of penetration the wedge is gendered male. And the wounded sphere is female. But as labial surface stroked by its active, possessing partner, the wedge reverses its sex, flipping into an unmistakable image of the genitality of the woman. Swish. Flip. Alter. Every alternation produces an alteration. And identities multiply. Lips. Testicles. Buttocks. Mouths. Eyes. Like clockwork. A clock every second of which marks the inversion of all its elements. Hetero-erotic . . . homo-erotic . . . auto-erotic . . . hetero-erotic . . .

Like clockwork.

It is too easy to think of *informe* as the opposite of form. To think of form versus matter. Because this "versus" always performs the duties of form, of creating binaries, of separating the world into neat pairs of oppositions by means, as Bataille liked to say, of "mathematical frock coats." Form versus matter. Male versus female. Life versus death. Inside versus outside.

Vertical versus horizontal. Etc. Chaos as the opposite of form is chaos that could always be formed, by the form that is always already there in wait for chaos.

Instead, let us think of *informe* as what form itself creates, as logic acting logically to act against itself within itself, form producing a heterologic. Let us think it not as the opposite of form but as a possibility working at the heart of form, to erode it from within. Working, that is, structurally, precisely, geometrically, like clockwork. The word in French that captures this is *déjouer*. The translation is given as something like "foil" or "baffle." But that suppresses the part of the action that has to do with games and rules and structure; with a structure destabilizing the game in the very act of following the rules. To create a kind of "mis-play," but one that, inside the system, is legal. The spring winding backward. Like clockwork.

11 *Jouer/déjouer I*. Here's the perfect example of a structure set up to generate "mis-play." In 1926 Bataille published *Histoire de l'oeil*. A pornographic novel, it is also a structurally closed system through which a formal logic is at work against the geography of the body, its order, its form.

The story of the eye is not about the novel's characters, but about an object—the eye—and what happens to it; and this "happening to," as Roland Barthes has shown, is a function of the rules of language, of metaphor and metonymy working to "decline" the object through an orderly succession of verbal states. As a globular element the eye is transformed through a series of metaphors by means of which, at any given point in the narrative, other globular objects are substituted for it: eggs, testicles, the sun. As an object containing fluid, the eye simultaneously gives rise to a secondary series related to the first: yolk, tears, urine, sperm. It is from the finite set of these two metaphoric series, as each crosses with the other, that a *combinatoire* is set up through which the course of the erotic action of the narrative is generated. The eye is round; its contents are white: the first erotic encounter is between the narrator and Simone who is sitting in (the cat's) plate of milk. The verbal fabric through which the story is told is also woven from the two metaphoric strands. The sun, metaphorized as eye and yolk, can, for example, be described as "flaccid luminosity" and can give rise to the phrase "the urinary liquefaction of the sky." What feels like a near infinity of images can be generated within the grid of these mutations. *Jouer*.

Is this the surrealist game for producing the image: the *chance* encounter of umbrella and sewing machine on a dissecting table? Nothing within a combinatory, Barthes reminds us, takes place by chance. Bataille's creation, he says, "is neither a wild image nor even a free image, for the coincidence of its terms is not aleatory." The action of cross-inseminating the two series is to take, for example, commonplace expressions associated with the various elements—like "to break an egg" or "to poke out an eye"—and to transpose their terms *systematically*. To produce "poke out an egg" or "break an eye" is at one and the same time to reorganize the terrain of the commonplace—of what is "proper" to a given linguistic term—and to reconstruct the body's territory—what is possible for a given organ. And to eroticize these possibilities. Systematic transgression. *Déjouer*.

But are the chains, in fact, the efflorescence of a single, master term, which, lying at the heart of the action, is more privileged than the rest? Is it a sexual fantasy that is the secret that will act as the key to this profusion of elements, giving it a hierarchy that progresses, ultimately, toward a unity that will totalize the tale? But the circularity of the substitutions, in which each term is always made the signifier of another term, does not secure genitality as the basis of the story. Just as the book's eroticism is never directly phallic ("It is a question," Barthes says parenthetically, "of a 'round phallicism'"), so it is never possible to decide whether it is the ocular or the genital theme that is originary. What this means is that *Histoire de l'oeil* succeeds in never being a profound work; it contains no hierarchy, encodes no secret. "What we are dealing with is signification without a signified," says Barthes, "(or something in which everything is signified); and," he adds, "it is neither the least beauty nor the least novelty of this text to compose, by the technique we are attempting to describe, an open literature which is situated beyond any decipherment and which only a formal criticism can—at a great distance—accompany."

12 *Labyrinth.* If art began in the caves, its starting point was not the space of architecture, with light differentiating vertical pillar from horizontal slab, but that of the labyrinth, with no light, no differentiations, no up, no down. Its master image is the Minotaur, not Narcissus. As Bataille was to insist over and over again, its cause was not form but alteration.

If insistence was necessary this was because Paris of the '20s had been swept up into a celebration of the origin of form as though it were set in these very caves. *The Creation of the World*, it was called for example, with music by Darius Milhaud and sets and costumes by Léger. Primitivism had become fashionable at the very same moment as the International

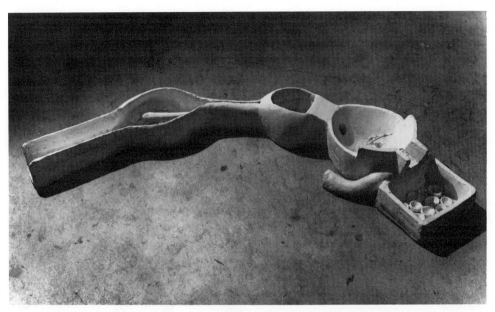

Alberto Giacometti, *Project for a Passageway (Labyrinth)*, 1930–1931.

Felled by the action of the informe *to collapse the vertical onto the horizontal axis . . . (p. 171)*

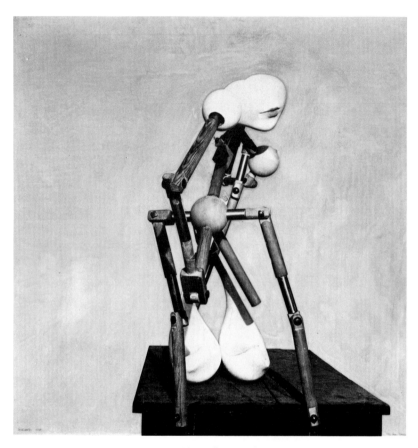

Hans Bellmer, *Machine Gunneress in a State of Grace*, 1937.

The praying mantis, totem animal of the '30s . . . (p. 171)

Style and Art Deco. This meant a convergence in the public *imaginaire* between the geometries of the Fang mask or the Dan spoon and the cubes and cylinders of chrome ashtrays or buildings cast in the mold of "steamboat modern."

That, indeed, is where Giacometti, fresh from the Grand Chaumière and an admiration for Laurens and Brancusi, had started. Black Deco had been his chic beginnings. But not for long. After 1928, when he had come in contact with Michel Leiris and Georges Bataille he began to rethink the meaning of the labyrinth as not simply another form but as a system for voiding form, for attacking it as *déclassé*. The vertical body—that staple of the sculptural imagination—now drops the ground, felled by the action of the *informe* to collapse the vertical onto the horizontal axis. A series of horizontal sculptures follow, one called *The Fall of a Head onto a Diagram*, another more directly titled *Labyrinth*. But these prone figures led to a further move into the terrain of undifferentiation and Giacometti imagined a sculpture that, instead of using the pedestal or base to lift the body off the surface of the space in which it stood, would be nothing but pedestal or base. It would be pure horizontal field, unlike any sculpture before it. Inassimilable to vision, inassimilable to form, it would inhabit the conceptual terrain of the labyrinth. It would go below the origins of form, below the gestalt.

13 *Mantis.* In 1937 Hans Bellmer makes a sculpture called *Machine Gunneress in a State of Grace*. Insectoid, robotic, the work opens onto the fantasmatic field that had been mapped out for the praying mantis, totem animal of the '30s. In it, automatism is rewritten by the insect, recast from the outpouring of libidinal energy into the unstoppable drive of the castrating machine, insentient and implacable. Caillois presents the creature in a chilling portrait of life's mechanical double, the android simulation of the living being. One of the uncanny qualities of the mantis, he begins, is that its defense against its predators is to "play dead." Rigid, immobile, wraithlike, the mantis's posture in life is to mime the inanimate. But its drive to imitate doesn't stop with the defense of its organism, he says. For even decapitated the praying mantis continues to function and thus to perform a hideously robotic dance of life. "Which is to say," Caillois writes, "that in the absence of all centers of representation and of voluntary action, it can walk, regain its balance, have coitus, lay eggs, build a cocoon, and, what is most astonishing, in the face of danger can fall into a fake, cadaverous immobility. I am expressing in this indirect manner what language can scarcely picture, or reason assimilate, namely, that dead, the mantis can simulate death."

In this sense of the double that stands at the border between life and death not as a barrier, a marker of difference, but as the most porous of membranes, allowing the one side to contaminate the other, the mantis, like the android, like the robot, like the epileptic in seizure, is a messenger of the uncanny, a harbinger of death. As, Freud says, is the doll.

And Bellmer, attending a performance of *The Tales of Hoffman* in the early 1930s, watching its hero maddened by his love for a doll who ends in dismemberment, found himself identifying with this story of identification, saw himself endlessly returning to this fantasy, this theater of castration.

Throughout the '30s Bellmer's great project became his two series of *Poupées,* each of which involved, like an eerily humanoid erector set, the assembling, dismantling, and reassembling of a demountable doll, each new assembly positioned and then photographed in a particular setting—kitchen, stairwell, bedroom, barn loft, woods—before being taken apart once more and reused. Staging, lighting, tinting the photographs to bracket their evidence within the space of fantasy, Bellmer casts the dolls again and again as phallic. The doll's hair may be tied in a bow, its feet shod in Mary Janes, but, armless, its torso aggressively swelling with a kind of pneumatic dynamism, it summons up the very image of tumescence. Or again, it is seen merely as two pairs of legs joined end to end, erectile, taut, straddling the trunk of a tree. This doll's body, coded /female/ but figuring forth the male organ within a setting of dismemberment, carries with it the treat of castration. It is the doll as uncanny, the doll as *informe.*

14   *Objective Chance.* Breton reads about the "omnipotence" of desire, about "wish fulfillment." He is electrified. There onto the black and white of psychoanalytic theory he is able to project a revolutionary program that will link the life of dreams to a radical change in the field of the real. By wishing. By wanting. By desiring. "Objective chance" becomes his term for the way the subject's unconscious thoughts will operate upon reality, recutting it to the measure of their desires. "Objective chance" is also the name for the seemingly happanstance return of this now refashioned world in the form of a revelation that will, like the message in the bottle, announce to the subject the hitherto buried nature of these phantasms. *Les vases communicantes* is the theorization of objective chance; *Nadja* is its novelization. For Nadja is the great heroine of the power of the desiring will, of prescience, of thought's omnipotence. She and Breton are sitting at a cafe table, the two of them looking across the square. "There will be a

Hans Bellmer, *La Poupée*, 1936/1949.

Two pairs of legs joined end to end, erectile, taut . . . (p. 172)

Hans Bellmer, *La Poupée*, 1938.

It summons up the very image of tumescence . . . (p. 172)

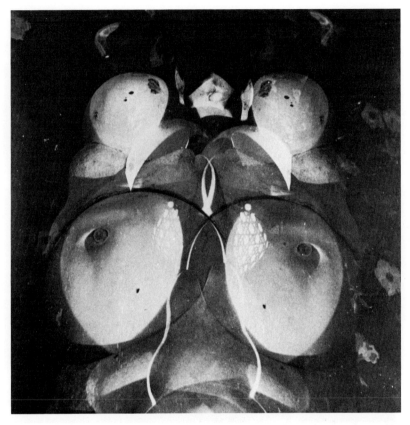

Hans Bellmer, *La Poupée*, 1938.

A messenger of the uncanny, a harbinger of death . . . (p. 172)

Hans Bellmer, *La Poupée (Idole)*, 1937.

The doll as uncanny, the doll as informe *. . . (p. 172)*

light in the window," she says, staring at a blank facade. A second later the window lights up. Breton is stunned. Out of such acorns, he is convinced, will the great oak of revolution grow.

Nadja, of course, is a love story. Since it is a narrative powered by desire, he thinks, what else could it be?

For almost a decade, however, Freud had been telling a different tale about the omnipotence of thought, and clairvoyance, one with a decidedly unhappy ending. Both the animism of primitive peoples and the narcissism of the infant, he notices, populate the world with extensions of themselves, with projections in the form of doubles or cast shadows (shades). The "double," Freud says, "was originally an insurance against destruction to the ego, an energetic denial of the power of death," which, he continues, "has its counterpart in the language of dreams, which is fond of representing castration by a doubling or multiplication of the genital symbol." But as infantile grandiosity yields to the all-too-obvious facts of helplessness, the subject's own creation becomes a Frankenstein monster. So that the ideas that "have sprung from the soil of unbounded self-love, from the primary narcissism which holds sway in the mind of the child as in that of primitive man," form the basis for a turn of events: "when this stage has been left behind the double takes on a different aspect. From having been an assurance of immortality, he becomes the ghastly harbinger of death." He becomes a ghost, a ghoul, a spook.

Freud is discussing this in the context of "The Uncanny" as he tries to grapple with the feeling, a function of adult life, of a sudden, uneasy "recognition" that one is confronted by fate. Often, he observes, this arises out of a sense that a seemingly chance occurrence has in fact been prepared for one, that behind the apparent randomness of coincidence there lies a message waiting to be read. The uncanniness that seems to surround certain repetitions of names, or numbers, or concatenations of objects within one's everyday life, "forces upon us," Freud notes, "the idea of something fateful and unescapable where otherwise we should have spoken of 'chance' only." The temptation to give a secret meaning to what seems like the obstinate recurrence of a number, for example, leads people frequently to read into these repetitions the language of destiny.

But Freud is speaking of the uncanny within a larger frame, the one he thinks of as a need to regress, a need to repeat what is prior, earlier, least developed within the self. Therefore this ascription of meaning to happenstance and this assumption of powers of clairvoyance (offhandedly referred to by his patients as their "'presentiments' which 'usually' come true") he understands as the reassertion within adult life of more psychologically primitive states, namely those related to the omnipotence of thoughts and belief in animism. "It would seem," he writes, "as though each one of us has been through a phase of individual development corresponding to that animistic stage in primitive man, that none of us has traversed it without preserving certain traces of it which can be re-activated, and that everything which now strikes us as 'uncanny' fulfills the condition of stirring those vestiges of animistic mental activity within us and bringing them to expression."

The collapse of the distinction between imagination and reality—an effect Breton courted with all of surrealism's resources, but one that Freud analyzes as the primitive belief in magic—animism, narcissistic omnipotence, all are potential triggers of that metaphysical shudder that is the uncanny. For they represent the breakthrough into consciousness of earlier states of being, and in this breakthrough, itself the evidence of a compulsion to repeat, the subject is engulfed by the idea of death.

Nadja, Breton thinks, is a love story, driven by the rebellious power of the libido, the pleasure principle, the imperious wish. But from the very first line, in the grip of the effects of objective chance, he writes it in the key of the uncanny, with its overtones of a drive toward death. "Who am I?" he begins. "If this once I were to rely on a proverb, then perhaps everything would amount to knowing whom I 'haunt.'"

15 *Photography.* It was in 1931, in his "Small History of Photography," that Walter Benjamin first used the term "optical unconscious." With the photographs of Muybridge or Marey undoubtedly in mind, he speaks of how the naked eye cannot penetrate movements of even the most ordinary kind. "We have no idea at all," he says, "what happens during the fraction of a second when a person *steps out.*" But photography, he exults, "with its devices of slow motion and enlargement, reveals the secret. It is through photography that we first discover the existence of this optical unconscious, just as we discover the instinctual unconscious through psychoanalysis."

Reading this, of course, we are struck by the strangeness of the analogy. True, the camera with its more powerful and even dispassionate eye can stand for the psychoanalyst, and the hitherto unseen visual data can operate as a parallel to those slips of tongue or pen, those parapraxes through which the patient's unconscious surfaces into view. But what can we speak of in the visual field that will be an analogue of the "unconscious" itself, a structure that presupposes first a sentient being within which it operates, and second a structure that only makes sense insofar as it is in conflict with that being's consciousness? Can the optical field—the world of visual phenomena: clouds, sea, sky, forest—*have* an unconscious?

Benjamin makes it clear both in this early essay and when he returns to the subject in the 1936 "Work of Art in the Age of Mechanical Reproduction" that for him the camera is an instrument that enlarges vision, much the way Freud spoke of it in *Civilization and Its Discontents,* where technological advances are viewed as a set of "prosthetic limbs" that expand the power of the individual. Benjamin likens the camera for example to the surgeon's knife that can operate dispassionately on the human body and by seeing it in fragments can enter more deeply into its reality. Freud, however, is clear that the world over which technical devices extend their power is not one that could, itself, have an unconscious. It may have a microstructure that lies beyond the range of the naked eye, but that structure is neither conscious/unconscious nor can it be in conflict with consciousness. This is why for Freud a sentence like Benjamin's "The camera introduces us to unconscious optics as does psychoanalysis to unconscious impulses," from the "Work of Art" essay, would simply be incomprehensible.

It is only at the end of the essay where Benjamin, speaking of fascism, writes that "mass movements, including war, constitute a form of human behavior which particularly favors mechanical equipment . . . [for] mass movements are usually discerned more clearly by a camera than by the naked eye," that we encounter some form of "unconscious" that the camera could intercept. If "gatherings of hundreds of thousands" are a fact that the human sensorium simply cannot register, such gatherings, which Freud also had in mind in his own essay on mass psychology, can indeed be thought to display a collective consciousness, leading to their analysis in terms of an unconscious. But the masses on the parade grounds at Nuremberg, though they may make patterns for the camera eye that can be organized within the optical field, are human masses, and if they have an unconscious, collective or not, it is a human unconscious, not an "optical" one.

My own use of *optical unconscious,* as it has been invoked in the pages of this book, is thus at an angle to Benjamin's. If it can be spoken of at all as externalized within the visual field, this is because a group of disparate artists have so constructed it there, constructing it as a projection of the way that human vision can be thought to be less than a master of all it surveys, in conflict as it is with what is internal to the organism that houses it.

16 **Rotten.** "Picasso's paintings are hideous," says Bataille in "Le jeu lugubre." Says it, you understand, admiringly. Indeed, it is from the fullness of this admiration that *Documents* moves in 1930 to issue its "homage" to Picasso. Bataille's contribution to it is titled "Rotten Sun." The text is a celebration of Picasso's decomposition of form. But as always, a notion of decomposition that works from within the very idea of formal achievement, of formal perfection. To shatter its unity. The very sun, says Bataille, that symbolizes loftiness, unity, productivity for an idealist culture, is the sun that is inherently double, violent, and wasteful. For the sun at its zenith, its most lofty, is precisely the sun at its most blinding, the sun our eyes approach only at their peril. The savagery that is there, materially, lodged at the very heart of the ideal, can be read in Icarus's story. As it can be seen in contemporary art. But only, strictly speaking, in the work of Picasso.

What must the owner of *Documents,* Georges Wildenstein, publisher and editor of the *Gazette des Beaux-Arts* as well, have thought of using *hideous* and *rotten* as terms of approbation? In the late 1920s in France it is clear, after all, what *rotten* means. Ozenfant is writing in *L'Esprit Nouveau.* About how modern society, fortified by its industrial base, has liberated vision from rot, from blur, from *flou,* and, clearing away this bewildering fog, has allowed the geometric basis of form to shine forth anew. He's been to the market where he's seen geometry at work in the display of food, in the turning of the organic into the abstraction of the commodity, releasing, as Walter Benjamin would say, "the sex appeal" of the inorganic. Ozenfant is nothing but ecstatic. "These monumental urban still lifes," he writes, "seen in relation to the picturesque still lifes by artists, make us turn our backs on Rembrandt's rotten beef."

It's right at the end of *Documents*'s brief run that Bloomsbury makes a curious appearance in the magazine. Clive Bell is writing about Constable's importance for French painting, for a romanticism that experiences itself as the release of color, the suppression of drawing, the transvaluation of form. But Bell, it seems, cannot warm to his task. He is only really thrilled by the emergence of structure from within the aesthetic object, which is to say, by the surfacing of form. "It would take an artist with far greater genius than Constable," he writes, "to know how to construct an absolute harmonic from the sole means of a direct transcription of nature." And, after all, it's only through this harmonic, this inner geometry, that land-

Raoul Ubac, *Portrait in a Mirror*, 1938.

"Perhaps everything would amount to knowing whom I 'haunt'". . . (p. 178)

Raoul Ubac, *The Battle of the Amazons (Group III)*, 1939.

Dispossessed and dispersed, we enter the picture . . . (p. 184)

scape could lay claim to being modern, says Bell, his thoughts silently racing toward Cézanne. Poor Constable. "All too frequently," declares Bell, "Constable is maladroit."

Bell has got his values *straight*. This is not a term of approbation. Bell's is an article that could have appeared in the *Gazette des Beaux-Arts*.

17 *Screen.* For Bataille the blur was categorical, heterological. For Caillois it was perceptual, or rather a function of the axis between perception and representation. The insect in the grip of a mimetic redoubling of its surroundings, a mimicry that dispossesses it so that it loses itself in a blur between itself and its background, is the insect that has been derealized. No longer a "subject," it is now a "picture." To be a subject, Caillois explains, is to feel oneself as the origin of the coordinates of perception. It is to experience one's toehold on the world as continually reconstructing one's place at the intersection between the vertical of one's body and the horizontal ground on which one stands. Through all the displacements of one's moving body, this toehold remains firm, because one carries the perceptual coordinates around with one; they are the baggage of one's subjective coherence, one's fixity. I stand fast; therefore I am.

But this very same ground plan is intersected at another point, one at a distance from oneself, by another vertical being, another object. A function of this remoteness, the distant object is no longer perceived in the tactile immediacy of the "toehold," but now, hovering on the horizon of experience, it can only, Caillois insists, be grasped as representation. "It is with represented space," Caillois then says, "that the drama becomes clear: for the living being, the organism, is no longer the origin of the coordinates, but is one point among others; it is dispossessed of its privilege and, in the strongest sense of the term, *no longer knows where to put itself*."

It was Jacques Lacan who would never forget this macabre image of the perspective diagram turned back on itself in a terrifying reversal. He would remember the consequences of no longer occupying "the origin of the coordinates," which is to say no longer being the eye positioned at the privileged viewing point of an optico-geometric mastery of space. The point that Caillois's insects inhabited was instead, like one of the little dots of color in a *pointilliste* painting, or one of the tiny tesserae in a Roman mosaic, an element in a picture seen by another, a picture into which the insect had no choice but to blend, camouflage-like, into a seamless invisibility: "one point among others."

To enter the picture, Lacan reasoned, was to be projected there, a cast shadow thrown onto the manifold of the world's image. And so instead of the perspective pyramid he imagined something more like a projector's lamp, an intervening obstacle, and a shadow cast onto the distant wall. Light, which is everywhere, surrounds us, robbing us of our privileged position, since we can have no unified grasp of it. Omnipresent, it is a dazzle that we cannot locate, cannot fix. But it fixes us by casting us as a shadow. It is thus that, dispossessed and dispersed, we enter the picture. We are the obstacle—Lacan calls it the "screen"—that, blocking the light, produces the shadow. We are thus a function of an optics we will never master.

18 *Third Term. Jouer/déjouer II.* Is Bataille's story of "The Big Toe" an account of fetishism? It turns, after all, on the eroticization of the foot. But since it insists that this is not a *displaced* erotics, a sexuality by proxy, it does not work along the logic of the fetish. It explicitly dismisses the play of substitutions. Of sublimations. Of foot = phallus. The foot, he says, seductive in and of itself, seduces us *basely*.

Bataille returns to this matter of the architecture of the human body, to the fact that, having raised himself onto only two of his feet, having assumed, that is, the vertical, man has no natural architecture (no "prow"). What there is instead is a structure of values imposed by the human subject: noble versus ignoble; notions about elevation, loftiness, ideals, as opposed to a space of viciousness and evil. The body is thereby inscribed within the logic of the paradigm, given formal meaning: noble/ignoble.

But if the upright body has no natural architecture, it has, we could say, a natural hinge. The pivot on which its original elevation turned, the lever that still plays that functional role, is the big toe—no longer prehensile, for wrapping itself around branches, but now rigidified, for bracing itself against the earth. And that, precisely, is its problem. For the toe still belongs to nature. Indeed its ground is that of the earth, of matter, of mud. Dirty, deformed, debased, the foot fails to leave the lowness of its place, and so failing does not enter the paradigm. It is not that man does not try to force it into the paradigm, to ennoble the foot, to give it form. In China it is bound; in the West it is shod with the highest of heels. Anything to dissemble the foot, to shape it. The foot repays this effort, however, by developing bunions, and corns, and calluses. It becomes splayed, bulbous. It refuses to be ennobled or even to be ignoble. It is, simply, base.

When the foot enters the erotic arena, it does so within the condition of the taboo. The nude foot is not supposed to be touched or seen, in Turkey, in China, in seventeenth-century Spain. The codes of modesty clothe the foot, withdrawing it from view. Is this enough to succeed in absorbing the foot within another paradigm of values, in this case the opposition modesty/immodesty?

Roland Barthes is analyzing "The Big Toe." One of his headings is "Déjouer." He wants to show Bataille's successful "baffling/mis-playing" of the paradigm due to the addition of the third term: *base*. In relation to the paradigm *noble/ignoble*, *base* is neither the complex (*noble* and *ignoble*) nor the neutral term (neither *noble* nor *ignoble*); welling up from the world of matter, *base* comes from outside the paradigm's formal construction of values to lodge within it as an irritant, as a disequilibrator, as an eccentric. It is an irreducible term, says Barthes, "the term of seduction *outside the* (structural) *law*."

But nonetheless, according to the system of "déjouer," it enters the paradigm, it allows itself to be vectored by form. "It is caught up," says Barthes, "in the paradigm *high/low*, i.e., in the simulation of a meaning, of a form, and hence it baffles [*déjoue*] the nature of matter *in itself*: '. . . contemporary materialism, by which I mean a materialism not implying that matter is the thing *in itself*' [Bataille]. In short, the true paradigm is one which confronts two positive values (*noble/base*) in the very field of materialism; and it is the normally contrary term (*ignoble*) that becomes the neutral, the mediocre (the negative value, the negation of which is not contradiction, but deflation)."

When Bataille places the erotics of the foot within the world of *modesty*, we expect him to invoke the force of what a legal, psychiatric institution asserts as its opposite: *exhibitionism*. But instead, Bataille invokes *laughter*: the untransformable ridiculousness of the toes, their grossness, their ungainly ugliness. This is the mark of a *base* seduction; laughter is a third term "that baffles Modesty, the *meaning* of Modesty." To introduce the third term is not, then, to destroy the paradigm as an apparatus of meaning, but to create within its very logic something eccentric, something scandalous in the operations of sense.

19 *Universal.* Here, then, is Le Corbusier describing the walks he took with his father, there in the Swiss Alps when, a child, he was still Edouard Jeanneret. "We were constantly on the summits," he says, "the immense horizon was quite usual for us. When the sea of mist stretched away to infinity it was just like the real ocean—which I had never seen. It was the most magnificent sight."

The sea of mist is below; the sky is above; one is, oneself, merely a point in an unarticulated immensity. A gravitationless field. A space that, defying the norms of the body, is verging on the almost purely abstract.

There is nothing of the void about this magnificence. Instead this space inside this cosmic envelope is everywhere vectored, scored by ordinate and abscissa, marking out the numberless sites of an always potential *Prägnanz*. For form is possible everywhere.

In art school young Edouard encountered the God of John Ruskin, and thus the moral purpose of an art that learned to read the message of creation. He was trained, therefore, to see nature as merely the distracting surface of an underlying harmonic whose most perfect expression was geometry. And so he undertook to reinvent the Alpine rocks and trees and clouds as a rhythmic network of interlacing shape, triangles spreading across the surface interlocked with circles, the negative rhomboids of the spaces-between emerging with the force of positive form. The task was to speak the language of ornament. Which was not the same as decoration. Ornament implied the possibility of chaining together a potentially endless lattice each unit of which (the motif) would imply the infinity of the extension. The ornamental unit would be a microcosm in which "everything" in the whole would be expressed. The triangle would be so charged that it would at one and the same time invoke the tree, the cone, the clouds, the solar rays, and the very dynamic of growth. Everything, in short.

From projecting these geometric structures into the disarray of nature it seemed an obvious step for Jeanneret to assume their preexistence. Thus he and Ozenfant speak of universal constants, the formal units that are foundational for vision, that underlie everything that gives itself to be seen. He cast himself as well into this grid of geometric purposiveness, as he described the way he also was tailored to the universal design: "It was a matter of occupying a particular square on the chessboard: a family of musicians, a passion for drawing, a passion for the plastic arts . . . a character that wanted to get to the heart of things."

20 *Value.* "Value," Barthes writes, "regulates all discourse." He is speaking of the system through which culture generates meaning not by naming things, but by opposing two values within a structure: S/S̄. In this, structuralism's logic is binary—yes/no. But with Bataille, and here once again Barthes is speaking of "The Big Toe," value, or meaning, "rests on a peculiar, anomalous paradigm, since it is ternary."

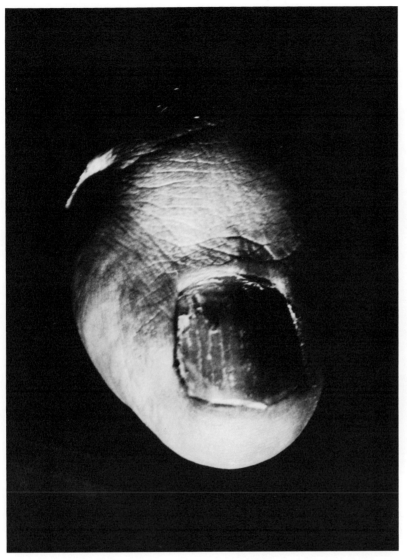

Jacques-André Boiffard, *Untitled*, 1929.

It is not that man does not try to force it into the paradigm, to ennoble the foot, to give it form . . . (p. 184)

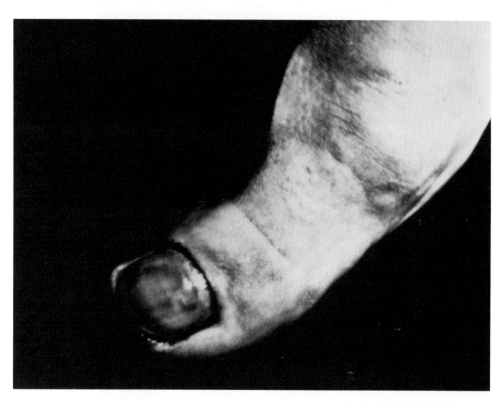

Jacques-André Boiffard, *Untitled*, 1929.

It is an irreducible term, says Barthes, "the term of seduction outside the *(structural)* law" . . . *(p. 185)*

Barthes does not explicitly graph the relations between the two terms of the paradigm (noble/ignoble) and the third term (low). But they could be so plotted, using, for example, Greimas's semiotic square. This structuralist graph, which its author extrapolated from the Klein Group, is, like the latter, a quaternary field within which a value is set in opposition not only to its contrary but to the contradictory term it also implies. In other words, "once any unit of meaning [S1] is conceived, we automatically conceive of the absence of that meaning [−S1], as well as an opposing system of meaning [S2] that correspondingly implies its own absence [−S2]." In distinguishing between the first binary, [S1] and [S2], and that of the implied second pair, Greimas's square plots the contradictory [$\overline{S1}$] as a complex term incorporating *both* S1 *and* S2; while $\overline{S2}$ is designated the neutral term, the expression of *neither* S1 *nor* S2.

It is possible to clarify and heighten the relationships implied by this square by mapping them onto the phenomenon that linguists call neutralization. In its simplest form, neutralization operates in relation to a binary that opposes marked and unmarked terms, the marked term understood as conveying more information than the unmarked one. Thus in the pair *old* and *young, young* is the marked term, since to say "John is as young as Mary" tells us more than does "John is as old as Mary," the latter simply conveying age, the former indicating age plus youthfulness. The unmarked term can then be neutralized into the complex condition of conveying both youth and agedness in the generalized term *old,* as in "thirty years old."

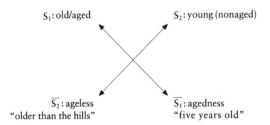

S_1: old/aged S_2: young (nonaged)

$\overline{S_2}$: ageless $\overline{S_1}$: agedness
"older than the hills"   "five years old"

That neutralization, in producing this generalized category, privileges the unmarked term over the marked one becomes more obvious if the pair in question carries a potentially charged content. Thus in the opposition *man/ woman* the marked term, *woman,* disappears within the neutralized complex form that combines both sexes into the categorical term, indifferent to gender: *man*. The conventional version of the square would then write the neutral term (neither man nor woman) as *humanity:*

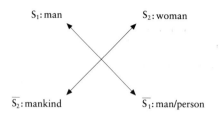

S₁: man   S₂: woman

S̄₂: mankind   S̄₁: man/person

But the neutral term need not be written in this way. Insofar as it stands to the complex term in a relation of opposition, the neutral term can be construed so as to generate a far more radical negativity, one that ultimately undoes "neutralization" by negating it. To place *she* in the fourth position, such that a marked term now becomes the generalized category, is to resist and disorganize the hierarchy coded into the purportedly neutralized term; it is to convey "the violence inscribed in the seemingly 'natural' and 'self-evident' use of *he* to mean 'person,' or *man* to mean 'humanity'."

190
four

It is then possible to analyze this displacement and overturning of neutralization as the very work we have come to call deconstruction. Speaking of the activity of the third term within Derrida's thought, one Greimasian scholar explains, "If the neutralizing term creates the order, then its denial deconstructs it, not with a new order, but an 'explosive' play and playing of forces. The 'graft' and 'trace' create this 'explosion': by using a marked term—'woman', 'writing', 'white', 'mark' itself—deconstruction conveys more information than neutralization permits. In this way it 'explodes' neutralization in the enunciation of its own intervention."

The enunciation that explodes neutralization in Bataille's "Big Toe" is, of course, the imposition of *low* as a third term:

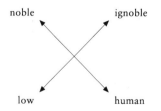

noble   ignoble

low   human

"Eccentric, full, irreducible," it is a form of this same radical negativity in which the *low* refuses that neutralization carried out by the paradigm through which the *human* is sublated into a system of values (*noble/ignoble*), insisting instead that the material term *low* is itself extrapolated from *human* as a function of Derrida's *"remainder* irreducible to the dominant force."* It is by means of this eccentric term that Bataille can then unseat or foul the paradigm by exposing its repressed material vectors, as when he ends his essay by saying "that one is seduced basely, without transpositions and to the point of screaming, opening one's eyes wide: opening them wide, then, before a big toe."

21 **Wind/unwind.** Winding the clock backward, Giacometti suspends a ball over the abyss of the *informe,* mounting an attack on form that lies within form, not outside it. Modernism dreams of rationalizing form, of making manifest the principles that subtend its merely perceptual presence. The gestalt is one way of thinking about the ordering and coherence of perception, of an already cognitive coordination within the perceptual plenum of figure plus ground. But modernism reaches beyond the complex term into the universalizing one: the neither/nor; the place where one looks for the very foundations of formalization itself. It finds it in the grid's generalization of order, in its condition as infinitely extensible generatrix of formal possibility:

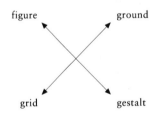

Suspended Ball reaches, however, for the third, the eccentric, the deconstructive term. Below the geometries of its elements—sphere/wedge—lies a body, a condition of carnality that refuses formalization. If the grid's system of intersection works to produce the universalization of difference—in a pure, abstract network of oppositions—each imagined swing of the work's pendulum resists the work of this work, fails to reinforce this difference, refuses the repeated production of the categorical relation (male/female). Instead the universal (difference) falls into the particular of *this body,* a particular that, as Giacometti works to make explicit, is, in its irreducible polymorphousness, radically nonsimple. Furthermore, if the grid's system constructs "form" within the general condition of synchrony, the deconstructive work of *Suspended Ball* is to formalize its production of the *informe* by placing diachrony at the heart of the system: the rhythmic beat the action of which is disruption, disarticulation, dysmorphia.

For modernism the neutral term—universalizing the general condition of form (gestalt)—comes increasingly to be understood as *grid. Suspended Ball* asks us to recognize an eccentric third term, one that refuses the assumption that *ground* can be generalized as an abstract plenum—neither figure nor ground, but their structural precondition. Its "third term" materializes *ground* as carnal and temporal, locating the preconditions of the visual elsewhere than in the transparency of the grid. The term *matrix* might be used for this refusal, *matrix* which means womb, or mold, or die, but also in Lyotard's usage, the unconscious.

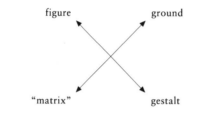

22 **X Marks the Spot.** Bataille's article of this name in *Documents* muses over a book on crime in Chicago and the forensic photographs of the victims of gangland murders. Benjamin would later agree that the photographic basis of aesthetic production in the new age of mechanical means would propel art into the role of documentation, so that all artists would echo Atget, who photographed Paris as though it were so many scenes of crime. But Brassaï was also interested in photographing the "scene of crime," and one more specifically about X-marking the spot. His series of graffiti images could have been programmed by Bataille himself, meditating on the relation between the art of the caves and the human need to dirty walls by leaving a mark: see *Caves,* above. See also chapter Six's discussion of graffiti, below.

23 **Zoology.** See *Double.*

Bibliographical Note

1 *Anamorph*. Salvador Dalí, "Objets psycho-atmosphériques-anamorphiques," *Le Surréalisme au Service de la Révolution*, no. 5 (May 1933), pp. 45–48.

2 *Base Materialism, and Gnosticism*. Georges Bataille, "Le bas matérialisme et la gnose," *Documents*, 2, no. 1 (1930), pp. 1–8; reprinted in Georges Bataille, *Visions of Excess: Selected Writings, 1927–1939*, ed. and trans. Allan Stoekl (Minneapolis: University of Minnesota Press, 1985).

3 *Caves*. André Leroi-Gourhan, "The Religion of the Caves: Magic or Metaphysics?," *October*, no. 37 (Summer 1986), pp. 6–17, and "The Hands at Gargas: Toward a General Study," *October*, no. 37 (Summer 1986), pp. 18–34. Georges Bataille, "L'art primitif," *Documents*, 2, no. 7 (1930), pp. 389–397, was a review of G. H. Luquet's *L'art primitif* (Paris: G. Doin, 1930).

For Bataille's relationship to primitive art, see Denis Hollier, "The Use Value of the Impossible," *October*, no. 60 (Spring 1992).

4 *Double*. The Salpêtrière photographs were published by Breton and Eluard to accompany their article "Le cinquantenaire de l'hystérie (1878–1928)," *La Révolution Surréaliste*, no. 11 (March 1928), pp. 20–22. The *con* in "convulsive beauty" is discussed in David Macey, *Lacan in Contexts* (London: Verso, 1988), pp. 66–68, 195.

Bataille's essay "The Old Mole and the Prefix *Sur* in the Words *Surhomme* and *Surréalisme*," written sometime in 1930 in response to Breton's "Second Manifesto of Surrealism," was never published. It is reprinted in Bataille, *Oeuvres complètes*, vol. 2 (Paris: Gallimard, 1970), pp. 93–109, and in Bataille, *Visions of Excess*, pp. 32–44.

Roger Caillois, "Mimétisme et psychasthénie légendaire," *Minotaure*, no. 7 (June 1935); and "Mimicry and Legendary Psychasthenia," trans. John Shepley, *October*, no. 31 (Winter 1984). Denis Hollier's phrase "subjective detumescence" is from his "Mimesis and Castration, 1937," *October*, no. 31 (Winter 1984).

5 *Ecstasy*. Dalí's photocollage *Le phénomène de l'extase* was published opposite a text of his by the same name in *Minotaure*, no. 3 (December 1933), pp. 76–77. Georges Bataille, "Bouche," *Documents*, 2, no. 5 (1930), p. 299 (and in *Visions of Excess*); "Informe," *Documents*, 1, no. 7 (1930), p. 382 (and in *Visions of Excess*). For a discussion of this projection of the *informe* through the rotation of the body, see my "Corpus Delicti," *L'Amour Fou: Photography and Surrealism*.

6 *Foundation*. Amédée Ozenfant, *Foundations of Modern Art* (1928), trans. John Rodker (New York: Brewer, Warren and Putnam, 1931).

7 *Game*. Georges Bataille, "Le 'Jeu lugubre,'" *Documents*, 1 (1929), pp. 369–372 (and in *Visions of Excess*).

8 *Geometry*. Ozenfant and Jeanneret, in *La peinture moderne* (Paris: Editions G. Crès, n.d.), devote a chapter to "Formation de l'optique moderne" (pp. 63–69). See also Ozenfant, *Foundations of Modern Art*, pp. 284–286.

9 *Hat.* Tristan Tzara, "D'un certain automatisme du goût," in *Minotaure,* no. 3 (1933), pp. 81–85.

Sigmund Freud, "Fetishism," *Standard Edition,* vol. 21, pp. 152–153.

10 *Informe.* Maurice Nadeau, *Histoire du surréalisme* (Paris: Seuil, 1945), p. 176. See the analysis of *Suspended Ball* in my "No More Play" (*The Originality of the Avant-Garde and Other Modernist Myths* [Cambridge: MIT Press, 1985]).

11 *Jouer/déjouer I.* Roland Barthes, "La métaphore de l'oeil," *Critique,* nos. 195–196 (1963), pp. 772–777; trans. Richard Howard, in Barthes, *Critical Essays* (Evanston: Northwestern University Press, 1972), pp. 239–248.

12 *Labyrinth.* In "No More Play" I discuss Giacometti's work in relation to the labyrinth and the production of sculpture as "bassesse."

13 *Mantis.* Roger Caillois, "La mante réligieuse," *Minotaure,* no. 5 (May 1934), pp. 23–26.

14 *Objective Chance.* Sigmund Freud, "The Uncanny," *Standard Edition,* vol. 17, pp. 234–235.

André Breton, *Nadja,* trans. Richard Howard (New York: Grove Press, 1960), p. 11.

15 *Photography.* Walter Benjamin, "A Small History of Photography" (1931), in *One Way Street,* trans. Edmund Jephcott and Kingsley Shorter (London: New Left Books, 1979), pp. 240–257; and "The Work of Art in the Age of Mechanical Reproduction" (1936), in *Illuminations,* trans. Harry Zohn (New York: Schocken Books, 1969), pp. 235–237.

Miriam Hansen discusses Benjamin's concept of the optical unconscious in her "Benjamin, Cinema and Experience," *New German Critique,* no. 40 (Winter 1987), pp. 207–211, 219–221.

16 *Rotten.* Georges Bataille, "Soleil pourri," *Documents,* 2, no. 3 (1930), pp. 173–174 (and in *Visions of Excess*). Ozenfant, "Formation de l'optique moderne," p. 65.

Clive Bell, "Constable et la peinture française," *Documents,* 2, no. 7 (1930), pp. 427–432.

17 *Screen.* Roger Caillois, "Mimicry and Legendary Psychasthenia."

Jacques Lacan, "What Is a Picture?," *The Four Fundamental Concepts of Psycho-Analysis* (1973), trans. Alan Sheridan (New York: W. W. Norton, 1978), pp. 105–119.

18 *Third Term. Jouer/déjouer II.* Georges Bataille, "Le gros orteil," *Documents,* 1, no. 6 (1929), pp. 297–302 (and in *Visions of Excess*).

Roland Barthes, "Les sorties du texte," in *Bataille,* ed. Philippe Sollers (Paris: 10/18, 1973), pp. 49–62; trans. Richard Howard, in Barthes, *The Rustle of Language* (New York: Hill and Wang, 1986), pp. 238–249.

19 *Universal.* Le Corbusier, as cited by William J. R. Curtis, *Le Corbusier: Ideas and Forms* (Oxford: Phaidon, 1986), pp. 17–18.

20 *Value.* This discussion of neutralization depends on that of Ronald Schleifer, *A. J. Greimas and the Nature of Meaning* (Lincoln: University of Nebraska Press, 1987), pp. 27–36, 50–56; and on deconstruction, ibid., pp. 166–182.

21 *Wind/Unwind.* For a discussion of Jean-François Lyotard's concept of "matrix," see chapter Five, below.

22 *X Marks the Spot.* Georges Bataille, "X marks the spot," *Documents,* 2, no. 8 (1930), p. 437.

Painting is stronger than I am. It makes me do what it wants.

—Picasso

five

And when we think about those '60s intellectuals in Paris, their eyes drawn to their television sets, their faces caught by a smile at once avid and knowing, their minds at work on the legitimation of their pleasure as they recode this quivering mountain of a man—in his tiny tights and ugly nail-studded belt, viciously kicking the head of his downed adversary over the protests of the referee—into the Scapin of their day, the grand figure of Treachery straight out of a morality play as old as the Greeks, do we imagine Barthes as cause or as symptom? What permission did he give by saying, just like that, that there's nothing vulgar about wrestling? "It is no more ignoble to attend a wrestled performance of Suffering than a performance of the sorrows of Arnolphe or Andromaque," Barthes had written.

And what about Picasso? Did he need such permission?

Picasso, after all, was the great source of his own authority. That's what they marveled at. The friends, the dealers, the photographers, the curators, the journalists, the collectors, the hangers-on, whoever had been allowed to enter La Californie in the 1950s, and now the massive farmhouse at Mougins to which he had retreated in the '60s, they watched enthralled as Picasso put on funny hats and fake mustaches and cavorted, bare-chested and in outrageously striped "convict" pants, on the terrace; as Picasso carelessly rolled and folded little pieces of paper over dinner so that before their eyes emerged a succession of tiny roosters and goats and Spanish dancers; as Picasso, surrounded by a wild mulch of objects—piles of every imaginable kind of paper, scatters of books and letters, profusions of masks and of plants, mobiles of sheet metal objects hanging from the masts of lamps, stacks of canvases twenty deep against the wall, clutters of ceramic pots, Spanish shawls, zebra skins, corrida posters, photographs—seemed to surface from amongst it all like a triumphant Triton, wreathed in seaweed and scallop shells and foam; as Picasso, the focus of every gaze, the magnet of every particle of attention, played with his courtiers' emotions like an impulsive Prince, now favoring them with a shaft of wisdom, now punishing them by his obstinate silence. He had needed no one's permission but his own after all to put a bicycle seat together with its handlebars and rename it a bull's head, to deform the female body in a thousand ways, from the fractured planes of cubism to the grand pneumatic tumescence of a reinvented classicism.

This house, itself a chaotic museum of its master's lifetime of inventions, was, it seemed to them, the perfect manifestation of Picasso's self-containment, of the way he demonstrated the complete autogenesis of the creative act, of the way painting comes from Painting, of the way Midas never had to leave his palace to turn everything to gold. This huge stone house, surrounded by vineyards and ancient olive trees, hung with cloaks of bougainvillea, seemed like a fortress erected against the world. A canal running below fed the pool onto which the terrace opened. "My Seine," Jacqueline liked to call it, reminding her listeners that she and Picasso had not left this stronghold for Paris for at least a decade.

So one would never imagine it there as well: the television set, riding the clutter of the main room on its unmistakable '50s pedestal, the one stolid eye that never turned toward the master.

Jacqueline hated the television set, hated Picasso's hours spent watching wrestling, his avidity for this thing that seemed to have no place within the carefully banked creative pyres of Notre Dame de Vie. Yet her obedience never flagged and, as her great friend Hélène Parmelin reports, she

Roberto Otero, photograph of Picasso's living room at Notre Dame de Vie, Mougins, from *Forever Picasso*.

The one stolid eye that never turned toward the master . . . (p. 198)

Pablo Picasso, *Bather with Beach Ball*, Boisgeloup, August 30, 1932.

The sheer buoyancy of Picasso's vision of the ripeness of her anatomy . . . (p. 201)

spent hours scouring the program guides to find the wrestling matches. "Wressing," Picasso pronounced it.

Hélène Parmelin imagines Picasso's enthusiasm for the spectacle: "All these guys who weigh a ton and yet move lightly through the air as though they were flying. Who thrust their feet everywhere, who rebound like rubber. And four-man wrestling! These little men who crisscross space like balls and always land on their feet? With or without it being staged, who cares, what athletes. What a show! How marvelous!" Which is to say she imagines Picasso reliving a part of his own aesthetic past: Marie-Thérèse at the beach, perhaps, floating above the sands on the sheer buoyancy of Picasso's vision of the ripeness of her anatomy. Rising curves billowing against a flat ground. That must be it.

Yet the more one considers it, the more the possibilities multiply. There's nothing in Barthes's analysis that wouldn't have appealed to Picasso. The notion of an exorbitant, but contemporary, *commedia dell'arte,* each character always true to type, each type corporealized with the same exactitude as Harlequin or Colombine, this theater is understood as staging and restaging the most primitive of morality plays: the demand for retribution. First there is Thauvin, Barthes begins, "a fifty-year-old with an obese and sagging body, whose type of asexual hideousness always inspires feminine nicknames," a figure who "displays in his flesh the characters of baseness, for his part is to represent what, in the classical concept of the *salaud,* the 'bastard' (the key-concept of any wrestling-match), appears as organically repugnant." After this *salaud,* there is the limp blond with disheveled hair radiating "the moving image of passivity," and the strutting queen who comes to the ring in a baby blue and pink dressing gown, the very picture of the "vindictive *salope,* or bitch." The spectacle these characters stage from one moment of exaggerated and carefully maintained "holds" to another is the great theater of Pain, Defeat, and Justice. "Wrestling presents man's suffering with all the amplification of tragic masks," Barthes says, adding, "But what wrestling is above all meant to portray is a purely moral concept: that of justice. The idea of 'paying' is essential to wrestling, and the crowd's 'Give it to him' means above all else 'Make him pay.'"

For the Picasso of the *Saltimbanques* or the *Three Musicians,* this telescoping of the tragic and the popular, this sense of the crowd's intimacy with the moral law as that is enacted in music halls and circus rings, in street theaters and sideshows, this display of popular justice so clearly captured by his beloved Charlot, none of this could be foreign.

Or, and equally plausibly, for the Picasso who enjoyed his own cruelty toward friends, lovers, business associates, what could be more appealing than this amazing exercise in inflicting pain, of pounding on the spine of one's temporarily grounded opponent, of grabbing the face of one's adversary and rubbing it into the mat, of entering totally into this machine for producing the image of torture under the cover of its self-description as "sport."

Or, and why not, there is the television set itself, this impassive eye that nonetheless exudes a constant visual beat since its image is produced by an electric current scanning upward along the hundreds of lines that cross the screen, generating an "image" through the continual renewal of its pulse, becoming all the more apparent when the set goes out of calibration and the whole image is wiped upward again and again as though pushed by an insistently reappearing black, horizontal bar. Why could it not be said that the screen's flicker, witness to its almost imperceptible mechanical pulse, provides the matrix, the formal support or "ground" against which these pounding, kicking, scratching, gouging "figures" of pain can be bodied forth to provide their full component of pleasure?

Yet it must be said that the collectors, the journalists, the friends, the curators would rally against this idea. What Picasso was happy to welcome at the manifest level of the content or "figure," they would point out, he was especially hostile to at the latent level of the formal support or "ground." The iconography of the popular—the clowns, the drunks, the waifs, the jugglers—was the *spécialité* of his particular *maison*. Its structure, on the other hand, the repetitive beat to which the bodies gyrate, the on/off binarism of the blinking signs, the mechanical spasms of the apparatus of the spectacle—whirring, spinning, shuttling, rattling—he found inadmissible.

Hélène Parmelin, ever willing, played the cat's-paw to his mounting annoyance in the late '50s and throughout the 1960s at what he could only regard as the inexplicable ascendance of Marcel Duchamp. There, through the narrow portal of Painting, was now pouring the whole detritus of the city—its neon signs, its hysterical sirens, its crawling metallic scrap heap, its entire mechanical ballet—as though someone had opened the floodgates and even then the dam had burst. The city, readymade, *kitsch*-ridden and monstrous, had breached the space of high culture. "They are ransacking Duchamp's warehouse and changing the packaging," Picasso fumed at the youngest generation. *Art and Anti-Art* was Hélène's little tract in the service of this exasperation.

Pablo Picasso, *Three Musicians*, Fontainebleau, summer 1921.

This sense of the crowd's intimacy with the moral law . . . (p. 201)

Max Ernst, *A Little Girl Dreams of Taking the Veil*, 1930: "Dans mon colombodrome."

And, inevitably, her dream will be pulsatile . . . (p. 209)

Hoping to match dada's cool with something of her own, the book is a shrug of the shoulders, a "sure, OK, terrific, why not?" She describes one of the May Salons: "Flying balloons and the most complex of electrical geometric labyrinths. Environments meant for architectural settings or for nothing at all. Rubber dolls that flop around on their beds, transparent plastic cages where indeterminate things are in motion, panels on which everyone is summoned to write, bits of sugar hung on strings, and all the bizarrenesses of neon, noise, movement."

"Sure," she says, "terrific, why not?" As long as they don't confuse this with Painting. As long as they drop their preposterous claim that because of this *painting* is dead. Her targets, one after another, are Fontana, Arman, Oldenburg, Buren. And, of course, Tinguély.

She has read in the papers somewhere that Tinguély has come forward with the proposition for a "lunatrack." This, according to the report, would be "a building 28 meters wide and 100 high, wholly of glass like any Mies skyscraper. Cost: 1 billion old francs. Beneath will be a garage, above a restaurant. Toboggans, shooting galleries, merry-go-rounds, ferris wheels, waterworks, dodge-em cars, parachutes, silly snack stands; it's the vertical concentration of the old Luna Park, enlarged with all kinds of technological gadgetry. The clever move is the facades . . . they will enliven 20,000 square meters of surface thanks to a permanent firing of brilliant colors." "OK, fine," Hélène retorts. "So what's holding things up? It'll be terrific!"

She shares Picasso's disdain for Duchamp. She labels all this stuff "the Concours Lépine of anti-art." She is just as mystified by the *Rotoreliefs* as she is by the slashed canvases of Fontana.

But on their face, of course, there is nothing "anti-art" about the *Rotoreliefs*. They participate in an iconography of abstraction into which could be placed the Orphic tondos of Delaunay, the cosmic figures of suprematism, the Newtonian disks of Kupka. Their "anti-art" comes at another level, the one where they make common cause with popular culture's own embrace of the media, of all forms of reproduction, here, most obviously, with the industry of recording. The *Rotoreliefs* with their pulsatile yet silent music evoke the listener's fascination with the spectacle of the turntable's monotonous spiral, with the sameness of its hypnotic beat whatever the melodic phrasing. What the *Rotoreliefs* throw in the face of Art and of Painting is not the image of another culture but a form, that of a pulse or beat, that the modernist artist senses all too well as the enemy of his

205

five

craft. For that pulse is devolutionary, destructive, dissolving the very coherence and stability of form.

In this, Duchamp was not alone in the '30s. The artists of the "optical unconscious" were particularly drawn to this beat, acknowledging the role it had begun to play in all forms of the popular.

From his outpost in the Ardèche at the end of the 1920s, Max Ernst would look through his pile of La Nature *dating from the 1880s and '90s, vicariously reliving the fascination its readership had had with whole ranges of optical devices—praxinoscopes, zootropes, phaenakistiscopes—through which an early version of the "movies" was then being imagined. The toys of children, the attractions at village fairs, the after-dinner amusements of middle class families, these had been the devices of visual prestidigitation: producing astonishing effects of three-dimensionality and of images in motion. But as he knew all too well, the movement, far from being fluid, was captive to the intermittence of, for example, the little slitlike openings along the drum of the zootrope. Through each of these slits you could see an image on the far side of the drum's inner wall, each one a single station in a sequence of positions, the frozen moment from within a recorded burst of motion. As the drum turned each new slit would uncover an additional position, the whole revolution revealing the entire arc of activity: a bird's wings dipping as its neck strains forward and then lifting upward as its head retracts. "Flight" would thus be captured in the circuit of the drum and giddily released for the onlooker.*

But "flight" was nonetheless syncopated by the march of the little openings passing before your fascinated gaze, separated as they had to be by stretches of blankness. Onto the effortless freedom of the bird's forward motion would thus be projected the stop-and-go flicker of these visual interruptions. This hiccup, this jerkiness, this twitch, would enter the projection of early films, from nickelodeons to silents, finally to be internalized in Chaplin's very walk, as hitching up his pants and bouncing his cane he imitated the tremor that constantly palsied the visual space of primitive cinema, everyone seeming to march to the sound of an invisible drummer.

Adoring these optical devices, drawn by the beat that coursed through their illusion, he would exploit them often. For an important image in his collage novel A Little Girl Dreams of Taking the Veil *he would place his heroine at the center of what she calls a dovecote but his viewer would recognize as the drum of a zootrope. He had lifted the image from the pages of* La Nature, *where the mechanism had been displayed from slightly*

Zootrope, *La Nature* (1888), p. 12.

The little slitlike openings along the drum of the zootrope . . . (p. 206)

Bronze figures representing eleven successive positions
of a pigeon in flight, *La Nature* (1888), p. 12.

The frozen moment from within a recorded burst of motion . . . (p. 206)

above so that you could see how each of the birds in the sequence was mounted on a little stand to bring it to the level of the slits in the drum. In a different illustration you were shown, as well, the separate models of birds in flight that Marey had had sculpted on the basis of his chronophotographic evidence. Here, in this serialized progression, was the "analysis" of motion, of which the "synthesis" could then be produced by the whirl of the zootrope's illusion.

From the pages of La Nature it was perfectly evident to him that the nineteenth-century audience of this magazine of popular science liked to play with both analysis and synthesis at the same time, wishing to be captivated by the appearance of the spectacle and, like the child in front of the clock he has just dismantled, wanting also to be connected to its inner works. The magazine had catered to this double pleasure. Ernst looks at an illustration in which such an audience is shown sitting spellbound in front of a screen onto which an anaglyphic image is being cast by means of a stereoscopic projector. Waistcoated, goateed, or in stays and flowered hats, each of the viewers is wearing glasses, one lens red and the other green, as he or she stares at the utterly enthralling display of a cow in 3-D drinking from the banks of a startlingly convincing stream. For the reader, looking on from outside, everything is labeled, the red beam, the green one, and, where they cross, the emergence of white light.

This both-at-once, this being caught inside the illusion and this looking on nonetheless from without, would, he understood, suit his purposes perfectly. It would manifest that peculiar feeling you have when you dream and even while captured by the emotions of its drama you can speak of yourself as someone else: "You're only dreaming, you know." So in his collage he will use the zootrope in such a way that, simultaneously inside the illusion and outside it, the little girl will dream of taking the veil.

And, inevitably, her dream will be pulsatile. The surge of the wings beating up and down from within the illusion will visually rhyme with the flickering staccato of the zootrope's motion, a rhythm connecting the interior image with the exterior "form." This is the rhythm that will simultaneously construct the gestalt and threaten it with dissolution, with a breakup into its separate, impotent fragments. And this is the rhythm, he knew as well, that will allow the erotic currents of the dream to surface.

Although Hélène is sitting on a rocking chair—his "throne," as he calls it—she remains carefully motionless, any movement, she realizes, threatening this fabulous stillness, this sense of being suspended, weightless, in an imperceptibly dilating, luminous void. Her thoughts seem infinitely to expand within the radiance of the enormous studio, their intensity matching that of the brilliant Midi sun. A sob almost catches in her throat as the very meaning of painting seems to flood her brain. "Everything," she thinks, "is clear to me. I am living one of those moments when the workings of the mind are at their keenest and one's intellect reaches out to meet the creator's which floods and gratifies it."

She is happy for once that Picasso isn't here, won't speak into this silence, won't rupture this concentration, scattering it with words no matter how brilliant. She thinks of the importance of this blazing sun for Picasso. She thinks of how he hates gray weather, rain, wind. "The sun here is a sort of charm," she muses, "protecting the illuminated silence of work."

The silence and the stillness go together, the stillness that is painting's hallmark, painting's genius. She remembers Picasso saying, "For me, Hélène, the role of painting is not to depict movement, to put reality into motion. Its role is rather, I think, to arrest motion. In order to freeze the image you have to outdistance motion. If not, you are always running behind. Only at that very moment," he would add, "do you have reality."

That very moment, she muses, is a paradox. That very moment involves the amazing speed of the eye as it outruns motion by synthesizing it into the single image of its "meaning." Photography's picture can never be anything but frozen movement, the gesture deprived of its inner life. Painting, she thinks, in its very stillness, its carefully structured immobility, is the true analogue of the visual completeness of this mastery by the gaze.

Silence, the silence of these studios in which Picasso obsessively works, the completeness of this silence, guaranteed by this baking, dazzling sun, is the necessary medium within which the blade thrust of this gaze which is both lightning-quick and timeless—hanging as it does in the perpetual suggestiveness of this race between the tortoise and the hare—will be able to swell to infinity.

She tears her eyes away from the painting mounted on its easel to look through the deep arches of the doorway-windows. Her gaze sweeps over the tops of the olive trees past the silhouettes of the distant buildings to the sea lying in wait in the background. Under the flaming sun the sea is molten, a buckling sheet of metal, its surface radiating waves of heat. She hears the cicadas' frenzy as they fill the air with a constant shriek. "There is this kind of invisible cloak of crazy heat," she thinks, "under which the whole of nature vibrates, the air trembles," as even the sound of the

Stereoscopic projections, *La Nature* (1891), p. 49.

Wishing to be captivated by the appearance of the spectacle . . . (p. 209)

Reynaud's projective praxinoscope, *La Nature* (1882), p. 357.

*This both-at-once, this being caught inside the illusion and this looking on
nonetheless from without . . . (p. 209)*

highway below—"this incessant *ronron,*" she smiles—completes the quality of the atmosphere in its almost hysterical pulsing, shimmying, beating, bopping . . .

She looks back at the painting on the easel, Jacqueline royally lounging on her green *chaise.* "The absolute silence of this place," she jots in her notebook, "its utter stillness, this perfect ambience for painting's timeless, motionless gaze."

Hélène Parmelin is, in this, nothing if not orthodox. She agrees with the art historian about painting's genius, painting's *truth.* She agrees that this is coextensive with the truth of the terms of vision. Those terms, she concurs, have their existence in a space that has nothing to do with sequence, with narrative, with movement through time. The terms of vision's truth are instead a function of what happens in the twinkling of an eye.

The visual pyramid on which classical perspective is built is a geometry, after all, by which the lines of sight and the lines of light are absolutely coordinated, a coordination that produces the identity (in mirror) between the vanishing point within the picture and the viewing point within the eye. And it is not for nothing that this geometry turns around the almost unimaginable limit of "infinity," a point that is literally reduced to nothing. Far from nothing coming from nothing, the truth that arises from this Euclidean meeting of parallel lines at that point beyond the limit of imagining is the solidity of the construction's basis in geometrical law. And the infinite smallness of this point in the eye from which the entire architecture is suspended is, as well, an infinite rapidity. If, in the art historian's perspective diagrams, the eye is always pictured open and fixated, staring into the pyramid's tunnel, that's because it is an eye that sees with such dazzling quickness that it has no need to blink. It sees in a twinkling, before the blink. And this twinkling, this infinite brevity or immediacy of the gaze, is the analogue for the picture's own condition in the all-at-once, for painting's ontological truth as pure simultaneity.

It is in this sense that painting is radically unassimilable to time. For it lives in a perpetual "now."

If the Renaissance had diagrammed the punctuality of this viewing point, it was modernism that insisted on it, underscored it, made the issue of this indivisible instant of seeing serve as a fundamental principle in the doctrine of its aesthetic truth. Modernism was to absolutize this "now," to insist that Painting exist within the indivisible present of the extremest possible perceptual intensity: the rush of pure color; the shock of light-on-dark as ground pulls level with figure; the reduction of the world to pattern. Nothing was to segment off the "now" from itself, not the chatter of narrative nor the distraction of description nor even the sense of a separation between the surface life of the image and the physicality of its support. The singleness of the pictorial datum was to be the mirror image of the form through which it was apprehended, it was to be the very picture of the instantaneity of vision-in-consciousness.

And even while the modernist artist had intuited the need for this speed, this visuality of the instant, Husserl had theorized it. Phenomenology had also needed this concept of punctuality, of the *now* as *stigmē*. In seeking to found the truth of consciousness in primordial intuition, in the fact of the immediate self-presence of lived experience as the mode of certitude and absolute necessity, Husserl fought the idea that consciousness needed to tell itself about what it was living. Consciousness did not have to be redoubled into an experience and a thought about, or an analysis of, that experience in order to breathe meaning into it. The existence of mental acts, Husserl insisted, does not have to be analyzed by the subject because their effects are immediately present to him in the present moment. And in this immediacy of self-presence the present, as lived intuition, is already fully meaningful.

The self-immediate is the unredoubled. It does not say "now you are going . . . ," "now you are doing . . . ," "now you are thinking. . . ." There is no time for that. If, Husserl argues, mental acts are not announced to themselves through the intermediary of analytical discourse, it is because they are "lived by us in the same instant" (*im selben Augenblick*). This instant, the instant of self-presence, is indivisible. It is as indivisible as a twinkling of the eye.

Thus the indivisibility of self-immediacy will go hand-in-hand with the indivisibility of a temporal present, characterized as "now." Jacques Derrida thinks about Husserl's need for this concept of "now," this point that, like the "infinity" of the perspective diagram, cannot be subdivided.

It is a fiction, he thinks. It is a myth. "It is a spatial or mechanical metaphor, an inherited metaphysical concept." He knows why Husserl must preserve this fiction, this myth of the instant as a point. He knows that if phenomenology's central concept of self-presence must be produced in the undivided unity of a temporal present, this is because it must have nothing to reveal to itself by what can only be the secondhand agency of signs. As

Husserl had written in *Ideen,* "between perception on the one hand and the symbolic representation by means of images or signs on the other, there exists an insurmountable eidetic difference."

But this is an eidetic difference, Derrida sees, that Husserl himself is forced to erode as, writing with the whole of nineteenth-century neurophysiology at his back, he is led to expand or dilate this "now," to make it continuous with something else. There can be no lived experience, in fact, in the absence of memory and expectation, or as the physiologist would term them, retensions and protensions. Husserl admits this. Listen to him saying, "the now-apprehension is, as it were, the nucleus of a comet's tail of retensions," adding that "a punctual phase is actually present as now at any given moment, while the others are connected as a retensional train." Husserl tries to get around the problem of this retensional train as something apart from the "now." If the now is primordial experience, retension is seen as a kind of primary memory that Husserl also wants to call primordial. It is immediate to the "now"; not secondhand like something remembered later, after the event.

Derrida leaps on this fact of retension, this nonpresent carried into the present, this not-now infecting the now. For it points to the very temporality of consciousness's putative "present" that phenomenology cannot acknowledge. "As soon as we admit this continuity of the now and the not-now, perception and nonperception," Derrida writes, "in the zone of primordiality common to primordial impression and primordial retension, we admit the other into the self-identity of the Augenblick; nonpresence and nonevidence are admitted into the blink of the instant. There is a duration to the blink, and it closes the eye."

Onto the screen of that closed lid, Ernst had projected the pulsations of the zootrope as an emblem of temporal distension and of the self-division of the dream: consciousness as decidedly not self-present in the present, consciousness crying out to itself from the depths of its spasm of fear or pleasure, "Now, that is you; and you are dreaming."

Ernst's dream shares with Duchamp's pulse, the pulse of the Rotoreliefs *and of the whole of Precision Optics, an attention to the forms of mass culture. Just as it shares a sense that this pulse is erotic. Indeed the dance staged by the* Rotoreliefs, *as the bump and grind of their gyrations pushes them from the illusion of one body part to the next, is Duchamp's version of a seven veils that is deeply exploitative of Husserl's "comet's tail," his "retensional train." The "now" of Husserl's self-presence might be utterly disincarnated—defined by the absence of that very body within which retensional memory could unfold—just as the disembodied "eye" of Leonardo's perspective diagrams is presented as a viewing "point," detached and abstracted. Duchamp's reliefs are fixed, instead, on corporealizing the visual, on restoring to the eye (against the disembodied opticality of modernist painting) that eye's condition as bodily organ, available like any other physical zone to the force of eroticization. Dependent on the connection of the eye to the whole network of the body's tissue, this force wells up within the density and thickness of the carnal being, as, tied to the conditions of nervous life, it is by definition a function of temporality. For the life of nervous tissue is the life of time, the alternating pulse of stimulation and enervation, the complex feedback relays of retension and protension. So that the temporal is mapped onto the figural in the space of Precision Optics as the specific beat of desire—of a desire that makes and loses its object in one and the same gesture, a gesture that is continually losing what it has found because it has only found what it has already lost.*

And it is time as well that Giacometti courts, placing it in the center of the cage of his Suspended Ball, *allowing the visual frame to be invaded by the emotionally disturbing disruption of a beat. As the pendulum of the cloven ball swings over the attendant wedge, this beat seems to measure out the oscillating determinations of genitality. The back-and-forth of the work's rhythmic arc operates as a temporal analogue to the shifting undecidability of its definition of gender, the sculpture thus asserting itself as a machine geared to the collapse of sexual difference. As Giacometti's little guillotine of castration works once again in relation to a beat, its pulse can be seen to be operating in a way that is deeply inimical to the stability and self-evidence of form, to the permanence—let us say—of the good gestalt.*

Form was what Hélène Parmelin had understood that day, as the meaning of painting rushed to her head with a conclusiveness that left her faint. Form—the gestalt—was what had presented itself to her as founding principle in the field of the visual: a sense that painting's meaning was to be found in the simultaneous separation and intactness of figure and ground, in the gestalt's operation as the concordance between absolute difference (figure versus ground) and complete simultaneity (no figure without ground). She had known, Picasso had indeed told her, that the field of good form has no need of motion; that motion comes from outside the domain of the visual. All those beats that surrounded the studio—the *ronron* of the highway, the trill of the cicadas, even the trembling of the heat—must logically be distinct from this visual field, can be nothing but interlopers from the domain of the temporal, the auditory, the discursive. No, she had thought, they cannot be the matrix within which the master works. And the pulse of the television's image also must be outside the "visual," must be external, eccentric to this world of form.

But this notion of outsideness, of the temporal as necessarily outside the visual, this idea of the separation of the senses on which modernism's logic is built, it is just this that the beat exploited by the artists of the "optical unconscious" contests. The pulse they employ is not understood to be structurally distinct from vision but to be at work from deep inside it. And from that place, to be a force that is transgressive of those very notions of "distinctness" upon which a modernist optical logic depends. Insofar as they insist that it is not temporal, the beat they employ must, in some sense, be figural—but of an order of the figure that is far away from the realm of space that can be neatly opposed to the modality of time.

The order of the figure. Modernism imagines two such orders. The first is that of empirical vision, the object as it is "seen," the object bounded by its contours, the object modernism spurns. The second is that of the formal conditions of possibility for vision itself, the level at which "pure" form operates as a principle of coordination, unity, structure: visible but unseen. That is the level that modernism wants to chart, to capture, to master. That is the formal order of the gestalt that Hélène, dizzy with comprehension, had grasped. But there is a third order of the figure, one that Jean-François Lyotard has decided to call *matrix,* by which he means an order that operates beyond the reach of the visible, an order that works entirely underground, out of sight.

He had started off, of course, from the position of Husserl, and of Merleau-Ponty, with a belief in a primordial intuition that is not in need of "concepts" in order to grasp its world. Nothing comes "before" to shape the aperture that perception opens onto the field of experience; nothing structures that opening in advance. That is why, he thinks, phenomenology's founding principle is not "intentionality" but passivity. Sure, Cézanne intended an experience in which *depth* would burgeon forth from the evidence of mountains and trees; but the background of this intention, Lyotard sees, was an extreme passivity, a voluptuous stillness through which Cézanne could allow this meaning-in-depth to happen. That passivity, he thinks, permits the body's own density to well up into the field of perception and to carry along with it not phenomenology's unconscious— a kind of primordial unity that is itself the subject of constitution—but a different unconscious, the one that is the object of repression. What Merleau-Ponty cannot address, Lyotard muses, is Cézanne's desire.

No matter, he thinks. He will address it. Though phenomenology's unconscious is not that of Freud, the two are compatible in their belief in a primordial spatiality. For the continuous extension within which the body's gesture unfolds its meaning is, after all, the same medium in which the complex dance of displacements and condensations occurs, a continuity hostile to the staccato break-up of the spatial medium which is that of speech. The transparent grid where signifiers are formed through the regulated action of spacing is an abstract, purely conceptual medium disjunct from the one through which the perceptual event unrolls or the impress of desire swells.

Lyotard thus begins with phenomenology's disdain for discourse, for language, for concepts, for the law. And to this he adds that of psychoanalysis. In their mutual opposition to language, libidinal and sensory meaning, he thinks, seem to map one onto the other. But it is in the realm of this "lived" space of experience that they also break apart. For phenomenology's world is forever that of the *partes extra partes,* of a space that unfolds progressively, constantly making room for the bodies that fill it. In this it is a space that is fundamentally *visible,* whether its organizing principle be seen or not. It is the space in which "form" will come into being; the space of good form, of the gestalt.

Psychoanalysis's space, the space of the unconscious, he comes to realize, disdains this fundamental notion of the coordinates of the real. In defiance of all probability it allows two, or three, or five things to be in the same place at the same time. And these things are themselves utterly heteroclite, not variations on one another but things in total opposition. This "space" is therefore quite literally unimaginable: a congealed block of contradictions. Not a function of the visible, it can only be intuited through the projection of various "figures" that surface from the depths of this "space": the slip of the tongue, the daydream, the fantasy. To this medium, lying below the level of the visible, he gives the name *matrix,* and he begins to follow its activity, which he recognizes as the production not of the gestalt but of bad form, the activity through which form is in fact transgressed.

Looking for instances of these "bad forms" in Freud's accounts of his cases, he thinks of the story of the young woman who, in a fit of paranoid fantasy, imagines her lover has photographed her lying with him on a couch. She "hears" a noise that she insists is the clicking of a camera's shutter. But Freud understands it otherwise. It is, he says, a repetition of that primal fantasy, so common in children, of watching their parents making love, a fantasy whose auditory component is simultaneously the sound of what is happening and a fear of making a noise that will betray their presence. Going even farther than this, Freud argues that the fantasy allows the young woman here to play the role of her mother, and having entered onto the stage of its sexual action, to produce the "click" of the camera as a paranoid denial of the pulse of her own excitement.

He likes the "click" as a figure. But, he concludes, there is not enough in what Freud relates here to be able to plot the workings of the matrix.

So he turns to the case called "A Child Is Being Beaten."

It is the story of a fantasy that several patients—filled with terrible shame—confess to Freud. "A child is being beaten," they think, as they find themselves shaking with pleasure. The single sentence is startling in its brevity. Freud probes. He discovers what he thinks must be an earlier version of the fantasy, one where the patient—one of four women whom, along with two men, he has analyzed—is able to say that an adult, yes, undoubtedly her father, is beating another child; she is looking on. So he has two sentences: "The father beats the (other) child"; and "A child is being beaten." Something has happened between the first sentence and the second, he notices. Active has turned to passive. This leads him to imagine an intermediary stage in which such a transformation could occur. It is a stage, he realizes, of utmost importance to the obsessional character of the fantasy, because it is that transition that gives it its erotic spin. The patient does not produce this stage; Freud reconstructs it, by ventriloquy, as it were. "I am being beaten by the father," it goes.

In his rebellion against what has come to seem to him the absolutism and ubiquity of an ideology of the "sign," of the rise and triumph of structural linguistics, and of semiology, Lyotard is filled with admiration for this move. Structuralism, grounding its own truth in the laws of opposition between binary pairs, is fond of the principle of commutability. In the abstract, logical space of the table in which S is contrasted with $\bar{S}$, it makes no difference if $\bar{S}$ were to precede its opposite. This commutability is an equally neutral affair for the linguist, who says that a transformation into the passive is correct if it changes nothing in the meaning; thus, "X beats a child" is the same as "a child is being beaten by X." But unlike the linguist, the analyst has seen desire sneaking through the space of this diagram, trying to escape attention by, of course—why not?—following

219

five

the rules. "At the very interior of this legitimate transformation wholly contained within the system of *oppositions,*" Lyotard marvels, "the thrust of an anal-sadistic regression toward masochistic pleasure is nonetheless 'represented.'" The analyst, caring nothing for the logic of commutability's "no change," has spotted the way desire has put the innocence of syntax to work so that the "neutral" fact of the passive voice might carry the psychic meaning implied by a retreat from action. The activity of "X beats the child" is genital, the expression of Oedipal desire, as the girl identifies with her father. But as the repression of this desire and its release of guilt transports the watching patient into the place of the (other) child, passive, she now assumes the role of victim. Yet the masochism of this position has its own rewards, as a spanking that is also understood as a caress hastens a regressive debasement in the libidinal nature of the drive. "The father beats the child" had been understood as "(Therefore) my father loves me," which was meant in the genital sense. "Owing to regression," Freud writes, "it is turned into 'My father is beating me (I am being beaten by my father).' This being beaten is now a meeting-place between the sense of guilt and sexual love. *It is not only the punishment for the forbidden genital relation, but also the regressive substitute for it,* and from this latter source it derives the libidinal excitation which is from this time forward attached to it."

"A Child Is Being Beaten" is everywhere filled with this logic of "but also." That is what Lyotard admires in it. For just as the beating is not only punishment for guilt *but also* a source of pleasure, every other element is similarly ruled by this wild ambivalence, this simultaneous holding of two wholly contrary positions. This simultaneity is the peculiar temporality of the matrix, the fact that within it, one "stage" does not progress beyond and thus supersede another; rather, the meanings of all the stages remain suspended within it, in the form of a "but also." Lyotard decides to call this "but also" a "difference" and to cast this notion of *difference* in the teeth of structuralism's rule of *opposition.* Opposition is what logically constructs the distributive distances within the diagrammatic space of structuralism, holding apart one thing from another and therefore at one and the same time establishing the elements of the system (what Lyotard calls "the products of separation") and the rules of their transformation ("the productive separations"). The lucidity of structuralism's space, the perfect transparency of, for example, the Klein Group, is a function of this continual separation of opposites, this maintenance of the law of noncontradiction.

The work of the unconscious, however, doesn't recognize this law, has no use for negation. It thus courts the transformation of everything into its opposite, holding both of these things together at once.

It amuses Lyotard to compare the matrix figure of the unconscious to the structuralist's system, since both, after all, share the properties of invisibility and synchrony. But the structuralist's invisibility is that of a virtual order working within the system to produce its intelligibility: the system as a producer of meaning. While the matrix's invisibility is a function of the repressive work of mutating everything into its opposite, thereby undermining the productive work of structure. The elements of the matrix, Lyotard thinks, do not form a system but a block. "If the matrix is invisible, it is not because it arises from the intelligible, but because it resides in a space that is beyond the intelligible, is in radical rupture with the rules of opposition. . . . It is its characteristic to have many places in one place, and they block together what is logically incompatible. This is the secret of the figural: the transgression of the constitutive intervals of discourse, and the transgression of the constitutive distance of representation."

As it blocks together active *and* passive, genital *and* anal, sadism *and* masochism, watching *and* being watched, "A child is being beaten"—the completed work of the matrix—overlays contradiction and creates the simultaneity of logically incompatible situations. Yes, Lyotard thinks, the fantasy is the perfect matrix figure, because "the statements one can project as layered within it that organize the goal (to beat), the source (the anal zone), and the object (the father) of one sentence are in their turn condensed into a single product formula—'A child is being beaten'—whose apparent coherence allows the psychic life to contain in a single manifold a multiplicity of logically incompatible 'sentences.' These do not form a system but a block. Thus the drive to be and to have the father is simultaneous; and the investment is both genital-phallic and sadistic-anal."

But there is one invariance in all of this, one constant. It is in a sense the matrix figure's own medium, the one that measures off all the oscillations of place and of direction, the one that then blocks them together on the rhythm of its particular action. That action is "to beat" and it is this pulse that remains unchanged from stage to stage. The contents of the fantasy may be in continual flux, marked by a constant instability. But underlying these contents is a form: a rhythm, a pulse. It is this form that works to secure the identity of the fantasy such that in each of its obsessional repetitions it will always return as the same. "The fantasmatic matrix," Lyotard thinks, "is evidently a 'form.'"

Lyotard is not happy. "How in general," he thinks, "can that which is form also be transgression? How can what is deviation, derogation, deconstruction, be at the same time form?" This pulse, he objects, is too easy to assimilate to musical intervals, to chromatic oppositions, to the diachronic rhythms of meter or even the synchronic rhythm of columns on a facade, in short, to the law of proportionality. "All the Pythagorean Platonists will burst into applause," he fumes, "if we are forced to grant that the order of the fantasy, the regularity within which the subject's unconscious is so to speak 'caught,' the formal matrix of its dreams and its symptoms, is obedient to a rationalizable proportion." Bum-bah, bum-bah, bum-bum. This pulse would seem to return us to the intervalic, and through "good form" to language. A kind of "fundamental iamb," he worries.

Then he thinks about *Beyond the Pleasure Principle* and the two different pulses that Freud weaves together there. One is the hum of charge and discharge as the pleasure principle operates toward the release of tension and the maintenance of the lowest levels of excitation. This rhythm, which is the on/off throb of $+ - + - + -$, or of the presence and absence of contact, can be seen as the metrical "figure" of *to beat:* its form. But the second pulse is not a principle of recurrence guaranteeing that an "on" will always follow an "off"; it maps the principle, instead, of interruption. It is a pulse that is rather to be figured as $+ 0$, which is to say existence followed by total extinction. It is thus a "beat" that does not promise the return of the same, but simply re-turn, the coming of nothing. This second pulse is not a good form, not a good gestalt. Rather, he thinks, "it is a form in which desire remains caught, form caught by transgression; but it is also the, at least potential, transgression of form." The anxiety that is part of the affect of "A Child Is Being Beaten," combining with its erotic pleasure, arises precisely from the force of rupture that is recurrent in the rhythm of the figure, a rupture that is not experienced as the onset of yet another contact but as an absolute break, that discontinuity without end that is death. Thus it is the death drive, operating below the pleasure principle, Lyotard sees, that transcodes this rhythm—as it beats with the alternation between pleasure and extinction—into a compulsion to repeat. The matrix is the form that figures recurrence.

The beating of the zootrope, cranking up to speed, the beating of the gull's wings within the imaginary space, the beating of all those mechanical devices through which the real appears to burst into life from the shards of the inorganic and deathly still, and the particular form of the pleasure

Pablo Picasso, *Déjeuner sur l'herbe d'après Manet*, 10 July 1961.

The variation on a theme is a complete thought about another complete thought . . . (p. 225)

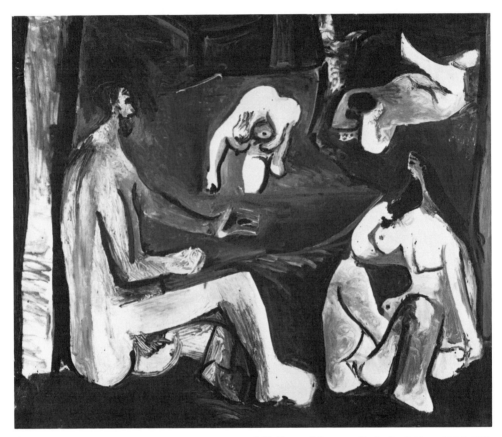

Pablo Picasso, *Déjeuner sur l'herbe d'après Manet,* 13 July 1961.

*Hundreds of preparatory studies by means of which the original could be
seen to be varied over the time of his creative attention . . . (p. 226)*

connected to that rhythm, all this became a resource for an artistic practice disinclined to obey the modernist law of the immobility of painting. Focused simultaneously on the unconscious ground of that pleasure and on its media form, which is to say its relation to mechanical reproduction, the artists of the "optical unconscious" were concerned with the vehicles of mass culture. It seemed to them that what was confirmed there was an order in which the neat separation of the senses—space logically segmented off from time—had been dissolved, deconstructed. That the beat summoned by these devices could not be understood as structurally distinct from "vision" but as operating from within it. They welcomed this beat, then, as a force that could transgress those very notions of "distinctness" on which modernism relies. The beat seemed to scatter the certainty of a statement like Picasso's: "For me, the role of painting is not to depict movement, to put reality into motion. Its role is rather, I think, to arrest motion."

The analysis of the gesture into its incremental displacements, so that the animation process can photograph the separate renderings of the same body each time ever so slightly reconfigured; the mechanical procedure of creating the minute variations that can subsequently be jerked into motion by their passage through the camera's gate or by the even cruder riffling of pages in the common flipbook: all this, as a resource of the beat, exists, it would seem, miles away from Picasso's studio. There his work was dedicated, for the last two decades of his life, to another process entirely: that of theme and variation.

How apt this procedure seems to his strictures against the admission of movement into painting. The variation on a theme is a complete thought about another complete thought, each wholly imbricated within the other, which is to say, within the confines of the pictorial frame, as neatly as if in a nest of Chinese boxes. As the variation secures its own pictorial unity both against and in relation to the unity of the theme, it becomes a declaration of the energies of the invention of its author, of the continual upsurge within his imagination of ever new ways of conceiving the original idea, no matter how powerful. A warrant of a fund of originality that seems never to be spent, the variation declares itself a resource of voluntary repetition, the outpouring of the controlled play of difference, wholly unlike the empty recurrence of the media forms. Deep into the later phases of the age of mechanical reproduction—television, discos, transistor radios—the austerity of the pictorial variation seems secure against the rhythmic pull of the "beat."

The *Femmes d'Alger,* the *Meninas,* the *Raphael and the Fornarina,* the *Déjeuner sur l'herbe,* all served as armatures for this process, through which the master spun out hundreds of preparatory studies by means of which the original could be seen to be varied over the time of his creative attention, each study sustaining and tracking the bursts of his imaginative energy. Even from within the fury of work, Picasso carefully located each element in the process, recording its date and, since the mere indication of a day would not suffice to distinguish the individuals in this multitude, its number. Thus it is possible to follow these creative strands, to reel up the thread of this fabulous abandon, and to try to enter the cave of the master's inspiration. It is in this vein that the art historian discusses the sketches leading toward one of Picasso's versions of the *Déjeuner sur l'herbe.*

"During the three days from the 7th to the 10th of July Picasso gave himself up to a period of intense creative work on the *Déjeuner,*" he reports. "In that short time he drew no less than 28 new compositional studies—18 of them in one day—and executed a second definitive variation in oils. These drawings reveal even more than those which preceded them the concentration of his thought." The historian describes the stutter with which the drawings announced repeated small corrections and revisions. From one to the next, "things are changed around ever so slightly," he observes, as "an arm or a leg will be moved for the sake of the general design." But no matter how seemingly transitory, the drawings are declared to be "masterly," and within them the historian sees Picasso "working with the fervor and conscientiousness of a Cézanne."

Cézanne, we remember, is the very personification of the phenomenologist's "now," the artist who was able to outwait appearances so that the meaning of depth could well up within him. He is the artist who was able so absolutely to synthesize the time of this waiting into a single, inextricable unity that he seemed to provide the very proof of the notion of the gestalt.

Picasso's drawings, however "masterly," are not syntheses in this sense. If he was able to produce eighteen in a day—something that would have been inconceivable for Cézanne—it was because, to a certain extent, he had a mechanical, reproductive basis for his process. The sketchbooks Picasso filled in the two and a half years of his work on the *Déjeuner* are produced in the manner of the animation film. For the drawing on each page—incised into its soft, thick paper with sharp penciled lines—in fact embosses its contours into the page lying beneath it. This trace, identical to the first, serves as the contour for a new drawing almost the twin of the one on the page above but for the fact that, as the art historian had noted,

Pablo Picasso, *Déjeuner sur l'herbe d'après Manet Sketchbook,* 4 July 1961 I.

In fact embosses its contours into the page lying beneath it . . . (p. 226)

Pablo Picasso, *Déjeuner sur l'herbe d'après Manet Sketchbook,* 4 July 1961 II.

"Things are changed around ever so slightly". . . (p. 229)

"things are changed around ever so slightly." With *this* now as the basis, the process then continues, as the new page etches its own configuration in turn into the succeeding level of the sketchbook, and so on. The mode of production Picasso can thus be seen to adopt is not that of the successive upsurge of renewed inspiration but that of the mechanically reproduced series, each member of which sustains those minute variations that seem to animate the group as a whole. And this animation cannot be thought of as a form of aesthetic vitalism; it is not on the order of the old organic metaphor applied to compositional unities. It is an animation that has humbler associations: the relative of the comics, of cartoons, of Disney. And indeed to explore successive layers of the sequence—as peeling them back one from the next we see the tiny anatomical shifts and swellings— is to have the impression not of watching an idea in development but rather of observing gesture in motion. Thus quite unexpectedly, Picasso places his viewer in the presence of a flipbook.

No one ever talks about this process to which the sketchbooks bear witness. No one ever says that it resembles the flipbook. Zervos reproduces the drawings in vertical columns, so that one would never know, one would never suspect, the manner in which they were in fact made. You would only know it if you had held them in your hands. You would have to have been able to turn their pages. And this you could only have done if you had been admitted to his studio. An intimate. Like Hélène Parmelin.

What is focused on, instead, when speaking of these compositions based on the work of others, is the freedom of Picasso's relation to the original, the liberty with which he enters and leaves it. "A painter of genius," it is typically said of him, "seems to have the capacity to surrender voluntarily to inspiration deriving from another work of art and then, escaping from it, find his imaginative strength renewed and capable of projecting an image of his own." This discussion of surrender and capture is interesting. Because, even though it is always climaxed by reassurances about the artist's freedom, it betrays, nonetheless, a kind of anxiety about Picasso's enterprise in these works, even while it utterly mistakes the nature of the "surrender" involved. For the surrender of the artist's imagination, the place in which it is caught by being given over to pleasure, is the function of a mechanical device—an apparatus of the spectacle—the production of a voluptuous passivity: the mechanism of the serial animation of the flipbook's beat.

Nowhere is this voluptuous succumbing to the unconscious productivity of the device clearer than in the sketchbook Picasso made as a kind of climax toward which all the others were leading, the sketchbook of August

2, 1962. Here the erotic investment in the scene is made as explicit as possible, as through nine successive pages the orgiastic subtext of the *Déjeuner sur l'herbe* is enacted, the important variations within this repeated appearance and disappearance of the scene being the migration of the actors' genitals to various sites on their bodies.

The display of the genitals within this matrix of the flipbook form can, moreover, be seen to be what much of the preceding 200 sketches had been preparing for. Picasso's long-held fascination with the figure of the woman bending over and seen from above—bending to tie her sandal, to dry herself, or as in the *Déjeuner,* to bathe—had already been at work within this series of variations to sexualize the image. The female figure viewed in this position is vulnerable to a transmutation that Picasso repeatedly performs on it, whether it occurs in the keening Magdalene from the *Crucifixion* or the bather from the *Déjeuner.* Bent to project below her breasts, the female head submits again and again to the same transformation, as it is recast as phallic signifier, the stand-in—mapped onto the nose and hair of the female face—for the genitals of an absent male.

That Picasso should have pursued this image over many years, that he should have had frequent and spectacular recourse to the depiction of sexual acts, means—one could object—that he certainly did not *need* the flipbook structure for permission to vent the erotic turn of his imagination. Yet even while agreeing that he did not need it, it is possible to think that as, at the end of his life, it became the medium of his activity, he did indeed become caught in its mechanism, his art becoming more and more a function of *its* pulse. And so though he did not need it he yielded to it, to the appeal of pure recurrence, to the seduction and the content of an endless pulse. The mechanically repeated and the erotically enacted seemed to have trapped him and he created the metaphors of this capture. In 1964 he made some ceramic tiles on each of which a priapic satyr pursues a nymph with the repetitive exactitude a template provides. He was showing Hélène Parmelin the dozen or so examples he had made and he asked her, "Wouldn't it be pretty to have entire rooms tiled like that?" She includes this remark in a section of her book titled "Picasso, the Moralist."

As witness to much of the theater of Picasso's variations, she remembers the sessions at night in his studio where they would all gather to marvel at the slides projected five times, ten times life-size onto the far wall of the room: Poussin's Massacre of the Innocents *grown to thirty feet high; Delacroix's* Entrance into Constantinople *an immense blaze of color. Other people might go to the movies, she would think. This is our spectacle!*

Pablo Picasso, *Raphaël et la Fornarina,* 4 September 1968 I.

*Even while it utterly mistakes the nature of the "surrender"
involved . . . (p. 229)*

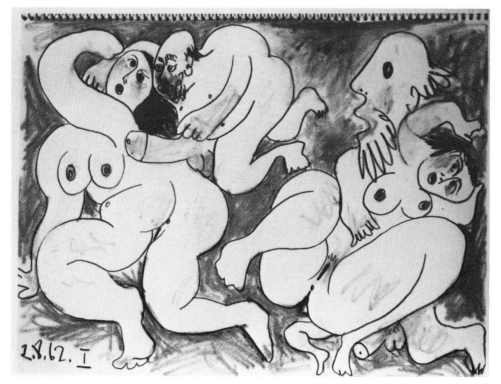

Pablo Picasso, *Déjeuner sur l'herbe d'après Manet Sketchbook*, 2 August 1962 I.

This voluptuous succumbing to the unconscious productivity of the device . . . (p. 229)

Pablo Picasso, *Déjeuner sur l'herbe d'après Manet Sketchbook*, 2 August 1962 II.

The display of the genitals within this matrix of the flipbook
form . . . (p. 230)

Pablo Picasso, *Untitled,* 15 November 1966 VI.

That Picasso should have pursued this image over many years . . . (p. 230)

But one time the spectacle is not so pleasant. It is a day at Vauvenargues Castle, massed at the foot of the Mont Sainte Victoire, with Picasso's mood as black as the day is crystalline. Nonetheless he invites his guests into his studio, offering to show them his own collection of the paintings of other masters. One of the pictures he shows them is a Cézanne of this very mountain, a painting no one has ever seen before. She enters deeply into the space of the work; her meditation so intense that his words barely reach her. "Why don't you get your camera, Hélène?" he is asking. "Why do you have one if you never use it? Why are you standing around doing nothing? You don't seem to realize what an occasion this is. You should be photographing the studio, photographing the pictures." She rises, stunned, to the surface of her silent concentration.

She gets the camera and it seems to her that with each "click" a knife is thrust into the freedom of her experience of the work, that at each slap of the shutter something live has just died. Suddenly Picasso wheels on her, enraged that "without his permission" she has photographed his Renoir. "His Renoir!" she thinks. She tears the film out of the camera and throws it in his face. "No one talks to me like that," she says.

In the weeks that pass Jacqueline tries to get her to return, to relent. "You know how he is!" she keeps repeating. And it is true. Hélène knows perfectly well how he is. Which makes her obstinance all the more interesting.

She keeps saying that Picasso had no right to violate her silence, to interrupt the completeness of her connection to the works, to scatter this to the winds as though it were so much trash. She couches her complaints to Jacqueline within the moralism of a defense of Painting, a modernist defense.

But of course she knows Picasso so well; had so often seen him conniving, manipulating, controlling; had herself been its victim. So it was not he who had violated her silence, provoking the extremes of this reaction. It had been the click that had troubled her, as it created its own rhythm within the immobility of the pictorial image.

Would Dr. Freud have had something to say about that click's content as—like the pure syntax of the passive voice—it could have acted to smuggle the beat of eros past the gates of repression?

"Picasso, the Moralist" could be the subtitle of almost every book on Picasso over the past fifty years, bringing one over and over again the message of art's assurance about voluntarism, intentionality, and freedom. Does anyone listen to Picasso himself as he speaks, in all innocence, of the way he is possessed by the *dispositif* he has constructed? Acknowledging that "with the variations on the old masters [Picasso] systematizes the process; the work is the ensemble of the canvases on the same theme and each one is only a link of the whole, a suspended moment of creation," one of the writers on this phase of his work quotes him as saying that what interests him "is the movement of painting, the dramatic push of one vision to the next, even if the push is not forced to its conclusion. . . . I have arrived at the point where the movement of my thought interests me more than my thought itself." The passivity of this interest comes out in another remark where he says, "I make a hundred studies in several days, while another painter might spend a hundred days on a single picture. In continuing, I will open windows. I will get behind the canvas and perhaps something will happen." "Quelque chose," he says, "se produira." The window will open and something will happen before the eyes of the painter who is caught there, fascinated—like the Wolf Man for whom the window opens onto that beyond where something takes place, as it displays for him the matrix figure of a scene in which he will be, for the rest of his life, entrapped.

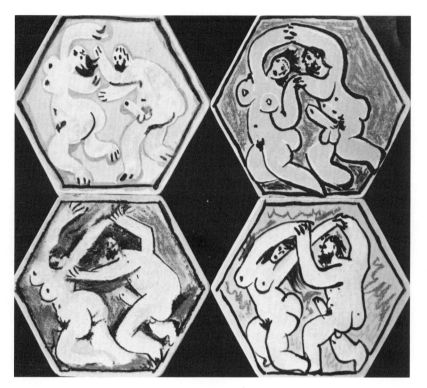

Pablo Picasso, *Untitled,* 14 August 1962.

"Wouldn't it be pretty to have entire rooms tiled like that?". . . (p. 230)

Sketch made by the Wolf Man, from Sigmund Freud,
"From the History of an Infantile Neurosis."

*"I will get behind the canvas and perhaps something will
happen". . . (p. 236)*

Roland Barthes's analysis is in "The World of Wrestling," the text that opens *Mythologies,* his essays on mass-cultural phenomena as depoliticized speech, collected as one volume in 1957 (*Mythologies,* trans. Annette Lavers [New York: Hill and Wang, 1972]).

Photographs of the television set in Picasso's living room at Notre Dame de Vie were published in Roberto Otero's *Forever Picasso* (New York: Abrams, 1978). The famous images through which we know Picasso in his various milieux are by David Doublas Duncan (*The Private World of Pablo Picasso* [New York: The Ridge Press, 1958]) and Edward Quinn (*Picasso avec Picasso* [Paris: Pierre Bordas, 1987]).

Hélène Parmelin, with her husband, the painter Edouard Pignon, became friends of Picasso's in the late 1940s and intimates of Picasso and Jacqueline Rocque during the turbulence of Françoise Gillot's break with Picasso. The three-volume work *Intimate Secrets of a Studio at Notre Dame de Vie* (New York: Abrams, 1966), *Picasso: Women, Mougins and Vauvenargues* (London: Weidenfeld and Nicolson, 1965), and *The Artist and His Model* (New York: Abrams, 1965), are the record of Hélène Parmelin's access to Picasso's studios, her reflections on what she saw there, and the conversations that she either had with Picasso directly or overheard between Picasso and others, mainly Pignon. The conversations, sometimes in direct quotation, sometimes summarized by her, were subsequently extracted from these volumes and consolidated in the more modest book, *Picasso Says* (London: George Allen and Unwin, 1969).

Voyage en Picasso (Paris: Robert Lafont, 1980), written by Parmelin as a more intimate portrait of Picasso, particularly during the time of his approaching death, describes the interior of Notre Dame de Vie, including the television set that sat at the foot of Picasso's bed during the last years (p. 201). She also gives an account of Picasso's passion for watching wrestling—*catch* in French, which Picasso pronounced *cache* (p. 202). Picasso's comment, "They are ransacking Duchamp's warehouse and changing the packaging," is from this book (p. 71), although Parmelin's *Art et anartisme* (Paris: Christian Bourgois, 1969) is a pamphlet-sized work committed to this idea, where she describes the May Salons in Paris (p. 25), Tinguély's lunatrack (p. 52), and the "Concours Lépine of anti-art" (p. 54).

Hélène's account of her emotions alone in Picasso's studios, as the meaning of art is revealed to her, is from *Women of Mougins* (p. 7), as are her descriptions of the sun and heat beyond the studio (p. 13), the sun protecting the studio's silence (p. 20), the sound of the highway in the distance (p. 20), and Jacqueline's calling the canal "my Seine" (p. 20). Picasso's comment about the nymph and satyr tiles is from *The Painter and His Model* (p. 153) and *Picasso Says* (p. 61). The discussion of the rapidity of the eye is from *Picasso Says* (p. 46), as are Picasso's strictures against painting's trying to depict movement (p. 39). In *Voyage en Picasso,* Parmelin tells about the incident at Vauvenargues when Picasso charges her to photograph works in his collection (pp. 31–35); about projecting slides on the studio walls at night, particularly Poussin's *Massacre of the Innocents* (p. 75); and once again the effect on her of the pulsing of the Midi heat around the house, coupled with the "*ronron* of the traffic," as she turns away from the work in the studios to the brilliance outside (p. 77).

Max Ernst published *A Little Girl Dreams of Taking the Veil* in 1930. The image of the zootrope comes from *La Nature* (1888), p. 12. The "Praxinoscope à projection" was pictured in *La Nature* (1882), p. 357; the "Projections stéréoscopiques" in (1891), p. 49; the hands serving as the basis for the cover of *Répétitions* is from (1887), p. 144; for *Oedipus Rex* (1891), p. 272; for *At the First Clear Word* (1881), p. 584. For the Schreber diagrams that appear in *Les malheurs des immortels*, see Dio Lewis, *The New Gymnastics, with a translation of Professor Schreber's Pangymnastikon* (Boston: Ticknor and Fields, 1862).

My discussion of Husserl's punctual moment (*im selben Augenblick*) follows that of Jacques Derrida, in *Speech and Phenomena*, trans. David B. Allison (Evanston: North-western University Press, 1973), pp. 60–69.

Lyotard's extraordinary analysis of the matrix figure, using "A Child Is Being Beaten" as its example, is from the section "Fiscours Digure," in *Discours, Figure* (Paris: Klinck-sieck, 1971), pp. 327–354: the discussion of the passive voice (p. 343); the comparison with the structuralist's structure (p. 339); blocking together of logically incompatible sentences (pp. 338–339); the matrix figure as "bad form" (pp. 349–350); the relation to the death drive (pp. 350–353). For his discussion of Cézanne's passivity, see p. 21. For "A Child Is Being Beaten" (1919), see Sigmund Freud, *Standard Edition,* vol. 17, pp. 177–204.

Douglas Cooper's account of the unfolding of work on the *Déjeuner sur l'herbe* variations is in Cooper, *Pablo Picasso: Les Déjeuners* (New York: Harry N. Abrams, 1963), where he describes how the drawings proceed (p. 19), comments on Picasso's escape from the influence of the older work (p. 23), and reproduces much of the work, omitting, however, the sketchbook from August 2. This latter object is catalogued as no. 165 in *Je suis le cahier: The Sketchbooks of Pablo Picasso*, ed. Arnold Glimcher and Marc Glimcher (Boston: Atlantic Monthly Press, 1986), where two images from this sequence are illustrated. The importance of the female head and breasts mapped onto the male genitals is brought out by Robert Rosenblum in "Picasso and the Anatomy of Eroticism," in *Studies in Erotic Art,* ed. Theodore Bowie and Cornelia V. Christenson (New York: Basic Books, 1970), see figure 198.

Marie-Laure Bernadac ("Picasso, 1953–1973: La peinture comme modèle," *Le dernier Picasso* [Paris: Musée National d'Art Moderne, 1988], p.49), quotes Picasso as saying, "The movement of my thought interests me more than my thought itself"; Douglas Cooper (*Les Déjeuners, p.* 33) quotes Picasso, although to support a wholly different argument, as saying, "I will get behind the canvas and perhaps something will happen."

Once the secondary elaboration of style has covered the wild form-play of art, never again can the human eye see its full effects, neither this generation, nor future generations.

—Anton Ehrenzweig

six

He's sitting there just as I remember him, next to the neat little marble-topped table, with its prim lamp in gilt bronze mounted by a simple white shade, and behind him a painting that might be by Kenneth Noland but is hard to identify in the tightly held shot that frames him. His face is much the same, flabby and slack, although time has pinched it sadistically, and reddened it. Whenever I would try to picture that face, my memory would produce two seemingly mismatched fragments: the domed shape of the head, bald, rigid, unforgiving; and the flaccid quality of the mouth and lips, which I remember as always slightly ajar, in the logically impossible gesture of both relaxing and grinning. Looking at him now I search for the same effect. As always I am held by the arrogance of the mouth—fleshy, toothy, aggressive—and its pronouncements, which though voiced in a kind of hesitant, stumbling drawl are, as always, implacably final.

"I first met Jackson Pollock in '42," he's telling the interviewer. "Came down the sidewalk and there was Lee Krasner whom I'd known of old and she was with a very respectable gentleman."

He hesitates so we can let it sink in, the coupling of Pollock's name with the words *respectable* and *gentleman*.

He begins again. "And I saw this rather nice-lookin' guy. Lee said to me, 'This guy's gonna be a great painter.'" Pause.

Then the singsong of his own reply: "Well. Uh. O-kay."

As the film cuts away from Clement Greenberg to the notorious photographs of Pollock painting, one of us is unable to hold back the question, "How many times has he told that story? One hundred? Two hundred? Three? How completely bored he sounds!"

But Clem is not bored, I think. If he's willing to broadcast the story over so many retellings, no matter how routinized and compressed, it's because he has a project, a mission. Lee had always said she introduced Pollock to him at a party, with dancing. Pollock, however, was never at his best at gatherings, alternately frozen with shyness and blustering with drink. So Clem's account labors to relocate their meeting: outside the customs house where he worked; therefore during the daytime; and thus the encounter with a sober Pollock—"respectable," a gentleman.

This, I think, is the process of sublimating Pollock. Of raising him up from that dissolute squat, in his James Dean dungarees and black tee-shirt, slouched over his paintings in the disarray of his studio or hunkered down on the running board of his old Ford. This is the posture, in all its lowness, projected by so many famous photographs, images recording the athletic abandon of the painting gesture but also the dark brooding silence of the stilled body, with its determined isolation from everything urban, everything "cultured." The photographs had placed him on the road, like Kerouac, clenching his face into the tight fist of beat refusal, making an art of violence, of "howl." Clem's mission was to lift him above those pictures, just as it was to lift the paintings Pollock made from off the ground where he'd made them, and onto the wall. Because it was only on the wall that they joined themselves to tradition, to culture, to convention. It was in that location and at that angle to gravity that they became "painting."

"He wasn't this wild, heedless genius," Clem continues. "No. He wasn't that. He looked. He looked hard; and he was very sophisticated about painting." His voice trails off, as though he were remembering.

And it's right there, in that brief paragraph, in that little clutch of sentences, that you have the whole thing, the full redemptive gesture, the raising of the work from off its knees and onto the grace of the wall in one unbroken benediction, the denial of wild heedlessness in order to clear a space for the look, the look that will (in its very act of looking) create order, and thus create painting—"sophisticated" painting.

This trajectory, moving ineluctably from disorder to order, can be tracked through the statements made by journeyman critics at the turn of the decade, as one after another they reversed themselves on the subject of Pollock's work. Before, they confessed, they could only see the wild heedlessness. Now, they say, they see the order. After the 1949 show, Henry McBride admits that previous works had looked to him "as though the paint had been flung at the canvas from a distance, not all of it making happy landings."

That's the language of *before.*

But now, he writes, "The spattering is handsome and organized and therefore I like it."

Which is to say that *before,* it was on the floor: "a child's contour map," "a flat, war-shattered city, possibly Hiroshima, as seen from a great height," "dribblings," "drooling," "a mass of tangled hair." And *now,* it's on the wall. Where it takes on order, and the sophistication of tradition: "elegant as a Chinese character," said the *Times,* while in *Art News* Pollock's use of metallic paint joins his work to Byzantium, to Siena, to all those sacred walls glittering with the illusioned light of transcendence: "Pollock uses metallic paint in much the same sense that earlier painters applied gold leaf, to add a feeling of mystery and adornment."

The welling up of this tide of benediction has a momentum of its own, carrying everything before it, even Greenberg. *Before,* the wall—the wall that was the guarantor for him of the work's condition as painting—the wall had signaled compression, concreteness, flatness; it had meant the transformation from the easel picture to the mural painting, the movement from illusioned depth to a declaration of the wall's impermeable surface in all the "positivity," as he said, of its observable fact. The wall, the mural, was about *thisness.* It was a vertical, bounded plane, an object that stood before the viewer's own vertical body, facing off against it. This object, he reasoned, this continuous, planar object could function as an analogue for another continuous object, namely positivist science's "space," the continuum of neutral observation, the space everywhere open to examination,

everywhere absolutely equal before the (scientific) law. "The picture plane as a total object," he had written, "represents space as a total object." And the extended plane of the mural-sized painting, he thought, will make this analogy into solid, pictorial fact.

But *now* the very verticality of that wall seemed to carry the force of transcendence.

Greenberg's first word for this was "hallucinated," as he began to search for a term that would capture the way this expansive vertical surface seemed to outrun the very world of facts, and the wall itself appeared to give way: "object" now rewritten as "field." "Hallucinated literalness," he first decided, would set up just the right kind of tension between the pictorial wall's flatness and the optical illusions it nonetheless released. He tried to characterize these illusions. The wall seemed to breathe, he thought, to exhale color. It took on a kind of radiance, a luminous openness, volatilizing substance. By the mid-1950s he was reading Pollock's drip paintings as a matter of creating the "counter-illusion of light alone."

The stolid neutrality of "space as an object," materialist and literal, would cede its place to the idea of the pictorial field as "mirage," which is to say a zone enveloped by the subjective possibility of error. But as such this weightless, hovering, exhaling plenum would now stand, Greenberg thought, as the analogue of "vision itself." It would be the matrix of a gaze that, cut loose from the viewer's body, was free to explore the dimensions of its own projective movement buoyed by nothing else but subjective reflection on its own form of consciousness. "To render substance entirely optical," he wrote, "and form as an integral part of ambient space—this brings anti-illusionism full circle. Instead of the illusion of things, we are now offered the illusion of modalities: namely, that matter is incorporeal, weightless and exists only optically like a mirage."

The vertical is not, then, just a neutral axis, a dimension. It is a pledge, a promise, a momentum, a narrative. To stand upright is to attain to a peculiar form of vision: the optical; and to gain this vision is to sublimate, to raise up, to purify.

Freud had told that story years before, had he not? "Man's erect posture," he had written, could in and of itself be seen to "represent the beginning of the momentous process of cultural evolution." The very move to the vertical, he reasoned, is a reorientation away from the animal senses of sniffing and pawing. Sight alone, enlarging the scope of attention, allows for a diversion of focus. Sight alone displaces excited humanoid attention away from its partner's genitals and onto "the shape of the body as a whole." Sight alone opens the possibility of a distanced, formal pleasure to which Freud was content to give the name *beauty;* this passage from the sexual to the visual he christened *sublimation.*

"Sight alone" was very much the province of gestalt psychology, which in those years was running fullback for Freud's fancy speculative passing plays in this matter of a psychohistory of the senses. The animal can see, the psychologists wrote, but only man can "behold." Its connection to the ground always ties the animal's seeing to touching, its vision predicated on the horizontal, on the physical intersection of viewer and viewed. Man's upright posture, they argued, brings with it the possibility of distance, of contemplation, of domination. "We are able to behold things in a plane perpendicular to the direction of our gaze," they wrote, "i.e., in the plane of fronto-parallel *Prägnanz* and of transparent distance." *Prägnanz* was the gestalt psychologists' term for the clarity of a structure due to its simplicity, its ability to cohere as shape. Beheld shape, they made clear, depended on being "fronto-parallel," which is to say, vertical.

The afterlife of the drip pictures continued to be conducted within this sublimatory, formal plane of the vertical. To that we have the testimony of the procession of artists who claimed themselves as Pollock's heirs: Helen Frankenthaler, Morris Louis, Kenneth Noland, Jules Olitski, Larry Poons. And the accounts of critics and historians—Michael Fried, William Rubin, T. J. Clark—do nothing if not concur. The drive of sublimation moves the paintings steadily away from the material, the tactile, the objective. By 1965 this drive had already reached a kind of climax when the next logical conclusion was drawn from Greenberg's claim that the volatilizing abstractness of Pollock's line "bounds and delimits"—in Michael Fried's paraphrase—"nothing—except, in a sense, eyesight." Turning his attention to those few paintings in 1949 where Pollock has removed figurative shapes from the optical web of the drip pictures by knifing out sections of canvas, Michael describes the result. It is a break, he says, although it is not experienced as a rupture in the physical surface of the painting so much as it is felt as a lacuna—a kind of "blind spot"—in the viewer's own field of vision. "It is like part of our retina that is destroyed," he urges, a part that "for some reason is not registering the visual field over a certain area." Evacuating the work altogether from the domain of the object and installing it within the consciousness of the subject, this reading brings the sublimatory movement to its climax. "In the end,"

247

six

Michael adds, "the relation between the field and the figure is simply not spatial at all: it is purely and wholly optical: so that the figure created by removing part of the painted field and backing it with canvas-board seems to lie somewhere within our own eyes, as strange as this may sound."

To Michael's good friend Frank Stella, however, it rang not only strange but false. The sublimated Pollock—the volatilized pigment, the patches of aluminum paint read out as a silver analogue for the gold grounds of Siena and Byzantium—raised a kind of skepticism in him. What he liked, instead, about Pollock's metallic paint, he told the interviewer in the film *Painters Painting,* was that it was "repellent." It repels the eye, as does much of the surface quality of the drip pictures seen up close, the coagulation of the paint in the areas where it had puddled and then shriveled in the process of drying, forming a disgusting film, like the skin on the surface of scalded milk. But Frank's objection went in large part unnoticed; and his own use of metallic paint would itself be gathered into the sublimatory embrace of "opticality."

Only three demurrals register within the afterhistory of the works that cannot be so assimilated, three refusals of the verticalization of Pollock, three reminders of the time when the drip pictures could still be thought of as having been "painted with a broom," a floorbound condition that elicited the comment that "a dog or cat could do better," the polite version of what both Thomas Craven and Tom Benton accused Pollock of in 1950: making the drip pictures by peeing on them. The three dissenting voices came from the practices of Cy Twombly, Andy Warhol, and Robert Morris. None of these was interested in the sublimated Pollock.

He's sitting there just as I remember him, next to the neat little marble-topped table, its prim lamp in gilt bronze mounted by a simple white shade, a painting behind him that might be by Kenneth Noland but is hard to identify in the tightly framed shot we see. His face is much the same, flabby and slack, although time has pinched it slightly and reddened it. There are two seemingly mismatched fragments, just as I remember them: the domed shape of the head, bald, rigid, unforgiving; and the flaccid quality of the mouth, slightly ajar in the physiologically impossible gesture of both re-laxing and grinning. As always I am held by the arrogance of the mouth—fleshy, toothy, aggressive—and its pronouncements, which though voiced in a hesitant, stumbling drawl are, as always, implacably final.

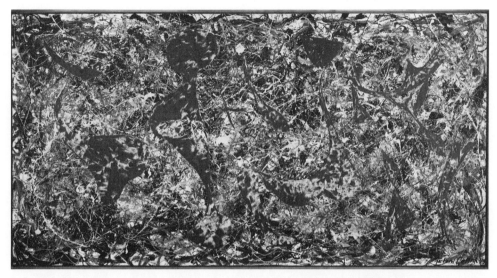

Jackson Pollock, *Out of the Web: Number 7*, 1949.

"It is felt as a lacuna—a kind of "blind spot"—in the viewer's own field of vision . . . (p. 247)

Jackson Pollock, *Echo: Number 25, 1951.*

*"After the '50 show," she would ask dramatically, "what do you do next?
He couldn't have gone further doing the same thing". . . (p. 255)*

I try to imagine his tone the time he told an interviewer that by 1952 Pollock had "lost his stuff." It was an expression I know he liked. I imagine him savoring the finality of it, its assaultiveness, the Middle English abruptness of the word *stuff*. He had given a lecture at the Guggenheim in the early '50s where he said that Dubuffet had "lost his stuff." And then, against the angry murmur of his audience, he added that de Kooning was another case "of an artist who has lost his stuff." He had, he claimed, said this to Pollock directly, at the same time in 1953 when he told him the paintings in his latest show were "soft" and "forced."

He smiles his slow, voracious grin. "Jackson knew he had lost his inspiration." He shrugs. "Jackson had a phenomenal ten-year run, but it was over."

I try to imagine him saying it: "All artists have their run; and yours, Jackson, is over."

He shrugs. Sooner or later all great artists lose their stuff, after which they just keep going in the day-to-day activity of the artist treading water, making derivative, minor painting, like Dubuffet after 1950, or de Kooning after the first bout of *Women*.

Pollock, however, didn't keep going. After he "lost his stuff" he was able to put together just three more shows before falling apart completely; in another year and a half, by August 1956, he was dead.

And where there's a corpse, you could say, there's a mystery.

It's often imagined that the enigma surrounding Pollock's work concerns the onset of the drip pictures, which is to say the invention of a procedure for making paintings more radical than anything else that had come before it. Out of what kind of inspiration did this arise, it is asked, out of what measure of formal intelligence? Was it the canniness of the master or just the result of happy accident? From whom did he copy it? Into what tradition did he imagine himself tapping? But this is surely the wrong question.

The scientist sets up an experiment. He has a hunch that if he does a certain group of procedures in a certain order he will get a certain result. And he knows he can repeat the experiment, that in subsequent tries he can widen the variables it will account for by altering it slightly. He is working by induction, from "case" to "rule," in a logic of relations that looks like this:

Induction

Case	These beans are from this bag.
Result	These beans are white.
∴ Rule	All the beans from this bag are white.

We can follow Pollock's experiment as he performed and reperformed it: laying the canvas down on the floor, building up the linear tracery that covered its surface with whorls and loops of liquid paint, varying the viscosity of the network and the size and format of the surface. We can follow the progression toward an increasingly open lattice and toward formats of less and less conventional dimensions, at first breaking with the traditionally vertical canvas by exploring exaggeratedly horizontal friezes, and then bursting the bounds of the easel picture itself by claiming extravagant amounts of surface: thirteen feet high, for example, by twenty feet wide. As he does this again and again he is, as *Art News* has already informed us, "painting a picture"; and although we may have questions about how and why he does it, it does not take the form of a mystery.

The mystery arises, rather, from what cannot be repeated, from what has been brought to an end, terminated, closed out. The murder mystery dramatizes this finality by producing a body: by giving finality the concrete form of the corpse. The mystery's form is the reverse of the scientific experiment, since its logic works backward from "rule" to "case," which is to say, from clue to cause. C. S. Peirce, to whom we owe the example of the beans in the bag, gave this logic the name of retro- or abduction:

Abduction

Rule	All the beans from this bag are white.
Result	These beans are white.
∴ Case	These beans are from this bag.

And a host of writers, fascinated by the retroactivity of the logic and attracted to the structure of the clue itself—whether that be called index, trace, or symptom—have supplied the names of famous workers in the field of retroduction: Sigmund Freud, Giovanni Morelli, Sherlock Holmes.

"The murderer always brings something to the scene of the crime," says the detective, his voice low and nasal and portentous, adding, "and, just as surely, he always leaves something behind."

Just so. It is obvious, a piece of street wisdom, a commonplace of the genre. Whether the "murderer" is repressive censor or forger or criminal, the clue is structured by this strange caesura that announces its break with the psychological fabric of intention. The clue is precisely what was not meant, what was never considered, what was inadvertent, unconscious, left by mistake. The clue is structured by the peculiar fact that though, as a trace, it is ineradicably connected to its "maker," its maker's connection to *it* cannot be said to have the same perspicuousness. And with this slackening of the criminal's grip on the "meaning" of his own clue, his story likewise passes out of his hands, becoming a newly born narrative. No longer the tale of the crime's commission, it is now the story of the deed's detection. As Holmes liked to explain to Watson, it becomes a matter of "reasoning backwards."

We could say that both clue and corpse announce this peculiar temporal structure, each in its own way. The corpse stands for finality, for what can never be repeated; the clue stands for a break in the chain of consciousness, for what was never intended. And the story, though focused on the past, is thus strangely delivered from it. For the narrative inhabits a present that is free to continue, to keep receiving the aftershocks of the crime, it is true, but also to keep forming its own new sets of events from which its interpretation of the crime will build.

So when the detective turns his leaden gaze on the frazzled housewife standing in the black and white glare of a Hollywood noon and insists, "Just the facts, ma'am," is he affirming Ranke's demand that the historian summon forth "things as they really were," thereby moving toward a truth contained in the past and unaffected by the present? Or is he rather just brushing aside *her* interpretation, *her* set of readings, the better to clear a space within which to discover his own? He wants the facts, and he wants them raw. But he does not think they will come bearing their own meaning. Interpretation is *his* job. And it occurs after the event. It happens now. According to the inexorable logic of the clue.

And what were the "facts," just the facts . . . ma'am?

In 1950, at age 38, Jackson Pollock was on a roll. He had made $5,800 from the 1949–50 gallery season—the result of record sales from his 1949 show and payments for a treasured mural commission. At a time when the average white-collar worker took home $3,500 a year, this was success measured in hard monetary terms. But success was not only financial. In large banner type, *Life* magazine had asked twelve million readers, "Is He the Greatest Living Painter in the United States?" And although the writers of the article's captions tried to tip the question over into derisive irony (the "drooling" business), the body of the story and the size of the reproductions did nothing but imply that the answer was "yes."

By 1950, Alfred Barr had purchased *Number 1, 1948* for the Museum of Modern Art and, though still wavering in his own assessment of Pollock, had given impressive space to his work in the American Pavilion at the Venice Biennale.

Beginning with the spring thaw, Pollock had opened the year's working season by embarking on a series of larger and larger paintings, climaxing in his four most ambitious and, to some, his most masterful works: *Lavender Mist, One, Number 32,* and *Autumn Rhythm.*

Deep into the summer Hans Namuth had begun a series of shooting sessions, photographing Pollock both in his studio at work and relaxing on the grounds of his house in Springs. Pollock seems to have found his reflection in the camera's gaze all of a piece with his newly consolidated fame. In any event he agreed to Namuth's next proposal, which was to make him the subject of a film and to train the camera on him at work . . . painting. The only other American artist he knew to have had a film made about him was Alexander Calder. So this put him in a league with the most established of artists and one moreover with important ties to Europe.

The filming began in September and finished on a cold day in late October. Pollock marked its completion by downing glass after glass of bourbon. During the dinner that followed he fought with Namuth, oblivious to the dozen or so other guests. "I'm not a phony. You're a phony," he kept saying. And then he upended the table, dinner and all. For four years he had stayed sober. Now he had fallen off the wagon.

He never got back on. As he wrote to his friend and supporter Alfonso Ossorio, his time in New York during and after his winter show represented "an all-time low." The "drinking and depression," he admitted, were "brutal." In the spaces between wave after wave of binges, the most he could do was to make some ink drawings on the pads of Japanese paper Tony Smith had given him. Back on Long Island in early spring these drawings, becoming ever more figurative, were soaked onto long stretches of canvas to constellate paintings with, as he once more wrote Ossorio, "some of my early images coming thru." This work, his 1951 black and white show, marking his definitive break with the drip pictures, signaled the beginning of the end of both his art and his life. And it is this ending, this revocation, this rupture that is the mystery, the shroud of the corpse.

For Lee, of course, there was no mystery. "After the '50 show," she would ask dramatically, "what do you do next? He couldn't have gone further doing the same thing."

The idea that Pollock refused to repeat himself, that he was too authoritative a master to sink into self-imitation, is part of the myth of Pollock's greatness. Michael Fried reverts to it in discussing the cutout pictures of 1949, with their stunning invention of the "blind spot," as he parries the entirely plausible question about why, if this solution were so important, Pollock had limited himself to exploring it only twice. But nothing, Michael attests, could be less surprising: "Among the important American painters who have emerged since 1940 Pollock stands almost alone in his refusal to repeat himself."

The idea of mastery as a refusal to repeat rings oddly hollow, however, amidst the actual practice of modernist art. What would we say about Mondrian, who, after having broken through to the invention of the neoplasticist grid, spent the next two decades "repeating himself"? Isn't repeating oneself precisely what painting allows one to do, especially once one has found one's particular language, the stylistic invention that will allow one to move inside it and inhabit it, growing and changing within the new syntax one can call one's own? That's what Clem praised in Pollock: the variety and drama latent within "what may at first sight seem crowded and repetitious. . . . One has to learn Pollock's idiom," he said, "to realize its flexibility." He looked at the great drip pictures of 1948, *Number 1, 1948*, for example. "Beneath the apparent monotony of its surface composition," he wrote, "it reveals a sumptuous variety of design and incident." But it was not just the variety within a given work that struck him; it was the range of feeling made possible by his newly invented idiom.

This is why for Clem, too, there was no mystery. At least not at first. In 1951 Clem greeted the black and white pictures as "a turn but not a sharp change of direction." At the time they merely seemed to confirm the suppleness, the range of possibilities offered by the new language. He ignored the "images coming thru" and looked instead at the development of Pollock's line, sinking as it did into the white cotton duck like ink into a blotter. "Now he volatilizes," Clem said, remarking on nothing more than a logical permutation within an ongoing series.

It was only later that he would return to this moment and reevaluate it, understanding it not as a progression but as a rupture and a breakdown. In 1955, situating *One* and *Lavender Mist* at the very frontier of painting's future, which is to say, at the very pinnacle of opticality, Greenberg would castigate the black and white pictures as having been, in fact, a massive recantation. "In 1951," he said, "Pollock had turned to the other extreme, as if in violent repentance." Gone was the optical radiance, the "vaporous dust of interfused lights and darks." In its place there was now "a series of paintings, in linear blacks alone, that took back almost everything he had said in the three previous years." Pollock took it all back, he wrote. Though he didn't ask why.

Into the explanatory gap of this mystery there have rushed a set of reasons based on Pollock's intentions. A few are art-historical, like the notion that Pollock turned to figuration in order to design a set of windows for a church project; but most are biographical. He stopped the drip pictures, one goes, because the 1950 show didn't sell, didn't even get reviewed. He stopped the drip pictures, states another, because he got tired of the accusations that what he was doing was undisciplined, meaningless. "No chaos, damn it," he had fired back to *Time* magazine in November 1950. He stopped the drip pictures, yet another speculates, because the only source of his inspiration was the set of childhood memories out of which he painted, supercharged memories whose images he "drew" in the air above the canvas letting the sprays of pigment fall where they might, in order to achieve the abstractness necessary to secure Greenberg's support, but memories which, increasingly, he no longer wished to veil. In this explanation Pollock's restlessness with the drip pictures' subterfuge had already become apparent in 1949; it only needed Tony Smith's urging in the spring of 1951—"Well, what you did was great, Jackson, but what are you going to do next? What is the *development?*"—to drop the veil.

But the very fact of the mystery—and the structure of the clue—should make us refuse this whole litany of intentions, this recital of "he no longer wished . . . ," "he got tired of . . . ," "he refused to repeat." We know what the detective has taught us, that the clue has already cut the act off from Pollock's control and in so doing has delivered it to another.

. . . Has delivered it to Cy Twombly, perhaps, meditating in the mid-1950s on the meaning of Pollock's art and constructing his own reading precisely on the clue's very nature.

By 1955 Twombly had stopped making paintings with the expressionist's loaded brush and had started using the sharp points of pencils to scar and

Cy Twombly, *Untitled*, 1956 (New York City).

He had begun, that is, down the attack route which is that of the graffitist . . . (p. 259)

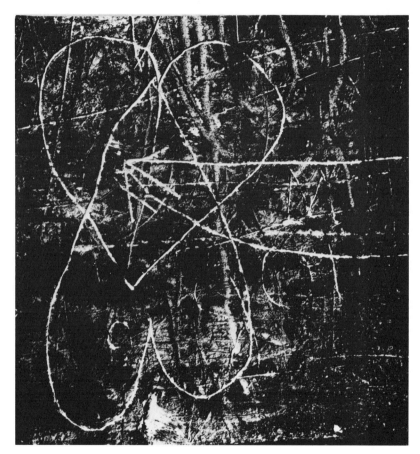

Brassaï, *Graffiti*, 1930.

Entering the scene as a criminal . . . (p. 260)

maul and ravage the creamy stuccoed surface of his canvases instead. He had begun, that is, down the attack route which is that of the graffitist, the marauder, the maimer of the blank wall. And he had made it clear that the maimer he had taken as his model was Jackson Pollock. It is not just the circularity of Twombly's marks and the loopy aimlessness of their tracks repeating over the canvas field that is addressed to the drip pictures. Rather it is the experience of the trace itself—the trace that composes the tracery of the drip paintings—as violent.

The violence that Twombly read in the traces left to mark the path of so many sprays of liquid thrown by Pollock from the end of stick or brush, the violence that he therefore "completed"—to invoke Harold Bloom's notion of the strong misreading—as graffiti, invested Pollock's traces with a form. For the formal character of the graffito is that of a violation, the trespass onto a space that is not the graffitist's own, the desecration of a field originally consecrated to another purpose, the effacement of that purpose through the act of dirtying, smearing, scarring, jabbing.

The graffitist makes a mark. Like all marks it has the character of a sign, structured thereby onto the double level of content and expression. Sometimes the content is a written message, "Kilroy was here," it says; sometimes it is the mere hiss of negation, the great big "X" that bruises the cleanliness of the wall, the slash that labels the surface "canceled." Whatever the content, however, the mark itself is its vehicle, its support, that which bodies the message forth. This is what the structuralists call the sign's level of expression, constructing it either through the medium of sound or that of image. But further, as the structuralists have taught us, each of these levels is itself subdivided, layered into a plane of form and a plane of substance. With the graffito, the expressive mark has a substance made up of the physical residue left by the marker's incursion: the smear of graphite, the stain of ink, the welt thrown up by the penknife's slash. But the form of the mark—at this level of "expression"—is itself peculiar; for it inhabits the realm of the clue, the trace, the index. Which is to say the operations of form are those of marking an event—by forming it in terms of its remains, or its precipitate—and in so marking it, of cutting the event off from temporality of its making.

The graffitist goes up to a wall. He makes a mark. We could say that he makes it to register his presence, to intervene in the space of another in order to strike against it with his declaration, "I am here." But we would be wrong to say this. Insofar as his declaration is a mark, it is inevitably structured by the moment *after* its making that even now infects the time of its making, the future moment that makes of its making nothing else than a past, a past that reads "I was here," "Kilroy was here." Thus even at the time the marker strikes, he strikes in a tense that is over; entering the scene as a criminal, he understands that the mark he makes can only take the form of a clue. He delivers his mark over to a future that will be carried on without his presence, and in so doing his mark cuts his presence away from himself, dividing it from within into a before and an after.

When Derrida would come to analyze this condition—the pure form of the imprint—to which he would give the name arche-trace, he would invent the term *différance* to account for the temporal disjunction internally fissuring this event. He would say of this form, "It is not the question of a constituted difference here, but rather, before all determination of the content, of the *pure* movement which produces difference. *The (pure) trace is différance.* It does not depend on any sensible plenitude, audible or visible, phonic or graphic. It is, on the contrary, the condition of such a plenitude." Unity, the unity of the sign, is thus preceded by multiplicity, or at least by the formal conditions of separation, of division, of deferral, which underlie the sign as its very ground of possibility. And this prior condition, intervening like a knife to cut into the indivisibility of presence— the presence of the subject to himself—is understood to be a form of violence. For if to make a mark is already to leave one's mark, it is already to allow the outside of an event to invade its inside; it cannot be conceived without "the nonpresence of the other inscribed within the sense of the present." This marking, which "cannot be thought outside of the horizon of intersubjective violence," is thus "the constitution of a free subject in the violent movement of its own effacement and its own bondage."

The index's violence is not, then, just a consequence of its being the residue of a crime, but is instead a condition of the structure of the marker's having been cut away from himself; it is as though he had gone up to a mirror to witness his own appearing and had smashed the mirror instead. Had thereby voided his own presence, leaving only his mark. "Kilroy *was* here," he writes in a present already invaded by the future.

Twombly acknowledges the structure of Pollock's mark, his drip, his clue, as the residue of an event. Clearly, however, it is not the event that Rosenberg had sketched in his essay on action painting. When Rosenberg had said that what was to enter the canvas's "arena" was "not a picture but an event," he had made it clear that what he had in mind was one in which "form, color, composition . . . can be dispensed with." Voiding "form," the canvas would become a mirror, a vehicle of "self-revelation";

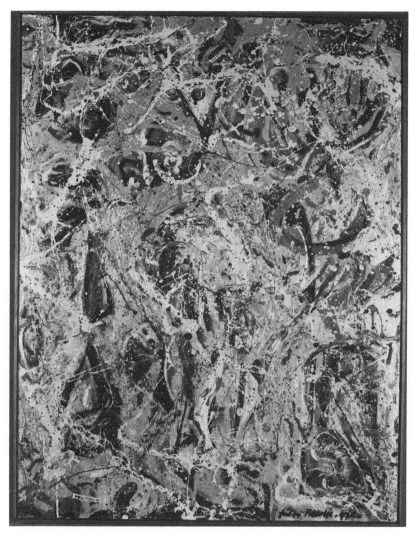

Jackson Pollock, *Galaxy*, 1947.

Pollock's first drip pictures were made indeed by striking at the figure, by effacing it . . . (p. 265)

Jackson Pollock, *Number 1, 1948,* 1948.

It is this schema that is then buried by the avalanche of the poured
skein . . . (p. 265)

Thomas Hart Benton, diagrams, published in "Mechanics of Form Organization in Painting,"
The Arts (November 1926), p. 288.

A relation to figurative art that was visible through its most diagrammatic mapping . . . (p. 265)

Cy Twombly, *Panorama,* 1955 (New York City).

His graffiti as a dispersal of abstract marks, white arcs and switchbacks
here scratched into gray . . . (p. 266)

it would be "of the same metaphysical substance as the artist's existence." Reflecting back to the artist the image of his own acts, it would allow the actor to look his own choices in the face, to judge the authenticity of his own claims to spontaneity, to self-invention.

Twombly does not buy into this idea of an escape from form through the presence of the mark to its maker, as though in a mirror. If Pollock's pictures can be said to have the structure of an "event" it is because they inhabit the condition of the trace and are formed by its violence against the very possibility of presence. They strike at the figure in the mirror. They smash it.

Pollock's first drip pictures were made indeed by striking at the figure, by effacing it. Below the early webs of *Galaxy* and *Reflection of the Big Dipper,* the images of human figures are clearly visible. The web of black line has been set up to efface those figures, to cancel them. Twombly has the sense that this striking at the figure is systematic within Pollock's operation of the trace, which is to say that it is in operation even where there are manifestly no "figures" in the underlayers of the painting.

In *Number 1, 1948,* for example, the sumptuous web that Alfred Barr bought for MoMA, one can barely make out an underdrawing that maps the surface with three more or less vertical poles, one at the center and the other two at either edge. It is this schema that is then buried by the avalanche of the poured skein, although the flurry of palm prints at the web's upper margin, made toward the completion of the painting, can be said to mark the sites of the schema, lying below.

The palm prints have led recent writers on the picture to make strangely representational claims for the painting, to insist that there really are figures underneath the tracery. But Pollock did not need "figures" in order to strike at the figure. Years of training in harness to Thomas Benton, analyzing Michelangelos and El Grecos by means of schematic plumb lines and implicit vectors, had left him a relation to figurative art that was visible through its most diagrammatic mapping. In 1948 he would spend evenings pouring over art books with his new friend and acolyte Harry Jackson, analyzing the structures of the work by means of their buried schemata. Jackson has described how Pollock "brought out *Cahiers d'art* and analyzed Tintoretto in great detail, explaining the composition of this and that; what he was doing was bringing me pure Tom Benton: Venetian Renaissance to Tom Benton. Tom to Jack, Jack to Harry."

In striking at the schema, the web cancels more than just this or that figure. It operates instead on the very idea of the organic, on the way composition can make the wholeness of the human form and the architectural coherence of the painting into analogues of one another, each repeating and magnifying the other's continuity. It strikes against the organic form's condition as unified whole, its capacity to cohere into the singleness of the good gestalt, its hanging together, its self-evident simplicity, its *Prägnanz*.

The form of the mark-as-graffito is, in its attack on presence, an attack on organicity, good form. Twombly would increasingly celebrate this aspect of the graffito's "content" in his own versions of the dispersed, disseminated body. If in *Panorama* (1955) he had stayed within the formula of the all-over web and maintained his graffiti as a dispersal of abstract marks, white arcs and switchbacks here scratched into gray, he had by the early 1960s felt the need to acknowledge that it was in fact the body that was at stake. The savagery of the mark does not let up but its crude violence is now the site of an obsessional formulation of bodily parts. Heart-shaped pudenda and barbell testicles, hairy penises and tick-tack-toe-like vulvas, many of them surrounded by the vicious emphasis of separate frames, coalesce within a work like *The Italians* (1961). Over the surfaces of his Roman paintings would thus appear so many cocks and cunts, so many wounds and scorings, so many tatters splayed over the surface of the work, the erotics of which is that its body will never be reconstituted, whole.

He's sitting there just as I remember him, next to the marble-topped table, its lamp in gilt bronze mounted by a white shade, a painting behind him that might be by Kenneth Noland but is hard to make out in the tightly framed shot we see. His face is much the same although time seems to have pinched and reddened it. Whenever I would try to picture that face, my memory would produce two seemingly mismatched fragments: the rigidly domed form of the head, and the slackness of the mouth. Looking at him now I am held, as always, by the arrogance of that mouth—fleshy, toothy, aggressive—and its pronouncements, which though voiced in a hesitant, Southern slur are, as always, implacably final.

In its flat compression, the story he's told about his meeting with Pollock is typical of Clem's resistance to any detailed accounts of other people. Whenever you would ask him about someone he would answer categorically: "He's a borderline," "She's a pathological liar," "He's a drunk." He would slam the lid shut on the past, as though looking back at the characters that filled it was simply not his affair. He only thought it respectable to talk about their art.

Cy Twombly, *The Italians*, 1961.

So many wounds and scorings, so many tatters splayed over the surface of the work . . . (p. 266)

Andy Warhol, *Do It Yourself (Flowers)*, 1962.

*The great artist as dead celebrity who had Pollock completely outdistanced
was Vincent Van Gogh . . . (p. 275)*

But over the years he had been led to speak about his and Pollock's friendship with somewhat greater specificity, at first to his confidants and later to the writers and scholars who came in increasing numbers. One of the stories he told was a demonstration of their intimacy, particularly in the glory days, at the height of Pollock's power, the summer of 1950. The two of them had left an East Hampton party one night in a common need for escape. "I didn't tell him I was depressed," Clem told an interviewer, "I didn't have to—he sensed it." And for his part he had seen Pollock's panic in the midst of the swirl of people who were now attracted to him in the light of his *Life* magazine notoriety. "They didn't see the man or the genius, they saw only a freak," Clem said. Pollock had driven them out to the dump, sited high on a bluff overlooking Gardiners Bay, and while for the most part they sat in companionable silence, Pollock had told Clem about the fear that now possessed him. "He said he'd had a terrible nightmare. He was at the edge of this cliff and his brothers were trying to push him off."

The terribleness of Pollock's nightmare was, apparently, in direct relation to the spectacular quality of his sudden fame. If Pollock had, as de Kooning called it, "broken the ice," so that collectors and museum people formerly known only for snubbing American painters now flocked to his openings, the publicity surrounding his work had also attracted the envy and rancor of his fellow artists. The brotherhood of the art world seemed to merge into the composite of his own family of five male siblings: he dreamed of "triumphing over them," but at the same time he winced in advance before their judgment, imagining their jealous hatred. He had said as much to Denise Hare: "They only want me on the top of the heap, so they can push me off."

When Pollock died in the car accident of 1956 his agony ended, but his fame grew exponentially. His was a famous car crash, second in media value only, possibly, to that, the year before, of James Dean.

Could Andy Warhol, obsessed by fame, not be fascinated by Jackson Pollock's? It was Warhol's custom in the late 1950s and early '60s to strike up conversations by asking his interlocutor if he or she ever thought about being famous. Whatever the reply Warhol would launch into his own fantasies. "He said he wanted to be as famous as the Queen of England," a report of one of these encounters goes. "Here was this weird coolie little faggot with his impossible wig and his jeans and his sneakers and he was sitting there telling me that he wanted to be as famous as the Queen of England! I thought that Andy was lucky that anybody would talk to him."

The jeans, the worn sneakers, and the tee-shirts Warhol affected through-out the 1950s were inspired by Brando's Stanley Kowalski and Dean's *Rebel without a Cause*. It didn't matter that the type was not his own, he was lost in admiration for the fame. And in the art world no one was as famous as Jackson Pollock for being famous.

His fascination with Pollock was not unmixed, since the machismo and the brutality were not his taste. But still he would pump Larry Rivers for personal details, and in 1962, barely established at the Stable Gallery, he would seek out Ruth Kligman, the "death car girl," to go around the art world with. "Andy was fascinated with de Kooning and Pollock, and through me, he wanted to be part of that lineage," she said. "He asked equally about their world and personalities." Years later when Kligman published *Love Affair,* her account of her connection to Pollock, Warhol briefly contemplated making the movie, with Jack Nicholson playing Pollock. If there were to be a movie about his own life, however, Warhol wanted to be played by Tab Hunter.

Warhol freely spoke of his admiration for Pollock's work—he had said, dismissing a late, abstract Siqueiros in 1972, "It's just action paintings. Anyway, Pollock was much better. Pollock was a great painter. I wish I had a Pollock"—but it's always hard to know how to separate the feelings about the art and the feelings about the fame. When Julian Schnabel boasted, "There are three great American artists in this century. Pollock, Andy, and me. And Andy would agree," Warhol's "agreement" carries its inevitable load of irony. For his posture was always meant to imply that greatness had far more to do with the breadth of the notoriety than the profundity of the work.

It was this double sense of "great" that worked as a strange control over many of Warhol's choices of themes, guaranteeing that the most *kitschig* image from the public *imaginaire* would also hook into the art of the museum, a resonance in which the utter banality and ubiquity of the one (flowered wallpaper for example) would perversely inflect the public reputation of the other (impressionism). "Andy liked his work to have art-historical references," Bob Colacello insisted, "though if you brought it up, he would pretend he didn't know what you were talking about." Colacello said this in the context of Warhol's most explicit reference to Pollock, the series of abstract expressionist look-alikes he made in 1977 and referred to as his *Oxidation Paintings.* But Warhol's early Pop pictures had also announced their connection to Pollock, and this in his more typical way of furtively marrying the lowest cultural associations to the

Installation view, *Andy Warhol,* Institute of Contemporary Art,
Philadelphia, 1965.

"I'd rather stand on my painting". . . *(p. 275)*

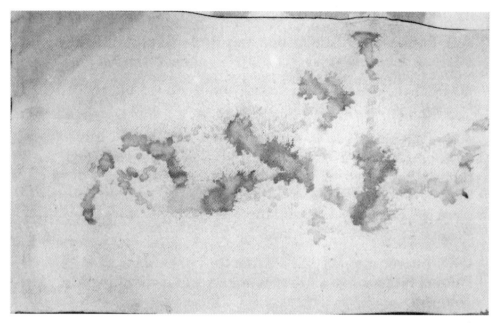

Andy Warhol, *Piss Painting*, 1961.

Warhol's formal reading of Pollock's act of branding his work as "horizontal"... (p. 275)

Hans Namuth, *Jackson Pollock*, 1950.

*One massive index of the position the pictures had had to be in during the
time they were being made . . . (p. 276)*

Andy Warhol, *Oxidation Painting*, 1978.

"Andy liked his work to have art-historical references" . . . *(p. 270)*

highest aesthetic ambitions. The car crashes Warhol began in 1962 were in this sense both the stuff of the most debased journalistic prying into the pain of anonymous lives and, though never announced as such, the celebration of famous deaths, for the two most important car crashes in Warhol's experience were those of Pollock and of James Dean.

In a certain sense, of course, the great artist as dead celebrity who had Pollock completely outdistanced was Vincent van Gogh, whom Warhol acknowledged in his 1962 *Do It Yourself (Irises)* but might also have been considering as the fame component in his decision to paint electric chairs, thus paying secret homage to the figure who had entered the hip art vocabulary of the early 1960s as the artist "suicided by society." But van Gogh did not, as did Pollock, inhabit Warhol's immediate art world horizon. And so Warhol's consideration of Pollock's work, for all its character of having been cathected by "fame," had a component that reached past the thematic surface and down into the structural level of *form*.

Take the *Dance Diagrams,* for example. The tacky image of the middle-aged rake trying to learn the rumba from the Arthur Murray instructor in a mass-cultural fantasy of Everyman his own Fred Astaire rises from these schematic renderings of dance steps lifted from the ads carried by supermarket magazines. But as footprint finds its way to canvas, its new context carries other resonances, and we seem to hear Pollock's famously defiant, "I'd rather stand on my painting," the possible double meaning of which *Time* magazine rushed to exploit in its well publicized sneer at Pollock's technique: "All it says, in effect, is that Jack the Dripper, 44, still stands on his work."

That Warhol exhibited the *Dance Diagrams* by laying the canvases on the floor of the Stable Gallery in 1962 made it clear that his own reading of Pollock was directed toward the unmistakable horizontality that had been, as far as he could see, branded into the very weft of the drip pictures. Even before Warhol had become a certified Pop Artist, even, that is, as "Raggedy Andy," the commercial artist, was casting around for a mode of entry into the art of the galleries, he had taken Pollock's example as one point of departure. In 1961 he had spread blank canvases in front of the door to his house so that people would have to walk on them, leaving a network of darkened tracks; and it was also in 1961 that he executed what he referred to as "the piss paintings," in materials specified in their later reproduction as "urine on canvas." It is in this convergence between the footprints and the urine that Warhol's formal reading of Pollock's act of branding his work as "horizontal" is made wholly explicit.

Abstract expressionism, for all the heated-up press about its release of transgressive means of applying paint, for all the sprays and showers and splatters of pigment, for all the viscosity and oily smears of wet-into-wet, continued for the most part to ratify the fact that the canvas field was a vertical facing the viewer, that the register of the image continued the age-old tradition of occupying the plane that transects the cone of vision, falling before the upright artist or viewer like a translucent veil or, for a far longer time, a transparent window.

In the work of de Kooning or Gorky or Kline, that is, the liquid paint registers the intensity and abandon of its application in runs and rivulets that, in responding to the pull of gravity, leave an indelible index of the picture's upright position over the course of its production. Pollock's application had also left an indelible index, but this time it was of the prone position of the canvas in relation to the artist who had worked above it. Whether it was in the puddles that massed in certain areas attesting to both the liquidity of the medium and the horizontality of the surface that received it, or in the throws of fluid lines leaving the trace of their fall in the halations of paler color soaking around them into the unprimed canvas, Pollock's drip technique was unique in being one massive index of the position the pictures had had to be in during the time they were being made. And unlike the other abstract expressionist works, his bore no telltale vertical runoff.

If, for Warhol, the pictures begged to be read as the residue of a liquid gesture performed by a man standing over a horizontal field, then peeing had become a way of decoding this gesture; and it was to this logical extreme that he carried his "interpretation" of Pollock's work in both 1961 and 1977. And whether it was true of the 1961 version, it was certainly the case that in 1977 the gesture had become, for Warhol, fully homoeroticized. He would not have needed anything as classy as Freud's peeing-on-the-fire footnote from *Civilization and Its Discontents* to make this association. Freud might have spoken about the first great feat of civilization as man's capacity to curb his impulse to pee on the fire, a desire Freud saw as arising from a primitive experience of the flames themselves as phallic, so that "putting out fire by urinating therefore represented a sexual act with a man, an enjoyment of masculine potency in homosexual rivalry." For Warhol the *Oxidation Paintings* were simply once again motifs that connected high and low culture—action painting and the world of the baths and their golden showers—along the vector of notoriety or "fame."

But if the *Oxidation Paintings* can and have been read as a homosexual decoding of the drip technique, it can also be said that they fail that technique and the mordancy of Warhol's other readings of it. Because with the bursts and clouds of color that bloom across their surfaces, the *Oxidation Paintings* give no manifest testimony to the situation through which they were made. Airborne on the canvases, the halated images have no perspicuous connection to either the horizontality or the liquidity of their production; and further, exploiting a Warholian "all is pretty" decorative instinct, and as a consequence leaving behind the sense of violence that Pollock's traces had carried, they bury the erotics of aggressive rivalry that was potential in the original, the very erotics that had probably attracted Warhol in the first place. For if the fixation on fame—as Warhol first wanted to be Matisse and then Picasso and then the Queen of England—and thus the attractions of rivalrous identification, was Warhol's very medium, then no one was better equipped than he to appreciate the psychodynamics of violence encoded in the drip technique.

If there is a vector that connects a banalized worship of fame—the paradox of thousands of teenagers asserting their individualities, for example, by wearing the mass-produced badge of a celebrity, so that in "wanna-being" Madonna as a way of sharing in fame's release from the crowd, they participate ever more resolutely in mass behavior—if there is a vector that connects this to mimetic rivalry, it surely moves along the course that René Girard maps as "metaphysical desire," just as it is surely powered by a unquenchable thirst for recognition in order to feel that one "is."

Metaphysical or triangular desire assumes that no desire is original, no wish spontaneous. Every desire is copied from someone else's desire; every desired object is lodged in the heart of a desiring subject by having been first spotted as the object of someone else's—the mediator's—quest. Thus there is always, in the universe of metaphysical desire, a necessary triumvirate, the subject, the object, and the mediator. Even in the sexual love between just two people, this triumvirate is in place. For the lover and the beloved are both in the position of desiring the same object, the body of the beloved, with each one serving as the mediator for the other's desire. This structure, which is that of double mediation, brings out the essentially rivalrous condition of triangulated desire. It is, Girard claims with Sartre, by this very rivalry, which leads the beloved to withhold the body the lover desires, that the beloved becomes ever more desirable, now clothed in the imagined majesty of a supposed autonomy and envied freedom; just as it is through the lover's persistent pursuit of the beloved's body that this otherwise disenchanted object becomes ever more precious in the beloved's own eyes, given luster by the lover's desire for it. That the triangle of desire between three—subject, mediator, and object—can, through the cat's cradle of mimetic rivalry over the same object, shrink the dramatis personae to two, makes no difference to the triangular *structure* of metaphysical desire. One has here simply the interlocking of the triangles, or double mediation. And it is also the case that the cast of characters can narrow to one, with the subject now in competition with itself.

If the psychoanalytic version of triangular desire casts its origin in the Oedipal scenario, which ends the rivalrous struggle by the subject's internalizing the mediator and identifying with his interdictions, then a post-Freudian attempt has been made to find an origin for this origin in a rivalrous identification of the subject with itself. The Kleinian depressive position is one such; the Lacanian mirror stage is another. In both, the model is a paranoid identification with one's rival such that by striking at that rival one is striking at oneself. If, Lacan argued, the ego can be seen to be formed in the mirror stage's labyrinth, then it is an ego constituted through the subject's emergence as its own first rival, forced to choose between the other and itself even though the other is itself. Although adult paranoia is this reflexive aggressivity writ large, it must, Lacan reasons, obey a structure of identification between subject and rival that "can only be conceived of if the way is prepared for it by a primary identification that structures the subject as a rival with himself." And this, then, is a primary rivalry that assures a primary violence.

Girard is clear about the violence inherent in metaphysical desire, driven as it is far more by rivalrous envy and hatred than by anything that could be called love for the object. He is also insistent about the degree to which this violence increases as the mediator comes closer and closer to the subject, no longer being, for example, the distant figure of the Knight that Don Quixote wants to imitate, but now merely the former schoolfellows that Dostoevski's underground man needs with all his might to force into recognizing him. And, further, since the rivalry between the subject and the mediator is, in most cases of triangular desire, between persons of the same sex, this intensity and focus can be thought, Girard says, as something to be decoded as latently homosexual. But "homosexuality, whether it is latent or not," he argues, "does not explain the structure of desire." Rather, he wants to claim, homosexuality is itself a function of a structure that produces a spectrum along which erotic value can be attached at one end to the object and at the other to the mediator. "This gradual transfer is not impossible," he writes, "it is even likely, in the acute stages of internal mediation, characterized by a noticeably increased preponderance of the

Pablo Picasso, *Girl before a Mirror*, Boisgeloup, 14 March 1932.

"He delved into the deepest recesses of the unconscious, where lies a full record of all past racial wisdom". . . *(p. 282)*

Jackson Pollock, *Masqued Image,* c. 1938–1941.

Picasso's object became Pollock's "own" desire . . . (p. 282)

mediator and a gradual obliteration of the object." But Girard also argues that as the mediator approaches ever more closely and the struggle is over the subject's very being, sexuality tends to drain out of the structure: "As the role of the *metaphysical* grows greater in desire, that of the *physical* diminishes in importance. As the mediator draws nearer, passion becomes more intense and the object is emptied of its concrete value." Or again, "The 'physical' and 'metaphysical' in desire always fluctuate at the expense of each other. This law has myriad aspects. It explains for example the progressive disappearance of sexual pleasure in the most advanced stages of ontological sickness."

Ontological sickness was not the name that any of his doctors or psychoanalysts or teachers gave to Pollock's drinking disorder. But the man who ricocheted between an obsession with greatness—"Everyone's shit but de Kooning and me"; "I'm the only painter alive"—and an increasingly overwhelming fear of nothingness—"I'm no damn good"; "I'm a fucking phony"—such that he could make these opposing claims was surely suffering from a malady of this sort.

That it was structured by mimetic rivalry is also not a difficult case to make. Pollock, after all, was the youngest of five brothers *all* of whom became artists. Within the family his most particular rivalry was with his oldest brother, Charles, whom he followed not just to New York and the Art Students' League but into the very studio where Charles had become the star disciple, and there, in a struggle for Thomas Benton's attention, he displaced Charles to become the trusted intimate of the Benton family. But it was not restricted to Charles. His brother Sande, who had worked in Los Angeles with Siqueiros, had communicated his enthusiasm to Jackson such that, in 1936 when the two of them briefly entered Siqueiros's studio in New York, it was Jackson who grabbed the master's attention. But several years later the mediator who entered Pollock's consciousness most deeply, to become a far more permanent and infinitely more dangerous rival, was Picasso.

That Pollock had begun by 1938 to imitate Picasso's current style as well as his image repertory—something that would intensify after the 1939 appearance of *Guernica*—has long been the stuff of art-historical accounts of Pollock's work. What has tended to be increasingly stressed more recently, however, is that this imitation had as its deepest goal a desire for what Pollock understood as Picasso's desire, namely, access to the unconscious. Perhaps Pollock did not need John Graham to reveal the secret of Picasso's desire, but Graham, who was Pollock's sole aesthetic and emotional support in the opening years of the 1940s, had dedicated a whole system and dialectic of art to this revelation. In 1937 he had publicly celebrated Picasso's conquest of the unconscious object. "He delved into the deepest recesses of the unconscious, where lies a full record of all past racial wisdom," Graham wrote. It was enough for Picasso to desire this object for it to take on unparalleled glamour, and the idea of the unconscious, to which Pollock had already been introduced in not one but two analyses—the first one Freudian, in summer 1938, in the asylum called Bloomingdales; the second Jungian, in 1939–1940, in his New York sessions with Joseph Henderson—now, having surfaced as Picasso's object, became Pollock's "own" desire.

His pursuit of this "object" led him into the places where it was claimed to be kept, led him to the whole discourse on automatism, beginning in 1939–1940 with the group experiments in automatic drawing with Baziotes and Kamrowski, to the lectures in 1941 on surrealism at the New School by Gordon Onslow-Ford, to the surrealist game sessions at Matta's house organized by Motherwell in 1942, and finally to the den of the surrealists themselves, the gallery of Peggy Guggenheim, in 1943. That he was puzzled and disappointed by the automatist *image* we know from Baziotes. The idea of the unconscious as a place from which to recover this or that figure, the idea of it as a kind of projective test, a "doodle reading," was clearly not what Pollock would accept as an answer. Because in his pursuit of the unconscious object what seemed consistently at stake was to do violence to the image. And the outcome of this pursuit seems to have been the drip pictures: the competition with Picasso over the unconscious won at last.

Although it is possible to speak of Pollock's mimetic behavior in specifically biographical terms—his imitation of the cowboy image as projected by his brother Sande; the impression he gave to so many as consistently acting a part, or many different parts: "a magpie," Rosenberg sneered at him— mimetic rivalry is, as Girard makes insistently clear, a structure. At a sociological level this structure clarifies something of the peculiar shape abstract expressionism took as it developed over the course of the 1940s into a multiplicity of signature styles announcing so many different identities in a rivalrous struggle over the prize for originality.

While the modern masters were in Europe acting as a set of external mediators, the American vanguard artists had a more or less homogeneous style, collectivized around the imitation of a limited formal repertory: a biomorphism that went from abstraction to cloisonnist Picasso. It was only when these adored models arrived in New York and settled down amidst their imitators that, in coming nearer, the mediation switched from external to internal, from distant to proximate. And it is this very proximity that, in leveling hierarchical distinctions, increases both the violence and the abstractness of metaphysical desire. Thus David Smith's lines could have been written by Girard himself when, in 1942, he spoke of Mondrian and Lipchitz. "We have met them and we have found that they were humans like we were and they were not gods," he said. De Kooning agreed as he compared himself to Léger: "One day I looked at what I was doing, and I said it's just as interesting as what they're doing."

In realizing that their rivals were not gods, the abstract expressionists were mistakenly basking in the very equality that is necessary to internal mediation's most desperate forms of rivalry, born of a need to create distinctions where no external hierarchies seem to establish them. Girard writes of the Proustian novel's capture of this new form of alienation arising "when concrete differences no longer control relationships among men." He also analyzes the tradition in American sociology to understand triangular desire, beginning with Thorstein Veblen's ideas of conspicuous consumption with its notion that the compulsion to buy is powered strictly by a value conveyed to an article based on a perception of the Other's desire. "David Riesman and Vance Packard," he writes, "have shown that even the vast American middle class, which is as free from want and even more uniform than the circles described by Proust, is also divided into abstract compartments. It produces more and more taboos and excommunications among absolutely similar but opposed units. Insignificant distinctions appear immense and produce incalculable effects. The individual existence is still dominated by the Other but this Other is no longer a class oppressor as in Marxist alienation; he is the neighbor on the other side of the fence, the school friend, the professional rival. The Other becomes more and more fascinating the nearer he is to the Self."

The rivalry unleashed among the Americans by the approach of the Europeans produced a rage for stylistic distinction and individuation that, it could be claimed, was *structurally* generated by the situation of internal mediation. Given at last the possibility of real competition with the mediators, the *form* the response took had the quality of finding a set of abstract marks of "uniqueness" to set each one off from his rivals. But in Pollock's case, we could say, the grip of internal mediation was all the more strengthened by the presence in his studio of Greenberg, whose entire critical vocabulary was that of rivalry and of American artists besting the Europeans, outwitting them in the battle for History. Whatever the structural conditions were, whatever Pollock's own inclinations to mimetic behavior, Greenberg's constant extending to him of the carrot of "the best American artist," over the last half of the 1940s, reinforced the socio-logic of the structure.

Caught up in this structure of rivalry—along with Rothko and Kline and Still and Newman and de Kooning and Gorky, only, one could argue, more so—Pollock was in a battle of hatred and envy with his particular mediator, Picasso, the desired object of which would be the "figure" of the unconscious.

At some point it became clear that that figure could only be approached through *bassesse,* through lowering, through going *beneath* the figure into the terrain of formlessness. And it also became clear that the act of lowering could, itself, only register through the vehicle of a trace or index, through, that is, the stain that would fissure the event from within into act of aggression and mark, or residue, or clue.

When Pollock began to dribble a network of line over the figures on the canvases of what became *Galaxy* and *Reflections of the Big Dipper,* this *bassesse* was suddenly in place: both the cancellation of the figure and the registration of the *beneath* in the unmistakable trace of the horizontality of the event. It was as if, in a way, he had solved the riddle of *She Wolf.*

Both *She Wolf* and *Stenographic Figure* date from Pollock's opening encounter with surrealist notions of automatism, most concretely explained, by Graham, by Baziotes, by Matta, as "automatic writing." Writing, which differentiates itself from pictorial images by orienting itself to the horizontal surface of the table rather than to the vertical field of vision, should, by all logic, go very far in defeating the "image." That it does not was a long-standing paradox of surrealist theory and something quickly observed by Pollock. For as soon as writing is "framed" it becomes an image: either "writing" turned into a decorative picture of itself, as in Breton's presentations of schizophrenic production, or a projective matrix within which to see images, as Polonius saw the camel in the clouds or Leonardo the figures in the fire. If writing stands to painting at the right angle of horizontal to vertical, it does so, as has been remarked, through an opposition of culture to nature, its horizontality removing it from the "natural" upright field of vision to the more culturally processed domain of the written sign. But that there is an axis along which these two planes can always be folded onto one another is a function of what Foucault would call the "commonplace" of representation. What matter "pipe" or [pipe],

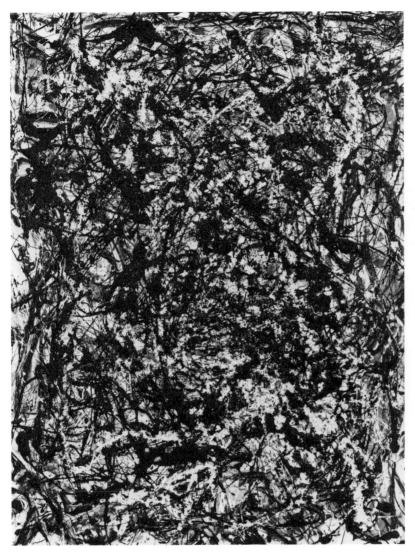

Jackson Pollock, *Sea Change*, 1947.

Both the cancellation of the figure and the registration of the beneath in the unmistakable trace of the horizontality of the event . . . (p. 284)

Jackson Pollock, *Stenographic Figure*, 1942.

Their supposed horizontality could not defeat the image, it could only join it . . . (p. 289)

DESSIN AUTOMATIQUE A LA PLUME.
(Th. Flournoy : *Esprits et Médiums*)

Illustration in André Breton's "Message Automatique,"
Minotaure (1933).

As writing is "framed" it becomes an image . . . (p. 284)

Jackson Pollock, *The She Wolf*, 1943.

But it carried nonetheless these vague, original associations with the ground . . . (p. 289) the language game of representation sets up an extraordinary continuity between the two. And thus it was not hard to see, as in *Stenographic Figure* for example, that the minute the written scribbles hit any portion of the painting, they were framed and thereby verticalized by that section of the image—becoming the "tattoos" on thigh or chest, the "patterns" on couch or bedclothes, the "grating" on wall or floor. Their supposed horizontality could not defeat the image, it could only join it.

In *She Wolf* of the following year this was even more so, since the random pattern produced by the all-over background of automatic doodling had in fact been expressly repackaged as an image. Onto this surface prepared by drips and spatters and sprays of color, Pollock produces an animal image by supplying a thickly painted frame that opaques out a contour around that part of the scrabbled field that will remain—left in negative as it were—as figure. Pollock had of course constructed images this way before, in the frenzy of work that spring in Siqueiros's studio as the May Day murals and floats and banners were produced by laying stencils down on the floorbound panels and spray-painting around them. As the process continued the floor itself had become a field in which the "negative" zones left by mists of spray would mark the place where the stencils had lain, zones now profiled by the opaque color that had landed beyond their edges. Like everything Siqueiros had been producing, *She Wolf* operated the "stencil" to achieve an image. But it carried nonetheless these vague, original associations with the ground, which had been encoded into the Siqueiros process. And everything else that Siqueiros had thought he was encoding: good riddance to bourgeois culture, death to easel painting, out to pasture with "the stick with hairs on its end," etc. Nothing that Siqueiros had managed had gone below "culture," of course, since he had continued to produce the image. But what was lower than both the pictorial image *and* the cultural plane of writing was, it could be seen, the floor, the ground, the beneathness of the truly horizontal. That was lower. That was out of the field of vision and out of the cultural surface of writing and onto a plane that was manifestly below both, below the body.

At the time Pollock made *She Wolf* he could not use this knowledge. It only came to hand when he was engaged in striking, or canceling, the figure.

He's sitting there just as I remember him, next to the neat little marble-topped table, its lamp mounted by a white shade, a painting behind him that might be by Kenneth Noland but is hard to read in the shot we see.

Time seems to have pinched and reddened his face. Whenever I would try to picture it, my memory would produce two seemingly mismatched fragments: the domed shape of the head, and the slackness of the mouth. Looking at him now I am held, as always, by the arrogance of that mouth—fleshy, toothy, aggressive—and its pronouncements, which though voiced in a modulated, hesitant drawl, are, as always, implacably final.

He had made such a pronouncement when, much to her relief, he had told Lee that the black and white pictures bore out her contention that Pollock could indeed, "draw like an angel." But this angelism had a different meaning for him from the traditional gifts Lee thought it signified. Attached to the choo-choo train of history the angelic aspect of Pollock's use of line was, for Clem, registered in the flight it could take, the statement it could make against the realm of matter and substance, and thus the sublimation it could perform. "Now he volatilizes," he had said.

The meaning of Pollock's black and white drawing *for Pollock* was clearly different since it left him feeling strangely shaken and insecure. Ibram Lassaw said "he seemed terribly unsure of himself," confirming Carol Braider's sense that Jackson "was worried about the image having come back."

That the image had to be the dross to be left behind in order for Pollock's recent drawing to have any aesthetic significance within an era of abstraction was the position Clem acted on as he encouraged Helen Frankenthaler to follow the lead of Pollock's soaked black line into the antimatter field of the stained, nonobjective image. One after another Frankenthaler, Morris Louis, Kenneth Noland began to "draw" by staining. And one after another they "righted" Pollock's painting, declaring that the spumes and furls and sprays had all along been verticals, had all along declared an analogy to landscape. "Mountains and Sea," said Frankenthaler, smiling.

One doesn't, however, imagine Louis smiling, as he labored in his tiny suburban room to lift his vast sheets of canvas so that the colored pours of acrylic could course down the channels he made for them in order to constellate his own version of Pollock's linear bleeds. That he had "righted" Pollock's line is all too evident in his own indexes of the upending of the painting process, with the individual streams of pigment still legible even as they soaked one into the other, and the "cusps" of the excess liquid building up along the bottom edge of the canvas. That Louis's paintings are often generically referred to as veils attests to the verticalization they reconstitute as felt image. But even further, that these veils are often felt to be themselves composed of flames of color, such that what is also imaged

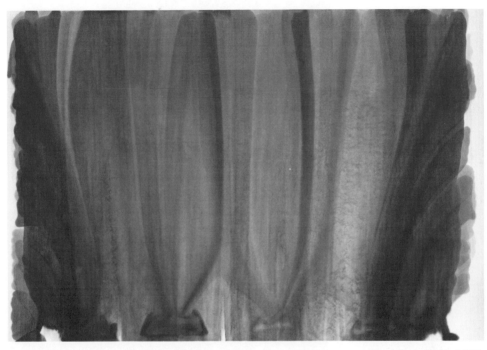

Morris Louis, *Saraband*, 1959.

The final, triumphant sublimation of Pollock's line . . . (p. 293)

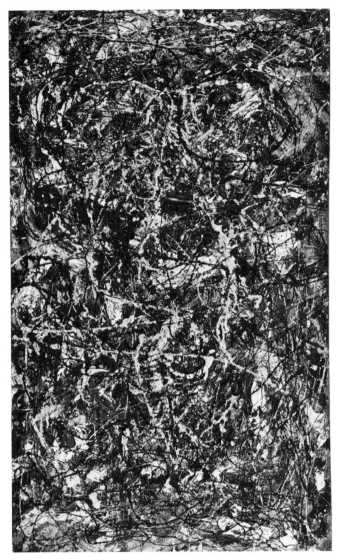

Jackson Pollock, *Full Fathom Five*, 1947.

Onto the surface he had thrown a heterogeneity of trash—nails, buttons,
tacks, keys, coins, cigarettes, matches . . . (p. 293)

forth is fire, is witness to the final, triumphant sublimation of Pollock's line. If peeing on the fire is the destructive barrier to civilization in an excess of aggression against a symbolically charged nature, the preservation of fire is, Freud contends, the first step toward mastering this aggression and producing culture. Louis reconstitutes the cultural artifact that Pollock had trampled, and in the place of his strike against the vertical body, Louis remakes and thus preserves—in the abstract, purified language that itself marks the field of sublimation—the fire.

For Pollock there had been other ways besides the liquid residue of the pour to construct the index of this horizontalization of the image that had definitively canceled and dispersed it. The residue of "dumping," for example, was another to which he had recourse early on, as in *Full Fathom Five*. There he had not only struck out the image by means of the black skein, he had also deposited great gouts of white lead and onto the surface he had thrown a heterogeneity of trash—nails, buttons, tacks, keys, coins, cigarettes, matches—to testify to the connection the work had had to have to the ground. The names he ratified for this first group of drip pictures also functioned to signal the fact of standing over the work and looking down: in addition to *Full Fathom Five* and *Reflection of the Big Dipper*, there were *Watery Paths, Sea Change, The Nest, Vortex*.

But the liquid gesture was perhaps the most efficient in that in one and the same stroke it canceled and testified, like the graffito mark, like the clue. Twombly had decoded Pollock's gesture in one way, Warhol in another. In the late 1960s when Robert Morris was to consider the logic of "Antiform," he would decode it in yet a third. For Morris did not look at the structural condition of the mark, nor at the thematics of the man standing over the supine field. He looked instead at the operations of gravity, of the way the horizontal is a force that pulls against the vertical, pulling it down.

Gravity, he saw in Pollock's work, had become a tool for the production of the work, every bit as much as the sticks from which the paint was flung or the arm's gestural reach as it flung it. Because of this, Pollock's work had constituted a "direct investigation of the properties of the material in terms of how paint behaves under the conditions of gravity." Gravity was what had combined with the liquidity of the paint to read through the finished work as a sign of *process*. "Of the Abstract Expressionists," Morris wrote, "only Pollock was able to recover process and hold on to it as part of the end form of the work. Pollock's recovery of process involved a profound re-thinking of the role of both material and tools in making." The rigidity imposed on most art materials—canvas is

stretched, clay is formed on internal armatures, plaster is applied to lath—
is a fight against gravity. So that ultimately what is conceived of as *form*
is what can maintain itself as vertically intact, and thus a seemingly autonomous gestalt. It's not, Morris reasoned, that what he was calling anti-
form—"random piling, loose stacking, hanging"—had no form, no edge,
no boundaries. It was that lacking rigid form it could not remain upright,
resistant to gravity.

When Greenberg had produced his own analysis of Pollock's dripped line,
his own scenario for why the artist had turned to this manner of drawing,
he had explained it as a way of avoiding the *cut*. "Pollock wanted to get
a different edge," he said. "A brush stroke can have a cutting edge that
goes into deep space when you don't want it to." For Greenberg the dripped
line avoided the edge that would cut into space, the edge that would
differentiate figure from ground, by isolating forms. By not cutting it would
allow the canvas to read as an unbroken continuity, a singular, undivided
plane. And that plane would then, according to the logic of opticality, yield
up an analogue of the immediacy, the unbrokenness of the visual field and
of the viewer's own perception of that field in an all-at-onceness of visual
reflexiveness. By avoiding the production of forms (cut out within the field)
the work would produce *form* itself as the law of the formulation of form.

But for Morris everything in Pollock's line had indeed to do with the cut,
with something slicing not into space but into the continuity of the canvas
plane as it conventionally stretches, rigid, across our plane of vision. The
lengths of felt Morris began to work with were submitted to a process of
systematic cuts, slicing into their pliant fabric surfaces, disturbing their
planar geometries even while the cuts themselves were geometrically regular
slashes. The irregularity came when, the work lifted onto the plane of the
wall, where it hung from hooks or suspended from wires, gravity pulled
open large gaps in the fabric surfaces, gaps that could be called neither
figure nor ground, gaps that somehow operated *below* form.

Gravity had also been what Hans Namuth had had to respect when plan-
ning for his film on Pollock. It was not enough merely to stand back from
the process as he had done in his still photographs, the upright body of
the photographer tracking and recording the gestures made by the upright
body of the painter. He wanted the connection of the flung paint to the
horizontal field to be absolutely manifest, something that could only occur
if one could see the painter's body and the result of the gesture conflated
onto the same visual plane. The answer to his dilemma, he said, came to

Jackson Pollock, *One (Number 31, 1950)*, 1950.

*Gravity was what had combined with the liquidity of the paint to read
through the finished work . . . (p. 293)*

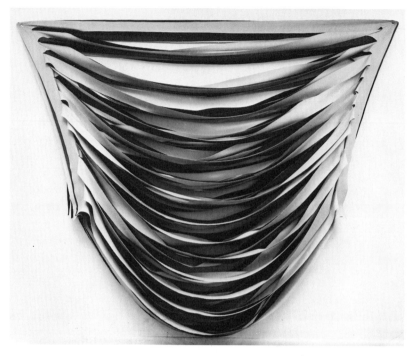

Robert Morris, *Untitled*, 1968.

*Something slicing not into space but into the continuity of the canvas plane
as it conventionally stretches, rigid, across our plane of vision . . . (p. 294)*

Robert Morris, *Untitled*, 1967–1968.

Gaps that could be called neither figure nor ground, gaps that somehow operated below *form . . . (p. 294)*

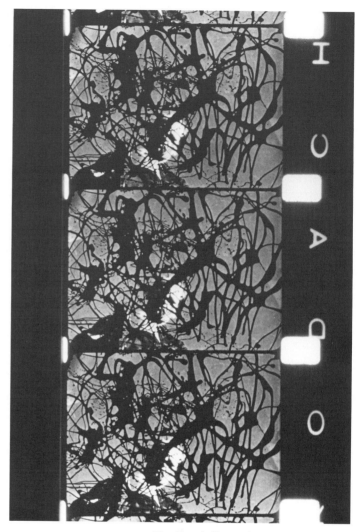

Hans Namuth, film strip from *Jackson Pollock,* 1950.

Suspended on the other side of two sheets of glass were two painters painting . . . (p. 301)

Gjon Mili, *Picasso "Drawing" with Flashlight, Vallauris*, 1949.

Picasso had come suddenly, frighteningly, nearer . . . (p. 301)

Jackson Pollock, *Number 7, 1951*, 1951.

*Drawing images across an imaginary "fronto-parallel," vertical
expanse . . . (p. 302)*

him in a dream. He decided to use a sheet of glass as Pollock's "canvas" and, lying below it, to take up the same absolute horizontal as Pollock's own pictorial surface, to shoot upward through the glass and onto the spectacle of Pollock painting.

But Namuth's dream had a name, of course. It was called Picasso.

As a European and a cosmopolite, Namuth knew what was happening in Paris and most particularly knew of the comings and goings of the most famous artist of his century. A filmmaker himself, he had to know of Paul Haesaerts's film *Visite à Picasso,* which was shot in 1949 and released in the spring of 1950. This, the first film to which Picasso had consented, is also determined to give its viewers direct access to the maestro at work. To this end it captures its image through the pane of glass on which Picasso obligingly paints. Of course in this case the transparent working plane is vertical and never more so than in the final shot when we see Picasso framed by a long French window inside the farmhouse at Vallauris as he fills its surface with a whimsical figure displayed for those of us looking on from without. He ends the film with his famous signature which he signs on another pane of glass in anticipation of the actual date when the film will be finished: "Picasso 50."

Namuth opens his film with Pollock signing his name. Although the shooting occurred in October 1950, Pollock is directed toward the date of its release. So he signs "Pollock 51." Perhaps the idea came to him in a dream.

But the encounter with Picasso across the medium of this film had, I would venture, more the character of a nightmare. For now, suspended on the other side of two sheets of glass were two painters painting, each one able in this strangely resemblant activity to be substituted for the other, to be slipped the one on top of the next. From being a distant rival, an external mediator, Picasso had come suddenly, frighteningly, nearer. This was now the arrival of the internal mediator, so close that he strangely doubles the subject. And the result, as Girard sees Dostoevski predicting, is a kind of poisoning of the will, a paralysis.

There are not one but two stories of Lee Krasner's hearing Pollock hurl a book of Picasso's work on the floor and rage about the fact that "that guy missed nothing." The first is located in New York, before they moved to Springs; the second in 1954 while Pollock was recovering from a broken ankle. Whatever the date of the incident, the two versions bracket the period of the drip pictures during which time Pollock had discovered something Picasso had not. But the revelation of the film was its creation of a condition in which the two of them can be seen to have discovered the "same" thing: the possibility of making an image by means of an airborne gesture through which one could see the body of the artist himself. Pollock would probably not have seen illustrations from Haesaerts's Picasso film (although Namuth probably would have). But he would most certainly have seen the next best thing: Picasso's *Space Drawings* photographed by Gjon Mili and not only widely published in 1950 but exhibited as well at the Museum of Modern Art. Looking through the extraordinarily authoritative pencil line of light that curves through open space to sketch the outline of the bull or the gesture of a figure running, one can see him there as well, bare-chested, in his all-too-familiar boxer undershorts, impishly grinning: Picasso—sucking all the air out of the space, taking up all the room. "Goddamn it, that guy has done everything. There's nothing left."

The scene Pollock carried out with Namuth just before he upended the table and dumped twelve dinners in the laps of his guests rings with this sense of outraged revelation at the sight of his own diminished stature and that of the bearer of bad tidings. "I'm not a phony," he kept saying to Namuth. "You're a phony." His sense of his own fraudulence never left him after that. He would say that there were three great painters in the twentieth century, Matisse, Picasso, and himself. And tears would course down his face. After the film Pollock had painted just one more full-scale exhibition, the black and white pictures, and then had barely been able to put together the five works he needed for the next show. The following year's exhibition had had to be a retrospective since, as everyone now knew, Pollock could no longer paint. A year and a half later he was dead.

After the film Pollock's work had simply lost its relation to gravity, and so even though he continued, in the black and white pictures, to make paintings by pouring liquid paint, these were now conceived as huge, representational drawings, and even his tools—basting syringes filled with black enamel instead of his old battery of sticks and encrusted brushes—resembled the draftsman's equipment of pen and ink, the better to form the image. And the image, resistant to gravity, floated above the canvas onto the plane of the vertical, just like the "pictures" that are formed by the myriad tesserae of Roman mosaics which, in constellating a figure from the zodiac on the floor, resurrect out of the ground itself an image of the sky above. Pollock's "volatilized" line cannot but act now like Picasso's light-pencil, drawing images across an imaginary "fronto-parallel," vertical expanse.

Even when Pollock tried to return to the abstractness of the drip technique, his way was now blocked by a rivalry that meant he was condemned to the plane, if not the letter, of the image. *Blue Poles* is the massive testimony to this confusion. Though parts of it look like the earlier dripped skeins, the work is also awash with great runs and rivulets of paint that stream like so much cream-colored rain "downward" along its surface, giving evidence to that part of the picture's execution done while the canvas was hanging vertical, on the wall. The "blue poles" that were added near the picture's completion only ratify both this commitment to the vertical and this resurrection of the schematized "body," as Tom Benton's diagrammatic vectors from his analyses of the world of Renaissance art now recompose themselves from their former dispersal in *Number 1, 1948* to constellate the traditional decorum of the processional frieze. "From Tom to Jack. From Jack to Harry."

The relation of Pollock's authentic drip pictures to gravity in the field of the real is different of course from the way the pictorial image—from within its virtual field—can come to visualize our own upright bodies and their relation to gravitational force. For gestalt psychology all vertical fields will—like a kind of mirror—already be structured according to the body's own organization, with a top and a bottom, a left and a right. The field, they say, is anisotropic. This internal differentiation lying *in potentia* in the very background within which the gestalt will appear already attests, then, to the features the brain will project onto the perceptual field in order to organize the gestalt: its simplicity, its hierarchy, its balanced dynamism. The gestalt will thus be, in a sense, a projective image of our bodies' own resistance to, their triumph over, the gravitational field.

Through the distance Pollock's drip pictures had traveled from this mirrored projection of the organization of the viewer's body, they had become anathema to the Gestalt psychologists, the very thing they loved to hate. What the works projected instead, as Rudolf Arnheim saw it, was the directionless monotony of "a kind of molecular milling everywhere." They were nothing but an attempt to make a picture out of mere background trivia, the very thing the human perceptual apparatus does not even see. The retina at the back of the eyeball may duly register background forms but, the gestaltists insisted, such forms have no psychological existence whatsoever. Since they are not included in the chosen gestalt (or figure), they are not perceived at all.

But if they are not perceived, Anton Ehrenzweig replied, it is because they are repressed. Speaking in 1948 in the service of what he chose to call *depth vision,* he thought of this domain of unconscious, primal sight as "gestalt-free, chaotic, undifferentiated, vague, superimposed." He likened its lack of differentiation to the perceptual field of the infant whose own Ego fills the entire world, running together inside and outside, making of all men, for example, "papa." He likened its superimposition and ambiguity to that of the dream or the fantasy. He likened the way it tended to project sexual imagery uniformly onto all parts of the visual field—as in the phallic profusion of both dreams and "primitive" sculptures—to the libidinal thrust of the unconscious and its drive toward pleasure, only to meet the stern resistance of the superego of *form.* He thought of the formless, gestalt-free products of depth vision on the analogy of the dream thoughts that, upon waking, are submitted to the censorship of the organizing principle Freud had called secondary revision, a force that creates the good form of a narrative where in the dream itself there has only been the Dionysian chaos of unrepressed affect. He thought of depth vision also as manifesting itself in the artist's unconsciously wrought technique—its linear meanders, the nervously erratic quality of its brush work—only to be made over, in its own kind of secondary revision, into the "form-control" of the "surface gestalt."

It was clear to Ehrenzweig, however, that the implacable force of the superego's will-to-form would mean that whatever had surfaced from "unconscious depth perception" would itself be denied through a need to impose order. In thinking about this phenomenon in the historical development of art, he saw two ways in which this imposition had been asserted. One had been to submit the ambiguous field to what he called "the constancy of thing-perception," or more simply put, to realism, and to accede thereby to the authority of science. Another form of denial had been, he said, "style perception," which takes the new way of seeing and rationalizes it by turning it into form. "All subsequent generations," he said, "will perceive the style instead of the gestalt-free symbol play, once the style formation is achieved." And he added, "Once secondary style elaboration has covered the wild form-play of art, never again can the human eye see its full effect, neither this generation, nor future generations."

Thus it was not only that Ehrenzweig could have predicted that what had initially been registered as Pollock's aggressivity—the work's "violence, exasperation and stridency"; its "Gothic-ness, paranoia and resentment"—would be made over into the "secondary style elaboration" of opticality; he could also have foreseen that even the psychologist's experience of all that wild "molecular milling" would be made over into the structural

Jackson Pollock, *Blue Poles,* 1952.

*Runs and rivulets of paint that stream like so much cream-colored
rain . . . (p. 303)*

Jackson Pollock, *Convergence*, 1952.

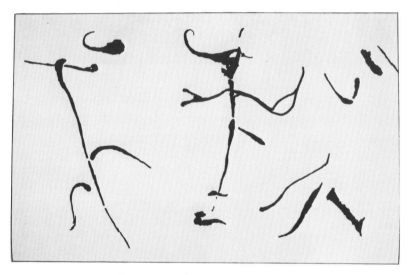

Diagram for *Convergence*, from Matthew Rohm, *Visual Dynamics in Jackson Pollock*.

Made over into the "secondary style elaboration" of opticality . . . (p. 304)

composure of gestalts. Thus a disciple of Arnheim, in service both to his gestaltist master and to the doctrine of opticality, now reads into Pollock's dripped pictures the very anisotropism of the vertical field's way of "mirroring the living organism." This latter-day interpretation thus sees Pollock as building the gestalt into the drip paintings both at the level of the "microstructure"—the drips themselves—and at that of "primary structural configurations"—the overarching forms Pollock is imagined as infusing into his dripped fields in order to achieve *Prägnanz*. The configurations that are listed by this strange intellectual hybrid, the optico-gestaltist, are the basic motifs of pole, butterfly, arabesque, and labyrinth. Although there is an attempt to read *Autumn Rhythm* itself in terms of the structural configuration of repeated poles, this breaks down into an admission that here the poles are strangely "exploded," "diffuse," and only vestigial. Instead it is to *Blue Poles* that the writer turns for unalloyed evidence of Pollock's looking to enforce the gestalt, to *Blue Poles* and to the other drip picture Pollock tried to make once his hold on his own mark had been broken: the 1952 painting *Convergence*. But these disastrous works are not happy examples to project back onto the drip paintings. Pollock had produced *Blue Poles* in an agony of desperation to retrieve something he had lost, but according to Clem, he knew it "wasn't a success. He knew it was over, that he'd lost his inspiration."

But Pollock's public "success" was made for him by a systematic misreading of his painting, by—to say the word—a repression of the evidentiary weight of its most basic and irrefutable mark. Pollock's "success" depended on a reading that overlooked the horizontal testimony of his line, a testimony that resonates indexically from within any other possible apprehension of it. For even as the dripped labyrinth permits an experience in terms of "interfused lights and darks," even as it evokes the luminous cloudiness that would seem to underwrite a name like *Lavender Mist*, the indexical mark can be read across and through that very ascensional axis, doing its work to *lower* and desublimate the perceptual field, doing the "job" that, two decades earlier, Bataille had given to the *informe:* to undo form by knocking it off its sublimatory pedestal, to bring it down in the world, to make it *déclassé*. Given the sublimatory force of the modernist reading, however, Pollock's thrown lattice was no longer seen as violent; it was now hallucinatory, a mirage. According to the principles of opticality projected within it, it had become a visual plenum in which nothing "cut" into space. Further, due to there being no inside or outside to the contours formed by this line, the continuum it seemed to project was now felt to resonate with that peculiar soothing and compensatory sense of indissoluble connection of the individual to eternity, "a feeling," Freud had said in another context, "as of something limitless, unbounded, something 'oceanic.'"

It was only in 1951, when Pollock had "lost his inspiration" and his relation to the miragelike, optical character of the oceanic could be thought to have failed, that he would once more be seen as "violent." With the black and white pictures, he took it all back, Clem had said, "as if in violent repentance."

If the oceanic feeling can be regarded as an analogue for modernist opticality, it is itself, however, a strangely slippery concept. In Freud's view, the oceanic feeling is at one and the same time the basis of religious sentiments *and* the ground of a limitless narcissism, the infant's experience of a total lack of difference between itself and its world. It is this very lack of difference that, Freud also asserts, allows for primitive man to see nature as an extension of himself and thus, in phallicizing the fire, to enter into aggressive, sexualized play with it. Civilization will deeroticize the fire, returning it to the reality of its naturalized, desymbolized difference from the human sphere. Civilization will strip the oceanic of this aggressive, undifferentiated lining, will repress it.

Against the "success" that a modernist reading had in store for them, however, the drip pictures can still be seen to retain the cutting edge of an indexical mark, one that slices the works lose from their purported verticality, by dropping them, visually, to the floor. It is a mark, as well, that cuts itself away from any intentional matrix to achieve its own isolation as "clue," the simultaneity of the visual present already thus fissured by time. And it is a mark that cuts loose the work it marks from any analogies with the gestalt of the body whole. Instead, in dispersing and disseminating the corporeal itself, it sets up a thematics of the sexual and the rivalrous that will return against the very "oceanic" condition of modernist aesthetics the aggressivity and formlessness of its repressed.

All this happens and is all recorded on the surface of the body without organs: even the copulations of the agents, even the divisions of God, even the genealogies marking it off into squares like a grid, and their permutations. The surface of this uncreated body swarms with them, as a lion's mane swarms with fleas.

—Gilles Deleuze and Félix Guattari, *Anti-Oedipus*

He's sitting there just as I remember him, next to the neat little marble-topped table, with its prim lamp in gilt bronze and its assortment of tiny ashtrays, one of them containing a heap of crumpled butts, the only disarray in this fanatically ordered space. I am across the room from him, perched on a long yellow sofa above which there hangs a dour Hans Hoffman, a brown surface of palette scrapings from which two squares of pure color have been allowed to escape with relative impunity, a larger one of vermillion, a smaller, acid one of green. As usual he is lecturing me, about art, the art world, people we know in common, artists I've never met. As always I am held by the arrogance of his mouth—fleshy, toothy, aggressive—and its pronouncements, which though voiced in the studied hesitancy of his Southern drawl are, as always, implacably final.

We have been talking about critics, one of whom has just presented her views in an attention-grabbing article about art he detests.

"Spare me smart Jewish girls with their typewriters," he laments.

"Ha, ha, ha," I reply, sparkling with obedient complicity.

I think of that now as I wonder how many of us there were in those days, in the mid-1960s, smart Jewish girls with typewriters, complicit, obedient, no matter what long streak of defiance we might have been harboring.

And I remember that as what Mark thought to mention first, picturing Eva Hesse to me from their days at Yale, starting off his description by telling me of her desire for instruction, of the way she faithfully jotted down the titles of books he referred to and the things he said about them. Though he had, perhaps, been drawn to her, what he immediately recalled was the air she often had of an obedient schoolgirl, the one that had made her a star in Josef Albers's class, far and away his favorite pupil.

Lucy Lippard is struck by this also and she remembers Eva's dutifulness in the role of wife, such that when they first knew her none of them really understood how seriously she took her art. Over and over her book on Hesse corroborates Mark's memory as she tells of Hesse's lists: the column of writers—Gide, Nabokov, Joyce, Dostoevski, Austen, Ortega—followed by the note confessing, "I have become a reader—the thing I've wanted most, but was in too great a conflict with myself to do"; the lists of word definitions, which became a habit all through the decade, aided by the huge thesaurus she finally bought as she searched for titles with the right degree of literacy for her work. Lippard tells how a list of possible titles with a somewhat poetic cast—"marking time, nice question, liar's dice, make sense, last not least, fairly fast, three of a kind, pride's profile"—was jettisoned to be replaced by quite another kind of roster, one filled with more "intellectual" words, "like those drawn from the thesaurus category 'circular motion' referring to the forms she was using: Circumnavigation/circumflexion/circuit/evolution/circumscribe/circuitous, devious/rotation, gyration, convolution/vortex, maelstrom, vertigiousness, vertigo/rotate, box the compass, gyrate/enfoldment, evolution, inversion/circle—cordon, cincture, cestuis, baldric/(complex circularity) convolution, involution, undulation, sinuosity/coil—labyrinth/wind, twine, twirl, entwine, undulate/meander, indent, contort/involved—labyrinthine/in and out/eccentric."

And here's another list: "Vertiginous Detour/ box the compass/baldric/labyrinth/Ennead/Several/ingeminate/biaxial/diadic dyadic/dithyletic/bigeminate/ingemination-repetition."

Standing back now and looking at those swarms of words zanily filling the page, producing the strange ululalia of a burble of off-rhymes—"wind, twine, twirl, entwine"—so dear to Artaud, we cannot help but think of Hesse's favorite term for her art, her highest critical encomium, the word "absurd." When she speaks of her "most important early statement"—the 1966 *Hang Up*—she justifies its centrality to her work by specifying, "It was the first time where my idea of absurdity or extreme feeling came through." And absurdity, Hesse was fond of pointing out, is one of the things repetition is effortlessly capable of producing. "My idea," she had said in 1970, speaking about the aesthetics of composition, of form, "is to counteract everything I've ever learned or been taught about those things, to find something else. . . . If something is absurd, it's much more exaggerated, more absurd if it's repeated."

Indeed, Hesse had made herself into the specialist of repetition-as-absurdity, which is to say repetition recast from the minimalist projection of

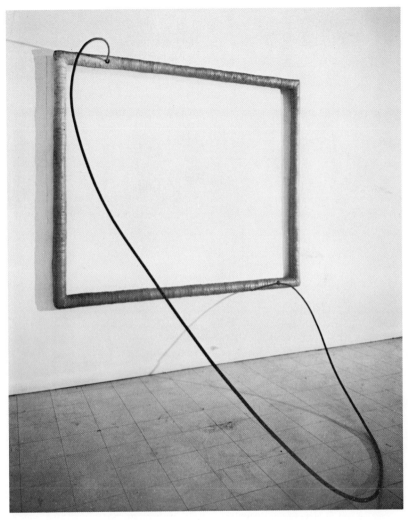

Eva Hesse, *Hang Up,* January 1966.

"And—oh! more absurdity!—it is very, very finely done . . ." (p. 313)

Eva Hesse, *Untitled*, 1967.

"Convolution, involution, undulation, sinuosity/coil—labyrinth/wind, twine, twirl, entwine, undulate . . ." (p. 310)

arithmetic, impersonal law—the grids, the serial expansions, the systemic progressions—into the disruptive subjectivity of an infantilized world of babble, of gurgle, of a viscerally conceived world of play. The exquisitely wrought drawings of hosts of concentric circles each graded from white through middle gray to dark, each placed on its own square within the compartment of a delicately inscribed grid, always managed to escape the realm of conceptual art's logic and to lodge themselves within the bodily and the obsessional, all the more so when, from the center of each targetlike circle, there would project the delicate filament of a length of clear plastic string—so many hairs marking the aureoles of so many nipples.

But Hesse would not have placed the lists copied down from the thesaurus in this domain of the absurd. Those lists came from a world of intellect it would not have occurred to her to challenge. This, we could say, was what marked her obedience.

The other thing that marked it was her adherence to painting, to its problematic, which is that of the vertical field: bounded, image-filled, wall-oriented, the vehicle of "fronto-parallel" address. Although she had decided to contest its rules, and that in the most subversive way possible, she had not simply walked out of its discursive space and slammed the door. She had not, that is, as so many of her critics suppose, become a sculptor.

Indeed, when she returned from her year in Kettwig, Germany, during which she had lifted the imagery of her painting into the realm of bas-relief, she thought she was headed into the three dimensions of the world of sculpture. So she made *Laocoön*, undoubtedly naming it in a rededication of her art to a new medium. But the work is a disaster—literal, awkward, depictive: a big jungle gym with a lot of snakes. No, the "absurd" work of the same moment is *Hang Up,* an enormous, empty picture frame, the site of painting declared and defied at the same time: "It sits on the wall," Hesse said, "with a very thin, strong, but easily bent rod that comes out of it . . . and what is it coming out of? It is coming out of this frame, something and yet nothing and—oh! more absurdity!—it is very, very finely done. The colors on the frame were carefully gradated from light to dark."

Hang Up not only marks Hesse's convocation of her art to the realm of the absurd, it declares her refusal or her inability to leave the territory of painting. She bridled at Albers's limitations, his rules, his dicta, at the monomania of an art "based on one idea." She wondered, "How much more can be done with this notion?" She said, "There isn't a rule . . . I don't want to keep any rules. I want to sometimes change the rules." But the same docility that led her to buy the thesaurus kept her fixated on the pictorial.

Do we need examples to drive this point home? She invented a new support, rubber and fiberglass over cheesecloth, and from this she made *Contingent* (1969), hanging, veil-like, perpendicular to the wall, or as *Expanded Expansion* (1969), propped directly against it. The huge scale of the latter, or of the propped fiberglass poles of *Accretion* (1968) or of the fiberglass boxes of the wall relief *Sans II* (1968), orients itself to the heroic scale of abstract expressionism, to its claims to mural status, to its bluster and scope. Just as the medium itself in its translucence and relative weightlessness proclaims its proclivity toward the "optical." "What Eva was able to do," Mel Bochner would later say, "was to work directly with light; she was able to make light a medium of sculpture." But surely it was the other way round? By infusing the rigid materials normally associated with sculpture with this effulgent luminosity, and connecting this radiance to the wall, she had reassociated them with painting and with the problematic of two dimensions, not three.

And then there is the glittering fiberglass bramble of *Right After* (1969), with its later *Untitled* version in a skein of latex-covered rope, and the last work she completed, the seven hanging, fiberglass-covered poles (1970). The relationship of all of these to Pollock is wholly explicit. Hesse herself spoke of this to *Time* magazine. Referring to the rope piece, she said, "Chaos can be structured as non-chaos. That we know from Jackson Pollock."

This knowledge is projected within the vertical domain of painting; it is suspended, it is airborne, it is optically displayed. And yet the knowledge itself is understood as transgressive. Hesse's complicity is here at work in the most corrosive of ways, burrowing from within the pictorial paradigm to attack its very foundations . . . like the L Schema tunneling away from within the inner core of the Klein Group. For Hesse had come to have a very particular take on the domain of painting, the shorthand name for which—although she would never have called it this—is *bachelor machine*.

It surely was fortuitous that in May 1965, almost at the end of Hesse's year in Germany, she and her husband, Tom Doyle, would travel to Bern for a show that included objects by Marcel Duchamp. All during the spring Hesse's work had been changing, projecting outward from the picture plane into a kind of low relief built up of papier-mâché, plaster, rope, and sometimes metal. In their strange connection of the organic—she described one as comprised of breast and penis forms—to the mechanical—"Thus they look like *machines,* however they are not functional and are nonsense," she wrote—the works move toward the domain that Duchamp had mapped in the *Large Glass.* One, called *Eighter from Decatur,* has the look of an electric fan, its wire blades projecting from a panel inscribed with the arcs of what reads as a partial spiral: the form and motion of the *Rotoreliefs* reconceived in the contemporary language of early '60s "funk." Another, called *Top Spot,* is strangely predictive of what was to come once Hesse had returned to New York. On a white masonite board that announces the ground or plane of the relief there swarms a strange assemblage of tubes and porcelain connective sockets, forming a series of aberrant machines hooked, daisy-chain-like, one to the other, all of them clinging precariously to the blankness of the flat surface. What Hesse would abandon once she got back to New York was the funky quality of the forms, the obviousness of their dada disorder. What she would keep was the system: the hook-up of the bachelor machines and their underlying meaning as "desiring production"—which is to say, *pure process*—distributed over the transparent glass surface, a territory—that of painting—to which they cling but which they can never articulate. For painting has now become what Deleuze and Guattari were soon to define as "the body without organs."

It is as anachronistic to read Hesse through the *Anti-Oedipus,* published two years after her death, as it is to read Pollock through the *Oxidation Paintings* or Morris's felt pieces. Because although Hesse may have felt a connection between her work and something of what Duchamp meant to the 1960s art world, she cannot have known or intended anything like the theorization Deleuze and Guattari would develop on the basis of the bachelor apparatus. Yet the model projected by that theory maps directly onto her work, describing it with a strange exactitude, capturing the schiziness of its autoeroticism coupled with its fanatical order, projecting the cunning of its enormous ambition trapped inside the autistic limits of a fixed convention.

Deleuze and Guattari begin with the body understood as a series of part-objects—breast, mouth, stomach, intestines, anus—each of which is a machine. But unlike the world of mechanical production, where a machine is one thing and its product is another, removed from it, discrete, separate, the desiring production of the part-objects is a process in which there is no distinction between production and product. For the flows produced by one machine, the breast, say, provide the continuum into which the next machine, the mouth, can cut, thereby setting up the precondition of the mechanical, which is to articulate matter. As each machine cuts into the continuity of the flows produced by its neighbor only to produce a new flow for the next machine to cut into in its turn, all are organized in relation to three principles. The first is repetition, for as Deleuze and Guattari say, "although the desiring machines make us into an organism, at the very heart of this production the body suffers in being organized in no way at all"; the second is continuity, for which the operative term is *process;* the third is desire, or the connective "labor" that drives libido toward producing/product.

Since the model of the *Anti-Oedipus* derives from Melanie Klein, it is not surprising that it should include that other aspect of the paranoiac-schizoid scenario of early development: the infant's body experienced as invaded by the part-objects that persecute and attack it and that the infant tries to pulverize and attack back. If the part-objects are rebaptized *desiring machines,* the threatened, paranoid body is now labeled the *body without organs.* This body, static, nonproductive, is also the body without an image, the gestaltless body, or the body without form. And it is over this body, locked in a relation of attraction/repulsion, that the desiring machines are distributed, although they can never articulate this body, for which the term Deleuze and Guattari invent is "deterritorialized." Nonproductive, formless, the body without organs is instead the site of inscription or recording, it is the place through which signs circulate in an effort to decode the flows of desire, at the same time setting up the illusion that they themselves are the agents of production. "When the productive connections pass from the machines to the body without organs (as from labor to capital)," they write, "it would seem that they then come under another law that expresses a distribution in relation to the nonproductive element as a 'natural or divine presupposition' (the disjunctions of capital)."

When Hesse came back to New York she discovered process, which is to say she came to understand the logic of flows of material—latex, fiberglass, rubber tubing—that would produce a continuum, a flux, into which the moldlike machines of her work could cut. And each mold, each cast element—sphere, tube, sheet, open box—by being repetitively set in series, would in its turn produce a new flow, a new continuum that would offer itself to the next act of cutting. Thus she no longer needed to fashion objects that looked like machines in the manner of the German reliefs. She had constructed the system of desiring production instead. Far more abstract and morphologically noncommittal, it was far more disturbing and, in its Beckett-like ingeniousness, far more "absurd."

Eva Hesse, *Untitled,* completed March 1970.

"Chaos can be structured as non-chaos. That we know from Jackson Pollock . . ." (p. 314)

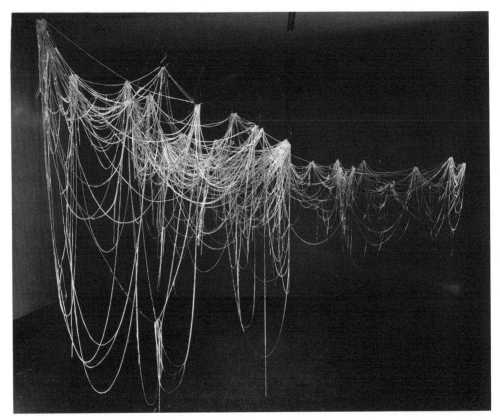

Eva Hesse, *Right After*, 1969.

A kind of amorphousness, the threat that a body "that suffers in being organized in no way at all" lies behind the surface . . . (p. 320)

And these machines are, as I have said, always deployed in relation to the planarity and verticality of that territorial convention called painting. It is thus that when Hesse "reads" Pollock's work in *Right After* and the "rope piece," she locates her reading in the sublimated, fronto-parallel plane of modernist opticality, the skeins dancing weightless before our eyes. But though she locates this plane by means of her own insistence on uprightness, and of the wall as a kind of backdrop or support for the image, she also defies the *meaning* of the plane, its existence as a precondition of *form*. The bounded, flattened plane of painting, after all, functions like the mirror described by Lacan, reflecting back to the subject the flattering picture of *Prägnanz*, of the organization and order of the good gestalt always there in potentia and, by means of its reflection, always assuring the viewing subject a concomitant logical and visual control. Hesse replaces this plane. In its stead, the implicit support of her images is the body without organs. Which is to say the plane has been redefined as the "uncreated body" over which the process-machines of her work swarm "as a lion's mane swarms with fleas."

In 1966 Lucy Lippard instigated *Eccentric Abstraction,* an exhibition tailored to, among others', Hesse's new work, which she saw as a collection of bulbous, organlike, erotico-abstract forms, an aggressive challenge to minimalist sculpture. But Hesse surprised her by submitting *Metronomic Irregularity,* a bramble of cotton-covered wire projected from the relief plane of three square panels. That it was not a provocation for sculpture but rather organized itself in relation to painting was leapt on at once by Hilton Kramer, who denounced its vocabulary as "second-hand," since, he pointed out, it "simply adapts the imagery of Jackson Pollock's drip painting to a three-dimensional medium."

Kramer went on to attack this move as yet another example of what Donald Judd had announced in 1965 as the strategy of "specific objects," that attempt to void the convention of painting, with its forms tucked away safely behind the plate glass of the surface and cosseted within illusionistic space, by producing these forms *literally,* in real space, thereby rendering painting itself obsolete. "What was formerly part of the metaphorical and expressive fabric of painting," Kramer lamented, "is now offered as a literal *thing.* A kind of technological positivism triumphs, but at the expense, I think, of a genuine imaginative probity. . . . Here, as elsewhere, the prose of literal minds effectively displaces the old poetry."

Lippard's response to this was to point to the way imagery used up in one medium can take on new power in another and so while she admitted the pictorial character of Hesse's work, she insisted that in the end it should be evaluated as sculpture, going so far as to liken it to the problematic, begun by Gonzalez and elaborated by David Smith, of "drawing in space." Thus by beginning with her admiration for Eva's subversiveness—a feeling that resonates on nearly every page of her superb book on Hesse—she ends by bringing her into the safe harbor of a three-dimensionality that poses no problems for painting, that ignores the notion of "want[ing] to sometimes change the rules."

The rules of painting are clear, as transparent as a diagram is to the logic of its relations, as bounded as a frame is by the law of exclusions that render it a terrain of self-contained autonomy. We know this logic. We have seen its picture.

By projecting the pictorial plane into real space, Hesse confronted it with a kind of amorphousness, the threat that a body "that suffers in being organized in no way at all" lies behind the surface of that mirror seemingly "pregnant" with its own gestalt. For the logic of relations she substituted the flux of process, and for the transcendental signified that projects *meaning* onto these relations she presented the dispersed, disorganized subject who is merely the sum of the apparatus. By being redefined as the body without organs, the convention called *painting* is projected as a paranoid space incapable of further articulation, a surface that merely multiplies more and more attempts to decode desire, while all the time the machines keep laboring in their parallel circuit, producing and intersecting flows.

The circuit of the L Schema maps onto the grid of the Klein Group, undermining it from within. Just so does Hesse's *process* elaborate the space of painting with its modernist laws, only to sap it from its very center: yet one more avatar of the optical unconscious.

Greenberg's account of his meeting with Pollock is part of his contribution to the PBS/
BBC-IV television series "Art of the Western World (Part 9)," made in 1989. He gave
the same account to Steven Naifeh and Gregory White Smith for their book *Jackson
Pollock: An American Saga* (New York: Clarkson Potter, 1989), p. 398, although Lee
Krasner provided them with her own, different version (p. 857).

The monographs on Pollock I have consulted are the Naifeh and Smith book; *Jackson
Pollock: Catalogue Raisonné of Paintings, Drawings, and Other Works*, ed. Francis V.
O'Connor and Eugene Thaw (New Haven: Yale University Press, 1978); Francis V.
O'Connor, *Jackson Pollock* (New York: Museum of Modern Art, 1967); B. H. Friedman,
Jackson Pollock: Energy Made Visible (New York: McGraw-Hill, 1972); Ellen Landau,
Jackson Pollock (New York: Abrams, 1989); Elizabeth Frank, *Jackson Pollock* (New
York: Abbeville Press, 1983); Matthew L. Rohn, *Visual Dynamics in Jackson Pollock's
Abstractions* (Ann Arbor: UMI Research Press, 1987).

Greenberg on Pollock

Clement Greenberg's analyses of Pollock's work have been drawn both from his published criticism and from interviews with him as cited in Naifeh and Smith. In the first
connection his statement about painting and positivist space is found in his "On the
Role of Nature in Modernist Painting," 1949 (reprinted in Greenberg, *Art and Culture*
[Boston: Beacon Press, 1961]); "hallucinated literalness" is from "The Later Monet,"
1956 (*Art and Culture*, p. 42); "the counter-illusion of light alone" is from "Byzantine
Parallels," 1958 (*Art and Culture*, p. 169); "optically like a mirage" is from the revised
version of "The New Sculpture," 1958 (*Art and Culture*, p. 144); the flexibility of
Pollock's idiom was discussed in Greenberg's review in *The Nation* (April 13, 1946)
(reprinted in *Clement Greenberg: The Collected Essays and Criticism*, vol. 2, ed. John
O'Brian [Chicago: University of Chicago Press, 1989, p. 75]); the variety "beneath the
apparent monotony" is from his February 1949 review of Pollock's show at the Parsons
Gallery in *The Nation* (reprinted in *Clement Greenberg: Collected Essays*, vol. 2,
pp. 285–286); his first assessment of the black and white pictures was "Art Chronicle,"
Partisan Review, 1952 (reprinted in *Art and Culture*, p. 152); his second view is from
"'American Type' Painting," 1955 (*Art and Culture*, p. 228); for the violence, paranoia,
and Gothic-ness of Pollock's art, see "The Present Prospects of American Painting and
Sculpture," *Horizon*, October 1947, (reprinted in *Greenberg: Collected Essays*, p. 166).

A useful close reading of Greenberg's evolving interpretation of Pollock's work is François-Marc Gagnon, "The Work and Its Grip," *Jackson Pollock: Questions* (Montreal:
Musée d'art contemporain, 1979), pp. 15–42. Gagnon convincingly demonstrates that
Greenberg continued to analyze Pollock's work in terms of the relatively traditional
value of organic structure (variety within unity) and to be hostile to the idea of all-over
composition, calling it "monotonous," until relatively late (1948). He also argues that
when in 1948 Greenberg related Pollock's composition to synthetic cubism, this was a
slip and he really meant analytic cubism, as he stated in his criticism from 1955 on.
Yve-Alain Bois contests this latter point in his "The Limit of Almost," in *Ad Reinhardt*
(New York: Rizzoli, 1991), pp. 16–17.

Naifeh and Smith report on Greenberg's telling either them or other interviewers about: Pollock's having "lost his stuff" (pp. 698, 731, 895); his contemptuous characterizations of others (p. 632), which my own experience of Greenberg throughout the 1960s confirms; his discussion with Pollock about Pollock's nightmare (pp. 628–629); on Pollock "drawing like an angel" (p. 678); on Pollock's drip line made to avoid cutting into deep space (p. 535); on Pollock's view that *Blue Poles* wasn't a success (p. 698).

Pollock and Modernism

After Greenberg's, the later modernist readings of Pollock's work are those of Michael Fried, in his *Three American Painters* (Cambridge: Fogg Art Museum, 1965), pp. 10–19; William Rubin, "Jackson Pollock and the Modern Tradition," in four parts, *Art-forum,* vol. 5 (February, March, April, and May 1967); and E. A. Carmean, Jr., *The Subjects of the Artist* (Washington, D.C.: National Gallery of Art, 1978), pp. 124–153.

Paradoxically, T. J. Clark's account of Pollock's work in his searching essay "Jackson Pollock's Abstraction" (in Serge Guilbaut, ed., *Reconstructing Modernism* [Cambridge: MIT Press, 1990], pp. 172–243) both supports and challenges the modernist reading of the drip paintings. In the essay Pollock's act of challenging "likeness" is seen as putting two conflicting images or metaphors into play: (1) a figure of unity (the pictorial wholeness or "Oneness" of the modernist reading), of a weightless transcendence of the terrestrial and of gravity; and (2) a figure of dissonance: of exasperation, interruption, and violent refusal of closure. Although the first (modernist) one is characterized as being dominant, it is the conflict or challenge posed by the second that destabilizes the reading in a canceling out of metaphor itself, one that undoes the work's relation to nature (p. 201). What is implied is that Pollock is trying to get below metaphor into a new, hitherto unimagined relation to the world, one in which the mark would manifest a premetaphorical sense of presence (see the section "The Indexical Mark," below). This picture of a struggle between two poles has some overlap with my own reading of Pollock's work as an oscillation between two axes—the vertical and the horizontal—with the optical axis invaded and undermined by the indexical reading of the mark, or trace. Where it differs (and that on the most basic level) is that for Clark the two conflicting poles are both "images," which is to say, the indexical is always understood representationally and never formally. This means that, as a "picture" of something, it occupies the domain of the vertical just as the image of "unity" or "harmony" does. Thus Clark's reading of the drip pictures, while it brings in those aspects of the paintings that are difficult to reconcile with the optical reading (the repulsive "skins" of puddled paint, the trash piled on the pictures, etc.), proposes no alternative reading that could undo the "dominant" one from within.

Our interpretations also diverge in Clark's desire to assess Pollock's own intentions in making the drip paintings. To this end he quotes extensively from Pollock's various statements. My own feeling is that since Pollock's statements can be shown to have been the result of a kind of ventriloquy practiced by his various mentors, starting with Benton and Graham and his psychoanalysts and going up to Greenberg and Krasner (and even, beginning in 1950, Michel Tapié), they give us no reliable sense of his own intentions, but rather a script of self-justification to which he had recourse. I don't feel that Pollock's "intentions" are recoverable in any useful sense.

Pollock's Biography

Accounts of Pollock's life in Naifeh and Smith concern: his finances in 1950 (p. 624)—although Tony Smith's version of Pollock's income for one year in the early 1950s was the figure $2,600 scribbled on the back of an envelope, which represented an experience of financial failure that, Smith claimed, accounted for Pollock's return to drink (in Friedman, *Energy Made Visible*, p. 199), a report that itself tends to undermine Smith's credibility as a witness for Pollock; the filming with Namuth (pp. 647–649), although where Namuth himself states that the shooting ended in late October ("Photographier Pollock," *L'atelier de Jackson Pollock* [Paris: Macula, 1978]), Naifeh and Smith place the ending and the scene of the dinner party in late November just before Pollock's post-Thanksgiving opening; Pollock's despair over the meager sales and lack of reviews from the 1950 exhibition (p. 656); Tony Smith's urging Pollock to do something new (p. 665); Pollock's analysis of old master art using Benton's method (p. 564); Pollock's dream of triumphing over his brothers (p. 642); Pollock's nightmare about his brothers pushing him off a cliff (p. 628); Pollock's boasts about being the greatest (pp. 617, 693); Pollock's fears about being a fraud (pp. 721, 763); Pollock's early experiences in automatism (pp. 415–417, 424–427); Pollock's mimetic behavior (p. 621; and see Harold Rosenberg, "The Search for Jackson Pollock," *Art News*, 59 [February 1961], p. 36); Pollock in Siqueiros's studio (p. 288); Pollock worried "about the images coming back" (p. 669); Pollock's rage at Picasso for having missed nothing, dated to 1954 (p. 737; in her interview with B. H. Friedman, Lee Krasner dates the incident to New York before they moved to Long Island [*Energy Made Visible*, p. 183]).

Contemporaneous Criticism of Pollock's Work

Journalistic praise of Pollock's drip painting includes Robert Goodnough, "Jackson Pollock Paints a Picture," *Arts News*, 50 (May 1951).

Dismissal of it as "a child's contour map" is from *Time*, 53 (February 7, 1949); as "drooling," from the captions to "Jackson Pollock: Is He the Greatest Living Painter in the United States?" *Life*, 27 (August 8, 1949); "Hiroshima seen from above" is by Henry McBride, *New York Sun* (December 23, 1950). The comments about painting with a broom as well as Benton's and Craven's remarks about peeing are from Naifeh and Smith (pp. 630–631). The "Jack the Dripper" article was in *Time*, 67 (February 20, 1956).

The comparison between Pollock and van Gogh as "sacrificial" victims was first made by Allan Kaprow in "The Legacy of Jackson Pollock" (*Art News*, 51 [October 1958], pp. 24–25, 55–57); Kaprow made the connection again in "Should the Artist Become a Man of the World" (*Art News*, 63 [October 1964], p. 35): "The modern artist is the archetypal victim who is 'suicided by society' (Artaud). . . . Cultured reactionaries . . . remind you that Rembrandt, van Gogh and Pollock died on the Cross (while you've 'sold out')."

The Drip Pictures and the Unconscious

John Graham, "Primitive Art and Picasso," *Magazine of Art*, 30 (April 1937), p. 260.

In his "Art for *Modern Man:* New York School Painting and American Culture in the 1940s" (Ph.D. thesis, Harvard University, 1988), Michael Leja argues: "Rather than being a conglomeration of unconscious material, Pollock's is a *representation* of that unconscious" (p. 176). This representation, he says, was itself determined by two discursive systems operating in American in the 1930s and '40s, both of which involved popularizations of depth psychology: a Jungian discourse on the one hand and an ego-psychological discourse on the other. Leja sees the turbulent sea of imagery of the pre-drip paintings as an employment of both Jungian motifs (the snake, the mandala, etc.) and an attempt to image forth the Jungian idea of unconscious struggle. He sees the drip pictures as a response to the ego-psychological model adopted from Freud, in which the unconscious is pictured as an electrodynamic building up of energies that are then released in bursts of activity. This latter model was employed in what Leja calls the "Modern Man" discourse to develop ideas about the importance of "integrated experience," and of the ego's growth toward stability and unity. That Pollock, under the impress of this discursive context, was trying to image forth such integration or unity accounts, Leja argues, for the visual integration of the drip paintings and Pollock's threefold use of the name "One" to mark such unity. Several aspects of such an account need noting: (1) whether it addresses the works of the early '40s or the period 1947–1950, this account is resolutely representational, based on the notion that the unconscious will be depicted according to received pictorial schemata (Leja acknowledges Gombrich for this conception, p. 186), which will express an idea through "pictures" of it; (2) it depends on a conception of the relation of the artist to the work that is based on traditional art-historical notions of "intention"; and (3) it leaves the modernist sublimatory reading of Pollock's drip pictures wholly intact.

The Jungian theories of the unconscious applied to Pollock's early work as a thematics of his art, which took up much space in the Pollock literature of the 1970s, have been analyzed by William Rubin in "Pollock as Jungian Illustrator: The Limits of Psychological Criticism" (*Art in America,* 67 [November 1979], pp. 104–123, and [December 1979], pp. 72–91).

Verticality, Erectness, Sublimation

Freud's discussions of man's assumption of an erect posture as the first step toward culture and as making possible a sublimated visuality are from "Civilization and Its Discontents" (1930), *Standard Edition,* vol. 21, pp. 99–100; and "Three Essays on the Theory of Sexuality" (1905), *Standard Edition,* vol. 7, pp. 156–157.

324

six

The gestalt psychological and phenomenological interpretation of the upright posture is from Erwin Straus, "Born to See, Bound to Behold: Reflections on the Function of Upright Posture in the Aesthetic Attitude" (1963), in *The Philosophy of the Body,* ed. Stuart Spicker (New York: Quadrangle, 1970), pp. 334–359; this is an elaboration of his earlier "The Upright Posture" (1948), in *Essays in Phenomenology,* ed. Maurice Natanson (The Hague: Martinus Nijhoff, 1966), pp. 116–192 (as cited by Michael Fried, "The Beholder in Courbet: His Early Self-Portraits and Their Place in His Art," *Glyph,* no. 4 [1978], p. 125).

Abduction

Analyses of Peirce's theories of abduction and their relation to the methods of Sherlock Holmes, Freud, and Morelli are collected in *The Sign of Three,* ed. Umberto Eco and Thomas A. Sebeok (Bloomington: Indiana University Press, 1983). The best-known of these essays is Carlo Ginzburg's "Morelli, Freud, and Sherlock Holmes: Clues and Scientific Method" (pp. 81–118).

The Black and White Pictures

Lee Krasner's assessment of the black and white paintings is published as "An Interview with Lee Krasner Pollock," by B. H. Friedman, in *Jackson Pollock: Black and White* (New York: Marlborough-Gerson Gallery, March 1969). Michael Fried's discussion of Pollock's refusal to repeat is in his *Three American Painters* (p. 18).

Opposing contentions that Pollock refused to repeat, E. A. Carmean mounts an art-historical explanation of Pollock's development, beginning in the summer of 1950 and continuing into the black and white paintings, based on repetition conceived on the pattern of traditional academic art's reliance on the precedents offered by earlier sources. Carmean tries to cast Pollock in this mold, arguing that in *Lavender Mist* Pollock began to reuse configurations offered by his own earlier work, in this case *Number 1, 1948.* What necessitated this, Carmean argues, is the fact that by 1949 and 1950 Pollock's paintings were so large and so heavy that the process of lifting them off the floor in order to view them hanging on a wall (Pollock's famous "get acquainted" interludes) was becoming more and more difficult (according to Lee Krasner [in an interview with Carmean, *The Subjects of the Artist,* p. 135]; the photographic evidence supplied by Namuth makes it likely that Pollock finished the big 1950s paintings without lifting them). Therefore, Carmean reasons, Pollock must have had a pregiven configuration from which to work, supplied to him from sources within his earlier drip pictures. Having adopted this mode of working, Pollock then went on in the black and white pictures to use his earlier, figurative drawings and paintings as such "sources" (see *The Subjects of the Artist,* pp. 129ff.). Subsequently Carmean enlarged his analysis of the black and white pictures to find sources in them from the history of religious painting and casting them as cartoons for the project for a private church on which Tony Smith was then working (see E. A. Carmean, "The Church Project: Pollock's Passion Themes," *Art in America,* 70 [Summer 1982], pp. 110–122). My own reply to this is "Contra Carmean: The Abstract Pollock," *Art in America,* 70 (Summer 1982), pp. 123–131, which I was led to write both because I thought that Carmean had a misguided notion of Pollock's process and because Lee Krasner discussed with me her own deep objections to the essay (which had originally appeared in the catalogue *Jackson Pollock* [Paris: Centre Georges Pompidou, 1982]) as well as her desire that it be publicly repudiated.

The theory that the black and white pictures emerged when Pollock stopped relegating the memory images of the drip pictures to a Greenberg-imposed abstraction, now letting them emerge from behind the veil, is from Naifeh and Smith, pp. 667–668. Their notion of the drip technique as a form of "unwinding images in three-dimensional space" above the canvases is on pp. 539–540, or, again, "the great tangled knowledge of his past . . . unwinding onto canvas," p. 567; their discussion of Pollock's supposed restlessness with the lack of figuration in the drip technique by 1949 is on pp. 616–617 and 665.

The Indexical Mark

The discussion of the arche-trace is from Jacques Derrida, *Of Grammatology,* trans. Gayatri Chakravorty Spivak (Baltimore: Johns Hopkins Press, 1974), pp. 62 and 132.

T. J. Clark's interpretation of the indexical trace within Pollock's work (the palm prints in *Number 1, 1948,* for example) understands the mark as a manifestation of the artist's own existential presence that can *also* be "seen as" a representation of "a hand, a hand out there, someone else's," through what Clark calls the metaphorical construal of the mark. He imagines Pollock as wanting to bring painting back to its own origins *before* metaphor in which the mark unequivocally instituted this kind of presence, thereby finding "some other means of signifying experience [that] might put itself in a different *sort* of relation to the world" (Clark, "Jackson Pollock's Abstraction," p. 197). In the discussion after his presentation Clark speaks of the Heideggerian tone inherent in his conception of Pollock's invocation of trace as presence (p. 240).

Rosenberg's action painting account of the picture-event as a mirror, in the realm, therefore, of presence, is "The American Action Painters," *Art News* Vol. 51 (December 1952), reprinted in *The Tradition of the New* (New York: Horizon Press, 1959), pp. 28–29.

Figures Below the Web

William Rubin stresses the figurative "underpicture" lying below both *Shimmering Substance* and *Eyes in the Heat* (both 1946) but does not speak of the continuing visibility of such underpictures in the beginning drip works ("Jackson Pollock and the Modern Tradition," part I [February 1967], p. 18). That there are actually figures below the web in *Number 1, 1948* is asserted by Serge Guilbaut, *How New York Stole the Idea of Modern Art,* trans. Arthur Goldhammer (Chicago: University of Chicago Press, 1983), pp. 197, 246. It is more subtly argued by Charles Stuckey in "Another Side of Jackson Pollock," *Art in America* (November 1977), pp. 81–91; and by Bernice Rose, *Jackson Pollock: Drawing into Painting* (New York: Museum of Modern Art, 1980), p. 9.

Thomas Benton's structural analysis of old master paintings using geometrical schemata was published as "Mechanics of Form Organization in Painting," *The Arts,* 10 (November and December 1926) and 11 (January, February, March 1927); the schemas most applicable to Pollock are in part I (November 1926), p. 288.

Warhol

Biographical information about Warhol comes from the following sources: Warhol's confession about the Queen of England (Victor Bockris, *The Life and Death of Andy Warhol* [New York: Bantam Books, 1989], p. 102); his dress in imitation of Kowalski (Bockris, p. 52); his conversation with Larry Rivers about Pollock (Andy Warhol and Pat Hackett, *POPism: The Warhol Sixties* [New York: Harcourt Brace Jovanovich, 1980], pp. 13–15); Kligman's report on their friendship in 1962 (Bockris, p. 118); thinking about making *Love Affair* into a film for Jack Nicholson (Bockris, p. 301); "I always wanted Tab Hunter to play me in the story of my life" (Bockris, p. 135); dismissing Siqueiros and wishing he had a Pollock (Bob Colacello, *Holy Terror* [New York: Harper Collins, 1990], p. 118); Schnabel's boast (Colacello, p. 475); Colacello on the *Oxidation Paintings* and Warhol's art-historical references (Colacello, p. 339).

A somewhat different account of the *Dance Diagram*'s relation to Pollock is given by Benjamin Buchloh in "Andy Warhol's One-Dimensional Art: 1956–1966" (*Andy Warhol: A Retrospective* [New York: Museum of Modern Art, 1989], pp. 45–46); information about the "piss paintings" from 1961 and the canvases outside his house comes from an interview with Warhol in *The Unmuzzled Ox,* 4, no. 2 (1976), p. 44, with a reproduction of one of the paintings (p. 45); on the *Oxidation Paintings* in relation to a gay context, see Colacello, p. 339; on their relation to a gay thematics of urination, see Jonathan Weinberg, "Urination and Its Discontents," an unpublished lecture, 1990.

Peeing on the Fire and the "Oceanic"

Freud introduces the "oceanic feeling" in "Civilization and Its Discontents" (*Standard Edition,* vol. 21, pp. 65, 72) and sets forth his theory about peeing on the fire (ibid., p. 90). Naifeh and Smith have recourse to an explanation by urination and repressed homosexuality as one aspect of their own account of the onset of the drip pictures (pp. 541–542); also see Jonathan Weinberg, "Urination and Its Discontents."

Leo Bersani's chapter "Theory and Violence" in *The Freudian Body* (New York: Columbia University Press, 1986) is a stunning analysis of the paradoxical logic of *Civilization and Its Discontents* in which aggressiveness is both set in opposition to the oceanic feeling and made synonymous with it in an erotics of the indistinction between the self and the world.

In discussions with Yve-Alain Bois on the material of this chapter he completed my own thoughts about Pollock's gesture by projecting the image of Morris Louis's work as not only having restored the vertical but simultaneously having (re)constituted the image of the fire.

Triangular Desire, Mimetic Rivalry

René Girard, *Deceit, Desire and the Novel,* trans. Yvonne Freccero (Baltimore: Johns Hopkins University Press, 1965): on "latent homosexuality," p. 47; on the disappearance of sexual pleasure in advanced stages of ontological sickness, pp. 85, 87; on the paralysis brought on by advanced stages, p. 87; on the rivalry over the body of the beloved, p. 105; on the increase of rivalry as external hierarchies diminish, p. 223.

Jacques Lacan, "Aggressivity in Psychoanalysis," *Ecrits,* trans. Alan Sheridan (New York: Norton, 1977), p. 22. Denis Hollier's important analysis of mimetic rivalry is "On Equivocation," *October,* no. 55 (Winter 1990), p. 9.

The sense of proximity of the European artists who had arrived in New York, as expressed by the Americans, is reported by Naifeh and Smith, pp. 420–421. The unfolding of Greenberg's conception of American painting's rivalry with Europe can be tracked in his post-1945 criticism. It is the subject, in large part, of Serge Guilbaut's *How New York Stole the Idea of Modern Art,* as it is of a whole literature on Greenberg's relation to Cold War diplomacy. William Barnett describes it as well in his *The Truants* (New York: Doubleday, 1982), pp. 148–152.

Jonathan Weinberg, in "Pollock and Picasso: The Rivalry and the 'Escape,'" *Arts,* 61 (Summer 1987), pp. 42–48, analyzes Pollock's work in terms of a rivalry with Picasso, although this analysis thematizes the rivalry in terms of an attempt to achieve a pictorial origin, emblematized by the fact that Pollock names three of his drip pictures "One," or "Number One."

Verticality/Horizontality

Leo Steinberg, in "Other Criteria" (*Other Criteria* [New York: Oxford University Press, 1972]), makes the important distinction between the horizontal dimension of culture and the vertical one of nature. For the purposes of art, he transcodes the first into what he terms "the flatbed picture plane" and the second into "the diaphane." Walter Benjamin has also contributed two texts to the phenomenology of the sign according to its vertical or horizontal orientation. See Benjamin, "Peinture et graphisme" and "De la peinture ou le signe et la marque," *La Part de l'Oeil,* no. 6 (1990), pp. 13–15, where they are presented by Yve-Alain Bois. Bois has made important use of the latter text in his own analyses (Bois, *Painting as Model* [Cambridge: MIT Press, 1990], pp. 178ff.). Michael Fried, in his "Realism, Writing, and Disfiguration in Thomas Eakins's *Gross Clinic*" (*Representations,* no. 9 [Winter 1985]), develops his own phenomenology of the distinction between what he calls the plane of writing (which he equates to the plane of perspective projection) and the plane of the visual (which he equates to the "pictorial"). The first, he asserts, is the dimension of piecemeal, affective identification with elements of a given painting; the second is the dimension of a more distanced, formal experience. It is in the horizontal, identificatory plane that he elaborates a thematics of violence and Oedipality in Eakins's *Gross Clinic.* If his analysis and mine are in agreement about the dimension along which aggression is projected, this is the only place in which such agreement might be mapped.

Michel Foucault proposes the idea of a language game that connects—at the deepest epistemic level—image and text (legend) together on the same plane (what he calls a *lieu commun*), such that in the space of the "common frontier" that binds the two systems together—"these few millimeters of white, the calm sand of the page"—are indelibly "established all the relations of designation, nomination, description, classification": see *This Is Not a Pipe*, trans. James Harkness (New York: Quantum, 1982), p. 28.

The extremely literary titles of the 1947 drip pictures were suggested to Pollock by the translator Ralph Mannheim in a naming session in preparation for their exhibition. But the plunging trajectory encoded in the names suggests that the experience of looking downward was apparent to Mannheim when he initially saw the works.

Horizontality has entered the Pollock literature primarily as a thematic issue (the expanses of the American West or the openness of the Atlantic Ocean) or as an historical source, particularly with regard to Pollock's interest in Navaho sand painting. See Hubert Damisch, "Indians!!!," in *Jackson Pollock* (Paris: Centre Pompidou, 1982). The extremely representational nature of sand painting imagery gives it the same character of verticality within the phenomenological field that Roman mosaic images have.

Process

Robert Morris, "Anti-Form," *Artforum*, 6 (April 1968), p. 34; and Morris, "Some Notes on the Phenomenology of Making," *Artforum*, 8 (April 1970), p. 63.

Namuth's Pollock Film

Namuth's contention that the idea to use glass came to him in a dream was reported by B. H. Friedman (*Energy Made Visible*, p. 163).

A still from Haesaerts's *Visite à Picasso* was reproduced in *Art d'Aujourd'hui* (October 1951), p. 27. A lavish spread of Gjon Mili's photographs of the *Space Drawings* was published in *Life*, 28 (January 30, 1950), pp. 10–12; they were also reproduced in *Art Digest*, 24 (February 1950), p. 15.

Gestalt Readings of Pollock and Their Antithesis

The Gestalt psychological dismissal of Pollock is Rudolf Arnheim, "Accident and the Necessity of Art," *Journal of Aesthetics and Art Criticism*, 16 (September 1957), pp. 18–31. The important attack on "form-control" in the name of "gestalt-free" depth vision is Anton Ehrenzweig, "Unconscious Form-Creation in Art," *British Journal of Medical Psychology*, no. 21 (1948), pp. 185–214, and no. 22 (1949), pp. 88–109. Robert Hobbes connects Ehrenzweig's later notions of "scanning vision" and "scotopia" to abstract expressionism in "Early Abstract Expressionism: A Concern with the Unknown Within," *Abstract-Expressionism: Formative Years* (New York: Whitney Museum of American Art, 1978), pp. 22–25. A modernist reading of Pollock that employs the very terms of Gestalt psychology by projecting patterns onto the drip pictures is in Matthew Rohn, *Visual Dynamics in Jackson Pollock's Abstractions* (Ann Arbor: UMI Research Press, 1987). That the labyrinth could possibly be classed as a gestalt (p. 46) is a peculiar view indeed.

Eva Hesse

In addition to Lucy Lippard's monograph *Eva Hesse* (New York: New York University Press, 1976), important documentation on Hesse has been published in "Order and Chaos: From the Diaries of Eva Hesse," selected by Ellen H. Johnson, *Art in America*,

71 (Summer 1983); and Cindy Nemser, "An Interview with Eva Hesse," *Artforum*, 8 (May 1970). My first written appraisal of Hesse's work was as a catalogue introduction to *Eva Hesse: Sculpture* (London: Whitechapel Art Gallery, 1979), in which I analyze her work in relation to painting, particularly the problematic connected to anamorphosis. For a range of contemporary critical responses to Hesse, see *Eva Hesse: A Retrospective* (New Haven: Yale University Art Gallery, 1992).

Lippard's early reaction to Hesse as "'Tom's wife' rather than a serious artist" is in her monograph, p. 23; her account of Hesse's raiding the thesaurus for titles, pp. 65, 204; of her writing down lists of authors, p. 12. Lippard publishes Hesse's letter to Sol LeWitt describing one of the Kettwig reliefs as "breast and penis" (p. 34); a letter to her friend Rosie Goldman describing the works as "machines" (p. 38); and the *Life* magazine quotation about Jackson Pollock and chaos disguised as non-chaos (p. 172).

Hesse's discussion of *Hang Up* is in the interview with Nemser (Lippard, p. 56), as is the statement about repetition heightening absurdity (Lippard, p. 5).

Hilton Kramer's review of "Eccentric Abstraction" appeared in the *New York Times* (September 25, 1966); it is quoted in Lippard (pp. 83, 188–189) and her defense, from *Sculpture of the Sixties* (Los Angeles County Museum, 1967) follows (p. 189); her discussion of the pictorial aspects and Hesse as a sculptor "drawing in space" closes the book (pp. 190–192).

See Gilles Deleuze and Félix Guattari, *Anti-Oedipus,* trans. Robert Hurley, Mark Seem, and Helen R. Lane (Minneapolis: University of Minnesota Press, 1983), pp. 8, 12, 16.

Adcock, Craig. *Marcel Duchamp's Notes from the "Large Glass": An n-Dimensional Analysis.* Ann Arbor: UMI Research Press, 1981.

Adorno, Theodor. "Looking Back at Surrealism." In *The Idea of the Modern in Literature and the Arts,* ed. Irving Howe, pp. 220–224. New York: Horizon, 1967.

Aragon, Louis. "Max Ernst, peintre des illusions" (1923). In *Les collages,* pp. 27–33. Paris: Hermann, 1965.

Arnheim, Rudolf. "Accident and the Necessity of Art." *Journal of Aesthetics and Art Criticism,* 16 (September 1957), pp. 18–31.

Bachelard, Gaston. *La psychanalyse du feu.* Paris: Gallimard, 1949.

Barbut, Marc. "On the Meaning of the Word 'Structure' in Mathematics." In *Introduction to Strucutralism,* ed. Michael Lane, pp. 367–388. New York: Basic Books, 1970.

Barthes, Roland. *Mythologies* (1957). Trans. Annette Lavers. New York: Hill and Wang, 1972.

Barthes, Roland. "The Metaphor of the Eye" (1963). In *Critical Essays,* trans. Richard Howard, pp. 239–248. Evanston: Northwestern University Press, 1972.

Barthes, Roland. "The Outcomes of the Text" (1973). In *The Rustle of Language,* trans. Richard Howard, pp. 238–249. New York: Hill and Wang, 1986.

Bataille, Georges. *Visions of Excess: Selected Writings, 1927–1939.* Ed. and trans. Allan Stoekl. Minneapolis: University of Minnesota Press, 1985.

Benjamin, Walter. *Illuminations.* Trans. Harry Zohn. New York: Shocken Books, 1969.

Benjamin, Walter. *Reflections.* Trans. Edmund Jephcott. New York: Harcourt Brace Jovanovich, 1978.

Benjamin, Walter. "A Small History of Photography" (1931). In *One Way Street,* trans. Edmund Jephcott and Kingsley Shorter, pp. 240–257. London: New Left Books, 1979.

Benjamin, Walter. "Peinture et graphisme" and "De la peinture ou le signe et la marque." *La Part de l'Oeil,* no. 6 (1990), pp. 13–15.

Benton, Thomas Hart. "Mechanics of Form Organization in Painting." *The Arts* (November and December 1926; January, February, March 1927), pp. 285–289, 340–342, 43–44, 95–96.

Bernadac, Marie-Laure. "Picasso, 1953–1973: La peinture comme modèle." In *Le dernier Picasso.* Paris: Musée National d'Art Moderne, 1988.

Bersani, Leo. *The Freudian Body.* New York: Columbia University Press, 1986.

Bersani, Leo. *The Culture of Redemption.* Cambridge: Harvard University Press, 1990.

Bockris, Victor. *The Life and Death of Andy Warhol.* New York: Bantam Books, 1989.

Bois, Yve-Alain. *Painting as Model.* Cambridge: MIT Press, 1990.

Breton, André. *Nadja.* Paris: Editions Gallimard, 1929.

Breton, André. *L'amour fou.* Paris: Editions Gallimard, 1937.

Breton, André. *Surrealism and Painting.* New York: Harper & Row, 1972.

Bryson, Norman. *Vision and Painting.* New Haven: Yale University Press, 1983.

Buchloh, Benjamin H. D. "Andy Warhol's One-Dimensional Art: 1956–1966." In *Andy Warhol: A Retrospective.* New York: Museum of Modern Art, 1989.

Buchloh, Benjamin H. D. "The Andy Warhol Line." In *The Work of Andy Warhol,* ed. Gary Garrels, pp. 52–69. Seattle: Bay Press and the Dia Foundation, 1989.

Buck-Morss, Susan. "The Flaneur, the Sandwichman and the Whore." *New German Critique,* no. 39 (Fall 1986), pp. 99–141.

Buck-Morss, Susan. *The Dialectics of Seeing: Walter Benjamin and the Arcades Project.* Cambridge: MIT Press, 1989.

Cabanne, Pierre. *Dialogues with Marcel Duchamp.* Trans. Ron Padgett. New York: Viking Press, 1971.

Caillois, Roger. "La mante réligieuse." *Minotaure,* no. 5 (May 1934), pp. 23–26.

Caillois, Roger. "Mimicry and Legendary Psychasthenia." Trans. John Shepley. *October,* no. 31 (Winter 1984), pp. 17–32.

Carmean, E. A., Jr. *The Subjects of the Artist,* pp. 124–153. Washington, D.C.: National Gallery of Art, 1978.

Clair, Jean. "Marcel Duchamp et la tradition des perspecteurs." In *Marcel Duchamp: Abécédaire,* pp. 124–159. Paris: Musée National d'Art Moderne, 1977.

Clair, Jean. *Duchamp et la photographie.* Paris: Chêne, 1977.

Clark, T. J. "Jackson Pollock's Abstraction." In *Reconstructing Modernism,* ed. Serge Guilbaut, pp. 172–243. Cambridge: MIT Press, 1990.

Clément, Catherine. *The Lives and Legends of Jacques Lacan.* Trans. Arthur Goldhammer. New York: Columbia Univerity Press, 1983.

Colacello, Bob. *Holy Terror.* New York: Harper Collins, 1990.

Cooper, Douglas. *Pablo Picasso: Les Déjeuners.* New York: Harry N. Abrams, 1963.

Copjec, Joan. "Favit et Dissipati Sunt." *October,* no. 18 (Fall 1981), pp. 21–40.

Crary, Jonathan. *Techniques of the Observer: On Vision and Modernity in the Nineteenth Century.* Cambridge: MIT Press, 1990.

Crow, Thomas. "Modernism and Mass Culture in the Visual Arts." In *Modernism and Modernity,* ed. Benjamin H. D. Buchloh, pp. 215–264. Halifax: Press of the Nova Scotia College of Art and Design, 1983.

Curtis, William J. R. *Le Corbusier: Ideas and Forms.* Oxford: Phaidon, 1986.

Dalí, Salvador. "Objets psycho-atmosphériques-anamorphiques." *Le Surréalisme au service de la révolution,* no. 5 (May 1933), pp. 45–48.

Damisch, Hubert. "The Duchamp Defense." *October,* no. 10 (Fall 1979), pp. 5–28.

Damisch, Hubert. *Fenêtre jaune cadmium: ou les dessous de la peinture.* Paris: Seuil, 1984.

Damisch, Hubert. *Le jugement de Paris.* Paris: Flammarion, 1992.

de Duve, Thierry. *Nominalisme Pictural.* Paris: Editions de Minuit, 1984.

Delaunay, Robert. *The New Art of Color.* Ed. Arthur Cohen. New York: Viking Press, 1978.

Deleuze, Gilles, and Félix Guattari. *Anti-Oedipus* (1972). Trans. Robert Hurley, Mark Seem, and Helen R. Lane. Minneapolis: University of Minnesota Press, 1983.

Derrida, Jacques. *Speech and Phenomena* (1967). Trans. David B. Allison. Evanston: Northwestern University Press, 1973.

Derrida, Jacques. *Of Grammatology* (1967). Trans. Gayatri Chakravorty Spivak. Baltimore: Johns Hopkins University Press, 1974.

Derrida, Jacques. "Freud and the Scene of Writing." *Writing and Difference,* trans. Alan Bass, pp. 196–231. Chicago: University of Chicago Press, 1978.

Didi-Huberman, Georges. *Ce que nous voyons, ce qui nous regard.* Paris: Minuit, 1992.

Duchamp, Marcel. *Salt Seller: The Writings of Marcel Duchamp (Marchand du Sel).* Ed. Michel Sanouillet and Elmer Peterson. New York: Oxford University Press, 1973.

Eco, Umberto, and Thomas A. Sebeok, eds. *The Sign of Three.* Bloomington: Indiana University Press, 1983.

Ehrenzweig, Anton. "Unconscious Form-Creation in Art." *British Journal of Medical Psychology,* no. 21 (1948), pp. 185–214, and no. 22 (1949), pp. 88–109.

Ernst, Max. *Beyond Painting.* New York: Wittenborn, Schultz, 1948.

Felman, Shoshana. *Jacques Lacan and the Adventure of Insight.* Cambridge: Harvard University Press, 1987.

Foster, Hal. "Armor Fou." *October,* no. 56 (Spring 1991), pp. 65–98.

Foster, Hal. "Convulsive Identity." *October,* no. 57 (Summer 1991), pp. 19–54.

Foucault, Michel. *This Is Not a Pipe.* Trans. James Harkness. New York: Quantum, 1982.

Freud, Sigmund. "Screen Memories" (1899). In *The Standard Edition of the Complete Psychological Works of Sigmund Freud,* ed. James Strachey. 24 vols. London: Hogarth Press and the Institute for Psycho-Analysis, 1953–1973. Vol. 3, pp. 301–322.

Freud, Sigmund. *The Interpretation of Dreams* (1900). Trans. James Strachey. New York: Avon Books, 1965.

Freud, Sigmund. "Three Essays on the Theory of Sexuality" (1905). In *Standard Edition,* vol. 7, pp. 156–157.

Freud, Sigmund. "Delusion and Dream" (1906). In *Standard Edition,* vol. 9, pp. 3–93.

Freud, Sigmund. "Leonardo da Vinci and a Memory of His Childhood" (1910). In *Standard Edition,* vol. 11, pp. 59–137.

Freud, Sigmund. "Psychogenic Visual Disturbance According to Psychoanalytical Conceptions" (1910). In *Standard Edition,* vol. 11, pp. 211–218.

Freud, Sigmund. "From the History of an Infantile Neurosis" (1918). In *Standard Edition,* vol. 17, pp. 3–122; Collier Books Edition: *Three Case Histories.*

Freud, Sigmund. "A Child Is Being Beaten" (1919). In *Standard Edition,* vol. 17, pp. 177–204.

Freud, Sigmund. "The Uncanny" (1919). In *Standard Edition,* vol. 17, pp. 234–235.

Freud, Sigmund. "Beyond the Pleasure Principle" (1920). In *Standard Edition,* vol. 18, pp. 7–64.

Freud, Sigmund. "A Note upon the 'Mystic Writing-Pad'" (1924). In *Standard Edition,* vol. 19, pp. 227–234.

Freud, Sigmund. "Fetishism" (1927). In *Standard Edition,* vol. 21, pp. 152–153.

Freud, Sigmund. "Civilization and Its Discontents" (1930). In *Standard Edition,* vol. 21, pp. 99–100.

Fried, Michael. *Three American Painters.* Cambridge: The Fogg Art Museum, 1965.

Fried, Michael. "Art and Objecthood." Published in 1967 in *Artforum.* Reprinted in *Minimal Art,* ed. Gregory Battock, pp. 116–147. New York: Dutton, 1968.

Fried, Michael. "The Beholder in Courbet: His Early Self-Portraits and Their Place in His Art." *Glyph,* no. 4 (1978), pp. 85–130.

Fried, Michael. "Realism, Writing, and Disfiguration in Thomas Eakins's *Gross Clinic.*" *Representations,* no. 9 (Winter 1985), pp. 33–104.

Friedman, B. H. *Jackson Pollock: Energy Made Visible.* New York: McGraw-Hill, 1972.

Fry, Roger. *Vision and Design.* New York: Brentano's, n.d.

Gagnon, François-Marc. "The Work and Its Grip." In *Jackson Pollock: Questions,* pp. 15–42. Montreal: Musée d'art contemporain, 1979.

Gallop, Jane. *Reading Lacan.* Ithaca: Cornell University Press, 1985.

Garnett, Angelica. *Deceived with Kindness.* London: Chatto & Windus, 1984.

Garnett, David. *The Flowers of the Forest.* London: Chatto & Windus, 1955.

Gateau, Jean-Charles. *Paul Eluard et la peinture surréaliste.* Paris: Droz, 1982.

Gee, Malcolm. "Max Ernst, God, and the Revolution by Night." *Arts,* 55 (March 1981), pp. 85–92.

Girard, René. *Deceit, Desire and the Novel.* Trans. Yvonne Freccero. Baltimore: Johns Hopkins University Press, 1965.

Graham, John. "Primitive Art and Picasso." *Magazine of Art,* 30 (April 1937), pp. 236–239, 260.

Greenberg, Clement. *Art and Culture.* Boston: Beacon Press, 1961.

Greenberg, Clement. "Modernist Painting" (1965). Reprinted in *The New Art,* ed. Gregory Battcock, pp. 100–110. New York: Dutton, 1966.

Greenberg, Clement. *Clement Greenberg: The Collected Essays and Criticism.* Vol. 2. Ed. John O'Brian. Chicago: University of Chicago Press, 1986.

Gregory, Richard. *Eye and Brain.* New York: World University Library, 1978.

Greimas, A. J. "The Interaction of Semiotic Constraints." In *On Meaning,* pp. 48–62. Minneapolis: University of Minnesota Press, 1987.

Guilbaut, Serge. *How New York Stole the Idea of Modern Art.* Trans. Arthur Goldhammer. Chicago: University of Chicago Press, 1983.

Hansen, Miriam. "Benjamin, Cinema and Experience." *New German Critique,* no. 40 (Winter 1987), pp. 179–224.

Helmholtz, Hermann von. *Helmholtz on Perception.* Ed. Richard Warren and Roslyn Warren. New York: John Wiley & Sons, 1968.

Hinton, Geoffrey. "Max Ernst: 'Les Hommes n'en Sauront Rien.'" *Burlington Magazine,* 117 (May 1975), pp. 292–299.

Hobbes, Robert. "Early Abstract Expressionism: A Concern with the Unknown Within." In *Abstract-Expressionism: Formative Years,* pp. 8–26. New York: Whitney Museum of American Art, 1978.

Hollier, Denis. *Against Architecture* (1974). Trans. Betsy Wing. Cambridge: MIT Press, 1990.

Hollier, Denis. "Mimesis and Castration, 1937." *October,* no. 31 (Winter 1984), pp. 3–15.

Hollier, Denis. "On Equivocation." *October,* no. 55 (Winter 1990), pp. 3–21.

Hollier, Denis. "The Use Value of the Impossible." *October,* no. 60 (Spring 1992).

Huot, Hervé. *Du sujet à l'image: Une histoire de l'oeil chez Freud.* Paris: Editions Univérsitaires, 1987.

Irigaray, Luce. *This Sex which Is Not One.* Trans. Catherine Porter. Ithaca: Cornell University Press, 1985.

Jameson, Fredric. "Imaginary and Symbolic in Lacan: Marxism, Psychoanalytic Criticism, and the Problem of the Subject." *Yale French Studies,* nos. 55/56 (1977), pp. 338–395.

Jameson, Fredric. *The Political Unconscious: Narrative as a Socially Symbolic Act.* Ithaca: Cornell University Press, 1981.

Jay, Martin. "In the Empire of the Gaze: Foucault and the Denigration of Vision in Twentieth-Century French Thought." In *Foucault: A Critical Reader,* ed. David Couzens Hoy, pp. 175–204. London: Basil Blackwell, 1986.

Jay, Martin. "Scopic Regimes of Modernity." In *Vision and Visuality,* ed. Hal Foster, pp. 3–28. Seattle: Bay Press and Dia Art Foundation, 1988.

Jay Martin. *Downcast Eyes.* Forthcoming from University of California Press.

Kaprow, Allan. "The Legacy of Jackson Pollock." *Art News,* 57 (October 1958), pp. 24–25, 55–57.

Kaprow, Allan. "Should the Artist Become a Man of the World." *Art News,* 63 (October 1964).

Klein, Melanie. "Psychogenesis of Manic Depressive States" (1935) and "Notes on Some Schizoid Mechanisms" (1946). In *Selected Melanie Klein,* ed. Juliet Mitchell. New York: The Free Press, 1986.

Köhler, Wolfgang. *Gestalt Psychology.* New York: New American Library, 1947.

Krauss, Rosalind. "Corpus Delicti." In *L'Amour Fou: Photography and Surrealism.* New York: Abbeville Press, 1986.

Krauss, Rosalind. *The Originality of the Avant-Garde and Other Modernist Myths.* Cambridge: MIT Press, 1986.

Kristeva, Julia. *Revolution in Poetic Language* (1974). Trans. Margaret Waller. New York: Columbia University Press, 1984.

Kristeva, Julia. *The Powers of Horror* (1980). Trans. Leon Roudiez. New York: Columbia University Press, 1982.

Lacan, Jacques. *Ecrits: A Selection.* Trans. Alan Sheridan. New York: Norton, 1977.

Lacan, Jacques. *The Four Fundamental Concepts of Psycho-Analysis.* Trans. Alan Sheridan. New York: Norton, 1977.

Landau, Ellen. *Jackson Pollock.* New York: Abrams, 1989.

LaPlanche, Jean. *Life and Death in Psychoanalysis.* Trans. Jeffrey Mehlman. Baltimore: Johns Hopkins University Press, 1976.

LaPlanche, Jean, and J.-B. Pontalis. "Fantasy and the Origins of Sexuality." *The International Journal of Psycho-Analysis,* 49 (1968). Reprinted in *Formations of Fantasy,* ed. Victor Burgin, James Donald, and Cora Kaplan, pp. 5–28. London: Methuen, 1986.

Legge, Elisabeth. *Max Ernst: The Psychoanalytic Sources.* Ann Arbor: UMI Research Press, 1989.

Leja, Michael, "Art for *Modern Man:* New York School Painting and American Culture in the 1940s." Ph.D. thesis, Harvard University, 1988.

Leroi-Gourhan, André. "The Religion of the Caves: Magic or Metaphysics?" and "The Hands at Gargas: Toward a General Study." *October,* no. 37 (Summer 1986), pp. 6–17, 18–34.

Lévi-Strauss, Claude. "The Structural Analysis of Myth." In *Structural Anthropology.* New York: Basic Books, 1963.

Lewin, Bertram D. "Sleep, the Mouth, and the Dream Screen." *Psychoanalytic Quarterly,* 15 (1946), pp. 419–434.

Lewin, Bertram D. "Sleep, Narcissistic Neurosis, and the Analytic Situation." *Psychoanalytic Quarterly,* 23 (1954), pp. 487–510.

Lippard, Lucy. *Eva Hesse.* New York: New York University Press, 1976.

Lyotard, Jean-François. *Discours, Figure.* Paris: Klincksieck, 1971.

Lyotard, Jean-François. *Les TRANSformateurs DUchamp.* Paris, Galilée, 1977.

Macey, David. *Lacan in Contexts.* London: Verso, 1988.

Maurer, Evan. "Images of Dream and Desire: The Prints and Collage Novels of Max Ernst." In *Max Ernst, Beyond Surrealism,* ed. Robert Rainwater, pp. 54–93. New York: New York Public Library and Oxford University Press, 1986.

Merleau-Ponty, Maurice. *The Phenomenology of Perception* (1945). Trans. Colin Smith. London: Routledge & Kegan Paul, 1962.

Merleau-Ponty, Maurice. "Eye and Mind." Trans. Carleton Dallery. In *The Primacy of Perception,* ed. James M. Edie. Evanston: Northwestern University Press, 1964.

Morris, Robert. "Anti-Form." *Artforum,* 6 (April 1968), pp. 33–34.

Morris, Robert. "Some Notes on the Phenomenology of Making." *Artforum,* 8 (April 1970), pp. 62–66.

Naifeh, Steven, and Gregory White Smith. *Jackson Pollock: An American Saga.* New York: Clarkson Potter, 1989.

Namuth, Hans. "Photographier Pollock." In *L'atelier de Jackson Pollock*. Paris: Editions Macula, 1978.

Nesbit, Molly. "The Language of Industry." In *The Definitively Unfinished Marcel Duchamp*, ed. Thierry de Duve, pp. 351–398. Cambridge: MIT Press, 1991.

O'Connor, Francis V. *Jackson Pollock.* New York: Museum of Modern Art, 1967.

O'Connor, Francis V., and Eugene Thaw, eds. *Jackson Pollock: Catalogue Raisonné of Paintings, Drawings, and Other Works.* New Haven: Yale University Press, 1978.

Ozenfant, Amédée, and Edouard Jeanneret. *La peinture moderne.* Paris: Editions G. Crès, n.d.

Parmelin, Hélène. *The Artist and His Model.* New York: Abrams, 1965.

Parmelin, Hélène. *Picasso: Women, Mougins and Vauvenargues.* London: Weidenfeld and Nicolson, 1965.

Parmelin, Hélène. *Intimate Secrets of a Studio at Notre Dame de Vie.* New York: Abrams, 1966.

Parmelin, Hélène. *Picasso Says.* London: George Allen and Unwin, 1969.

Parmelin, Hélène. *Art et anartisme.* Paris: Christian Bourgois, 1969.

Parmelin, Hélène. *Voyage en Picasso.* Paris: Robert Lafont, 1980.

Paz, Octavio. *Marcel Duchamp: Appearance Stripped Bare.* New York: Viking, 1978.

Rohn, Matthew L. *Visual Dynamics in Jackson Pollock's Abstractions.* Ann Arbor: UMI Research Press, 1987.

Rose, Bernice. *Jackson Pollock: Drawing into Painting.* New York: Museum of Modern Art, 1980.

Rose, Jacqueline. *Sexuality in the Field of Vision.* London: Verso, 1986.

Rosenbaum, S. P., ed. *The Bloomsbury Group.* Toronto: University of Toronto Press, 1975.

Rosenberg, Harold. "The American Action Painters." *Art News,* 51 (December 1952). Reprinted in *The Tradition of the New,* pp. 28–29. New York: Horizon Press, 1959.

Rosenblum, Robert. "Picasso and the Anatomy of Eroticism." In *Studies in Erotic Art,* ed. Theodore Bowie and Cornelia V. Christenson. New York: Basic Books, 1970.

Roudinesco, Elisabeth. *Histoire de la psychanalyse en France.* 2 vols. Paris: Editions du Seuil, 1986.

Rubin, William. "Jackson Pollock and the Modern Tradition." *Artforum,* 5 (February, March, April, and May 1967).

Rubin, William. "Pollock as Jungian Illustrator: The Limits of Psychological Criticism." *Art in America,* 67 (November 1979), pp. 104–123, and (December 1979), pp. 72–91.

Ruskin, John. *Praeterita* (1885–1889). Oxford: Oxford University Press, 1979.

Sartre, Jean-Paul. *Being and Nothingness* (1943). Trans. Hazel E. Barnes. New York: Washington Square Press, 1966.

Sartre, Jean-Paul. *Imagination, a Psychological Critique.* Trans. Forrest Williams. Ann Arbor: University of Michigan Press, 1962.

Schleifer, Ronald. *A. J. Greimas and the Nature of Meaning.* Lincoln: University of Nebraska Press, 1987.

Schwarz, Arturo. "The Alchemist Stripped Bare in the Bachelor, Even." In *Marcel Duchamp,* ed. Anne d'Harnoncourt and Kynaston McShine, pp. 81–98. New York: Museum of Modern Art; Philadelphia: Philadelphia Museum of Art, 1973.

Sedgewick, Eve Kosofsky. *Between Men: English Literature and Male Homosocial Desire.* New York: Columbia University Press, 1985.

Spies, Werner. "Une poétique du collage." In *Paul Eluard et ses amis peintres,* pp. 45–69. Paris: Centre Georges Pompidou, 1982.

Spies, Werner. *Max Ernst, Loplop: The Artist in the Third Person.* New York: George Braziller, 1983.

Spies, Werner. *Max Ernst: Les collages, inventaire et contradictions.* Paris: Gallimard, 1984.

Steinberg, Leo. *Other Criteria.* New York: Oxford University Press, 1972.

Straus, Erwin. "The Upright Posture" (1948). In *Essays in Phenomenology,* ed. Maurice Natanson. The Hague: Martinus Nijhoff, 1966.

Straus, Erwin. "Born to See, Bound to Behold: Reflections on the Function of Upright Posture in the Aesthetic Attitude" (1963). In *The Philosophy of the Body,* ed. Stuart Spicker, pp. 334–359. New York: Quadrangle, 1970.

Stuckey, Charles. "Another Side of Jackson Pollock." *Art in America,* 65 (November 1977), pp. 81–91.

Teuber, Dirk. "Max Ernsts Lehrmittel." In *Max Ernst in Köln,* pp. 206–240. Cologne: Kölnischer Kunstverein, 1980.

Tzara, Tristan. "D'un certain automatisme du goût." *Minotaure,* no. 3 (1933), pp. 81–85.

Waldberg, Patrick. *Max Ernst.* Paris: Jean-Jacques Pauvert, 1958.

Warhol, Andy, and Pat Hackett. *POPism: The Warhol Sixties.* New York: Harcourt Brace Jovanovich, 1980.

Warlick, M. E. "Max Ernst's Alchemical Novel: *Une semaine de bonté.*" *Art Journal,* 46 (Spring 1987), pp. 61–72.

Weinberg, Jonathan. "Pollock and Picasso: The Rivalry and the 'Escape.'" *Arts,* 61 (Summer 1987), pp. 42–48.

collection, Switzerland. © 1993 ARS, New York / SPADEM / ADAGP, Paris. *Page 55*

Kölner Lehrmittelanstalt catalogue, p. 142, detail. *Page 56*

Max Ernst, *Dada in usum delphini,* 1920. Present whereabouts unknown. © 1993 ARS, New York / SPADEM / ADAGP, Paris. *Page 59*

Max Ernst, *Souvenir de dieu,* 1923. Present whereabouts unknown. © 1993 ARS, New York / SPADEM / ADAGP, Paris. *Page 60*

Max Ernst, *The Virgin Chastising the Infant Jesus in Front of Three Witnesses: A. B., P. E., and the Artist,* 1926. Oil on canvas, 77 x 51 inches. Collection Madame Jean Krebs, Brussels. © 1993 ARS, New York / SPADEM / ADAGP, Paris. *Page 61*

Oskar Pfister, *Picture Puzzle,* 1919. Reproduced in Freud, *Leonardo da Vinci,* p. 116. *Page 62*

Max Ernst, *At the First Clear Word,* 1923. 93¼ x 65¾ inches. Kunstsammlung Nordrhein-Westfalen, Düsseldorf. Photo by Walter Klein. © 1993 ARS, New York / SPADEM / ADAGP, Paris. *Page 69*

"Illusion of Touch," *La Nature* (1881), p. 584. *Page 70*

Max Ernst, *La femme 100 têtes,* 1929: "Truth will remain simple, and gigantic wheels will ride the bitter waves." © 1993 ARS, New York / SPADEM / ADAGP, Paris. *Page 77*

Max Ernst, *La femme 100 têtes,* 1929: "The might-have-been Immaculate Conception." © 1993 ARS, New York / SPADEM / ADAGP, Paris. *Page 78*

Max Ernst, *La femme 100 têtes,* 1929: ". . . and the third time missed." © 1993 ARS, New York / SPADEM / ADAGP, Paris. *Page 79*

Max Ernst, *The Garden of France,* 1962. Oil on canvas, 44⅞ x 66⅛ inches. Musée National d'Art Moderne, Paris. © 1993 ARS, New York / SPADEM / ADAGP, Paris. *Page 80*

Max Ernst, *The Invention,* 1922. Present whereabouts unknown. © 1993 ARS, New York / SPADEM / ADAGP, Paris. *Page 83*

"Electrical Experiment, Carried Out on a Walnut," *La Nature* (1891), p. 272. © 1993 ARS, New York / SPADEM / ADAGP, Paris. *Page 84*

Max Ernst, *Répétitions* (cover collage), 1922. Present whereabouts unknown. © 1993 ARS, New York / SPADEM / ADAGP, Paris. *Page 85*

"The Magic Ball," *La Nature* (1887), p. 144. *Page 86*

Max Ernst, *Magician,* 1921. 5⅛ x 4½ inches. Galerie Dieter Brusberg, Hanover. © 1993 ARS, New York / SPADEM / ADAGP, Paris. *Page 89*

"The Multiplication of Eggs, the Magician Alber's Trick," *La Nature* (1881). *Page 90*

Marcel Duchamp, *Rotorelief* ("Montgolfier Balloon"), 1935. Cardboard, printed by offset lithography, 7⅞ inches diameter. The Museum of Modern Art, New York, Gift of the Riklis Collection of The McCrory Corporation. © 1993 ARS, New York / ADAGP, Paris. *Page 99*

Marcel Duchamp, *Rotorelief* ("Goldfish"), 1935. Cardboard, printed by offset lithography, 7⅞ inches diameter. The Museum of Modern Art, New York, Gift of the Riklis Collection of The McCrory Corporation. © 1993 ARS, New York / ADAGP, Paris. *Page 100*

Marcel Duchamp, *Rotorelief* ("Chinese Lantern"), 1935. Cardboard, printed by offset lithography, 7⅞ inches diameter. The Museum of Modern Art, New York, Gift of the Riklis Collection of The McCrory Corporation. © 1993 ARS, New York / ADAGP, Paris. *Page 101*

Marcel Duchamp, *Rotorelief* ("Corolles"), 1935. Cardboard, printed by offset lithography, 7⅞ inches diameter. The Museum of Modern Art, New York, Gift of the Riklis Collection of The McCrory Corporation. © 1993 ARS, New York / ADAGP, Paris. *Page 102*

Earle Loran, diagram from *Cézanne's Compositions. Page 105*

Earle Loran, diagram from *Cézanne's Compositions. Page 106*

The visual cone, from B. Taylor, *New Principles of Linear Perspective* (London, 1715). *Page 109*

Marcel Duchamp, *Etant donnés: 1° la chute d'eau, 2° le gaz d'éclairage,* 1945–1966, exterior view. Mixed-media assemblage, 95½ x 70 inches. Philadelphia Museum of Art, Gift of the Cassandra Foundation. © 1993 ARS, New York / ADAGP, Paris. *Page 110*

Diagram of Duchamp's *Etant donnés,* from Jean-François Lyotard, *Les TRANSformateurs DUchamp* (Paris: Galilée, 1977). *Page 115*

Marcel Duchamp, *Etant donnés,* view through the door. © 1993 ARS, New York / ADAGP, Paris. *Page 116*

Marcel Duchamp, *La mariée mise à nu par ses célibataires, même (Le grand verre),* 1915–1923. Oil, varnish, lead foil, lead wire, and dust on two glass panels, 109¼ x 69¼ inches. Philadelphia Museum of Art, Katherine S. Dreier Bequest. © 1993 ARS, New York / ADAGP, Paris. *Page 121*

Marcel Duchamp, *Cols alités,* 1959. Pen and pencil on paper, 12⅝ x 9⅝ inches. Collection Jean-Jacques Lebel, Paris. © 1993 ARS, New York / ADAGP, Paris. *Page 122*

Marcel Duchamp, *Rotary Demisphere (Precision Optics).* 1925. Motor-driven construction, 58½ x 25¼ x 24 inches. The Museum of Modern Art, New York, Gift of Mrs. William Sisler and Edward James Fund. © 1993 ARS, New York / ADAGP, Paris. *Page 129*

Wheatstone stereoscope, 1830. Reproduced in *Helmholtz on Perception. Page 130*

Marcel Duchamp, *Handmade Stereopticon Slide,* 1918–1919. Pencil over photographic stereopticon slide, each image 2¼ × 2¼ inches. The Museum of Modern Art, New York, Katherine S. Dreier Bequest. © 1993 ARS, New York / ADAGP, Paris. *Page 131*

The Müller-Lyer illusion. *Page 132*

Jacques-André Boiffard, *Gnostic Seal,* photograph from *Documents,* 2, no. 1 (1930). *Page 153*

Salvador Dalí, *Phenomenon of Ecstasy,* 1933. Photocollage, 11 x 7¼ inches. Manoukian Collection, Paris. © 1993 Demart Pro Arte, Geneva / ARS, New York. *Page 154*

Man Ray, *Anatomies,* c. 1930. Silver print, 9½ x 7 inches. The Museum of Modern Art, New York. © 1993 ARS, New York / ADAGP, Paris. *Page 159*

Diagram of Salvador Dalí's *Lugubrious Game* (1929), as published in *Documents,* 1, no. 7 (1929). *Page 160*

Man Ray, *Hat,* 1933. Silver print, 6¾ x 5¼ inches. Collection Rosabianca Skira, Geneva. © 1993 ARS, New York / ADAGP, Paris. *Page 163*

Alberto Giacometti, *Suspended Ball,* 1930–1931. Plaster and metal, 24 x 14¼ x 14 inches. Kunstmuseum Basel, Alberto Giacometti Foundation. © 1993 ARS, New York / ADAGP, Paris. *Page 164*

Alberto Giacometti, *Project for a Passageway (Labyrinth),* 1930–1931. Plaster, 6 x 50 x 17 inches. Kunsthaus, Zurich, Alberto Giacometti Foundation. Photo by Walter Drayer. © 1993 ARS, New York / ADAGP, Paris. *Page 169*

Hans Bellmer, *Machine Gunneress in a State of Grace,* 1937. Paint over photograph, 25½ x 25½ inches. San Francisco Museum of Modern Art. © 1993 ARS, New York / ADAGP, Paris. *Page 170*

Hans Bellmer, *La Poupée,* 1936/1949. Tinted silver print, 16⅛ x 13 inches. Musée National d'Art Moderne, Paris. © 1993 ARS, New York / ADAGP, Paris. *Page 173*

Hans Bellmer, *La Poupée,* 1938. Tinted silver print, 11 x 9¼ inches. Private collection, Paris. © 1993 ARS, New York / ADAGP, Paris. *Page 174*

Hans Bellmer, *La Poupée,* 1938. Tinted silver print, 5⅝ x 5⅝ inches. Private collection, Paris. © 1993 ARS, New York / ADAGP, Paris. *Page 175*

Hans Bellmer, *La Poupée (Idole),* 1937. Tinted silver print, 5½ x 5½ inches. Private collection, Paris. © 1993 ARS, New York / ADAGP, Paris. *Page 176*

Raoul Ubac, *Portrait in a Mirror,* 1938. Silver print, 9½ x 7 inches. The Metropolitan Museum of Art, New York. © 1993 ARS, New York / ADAGP, Paris. *Page 181*

Raoul Ubac, *The Battle of the Amazons (Group III),* 1939. Silver print, 10¾ x 15⅝ inches. Galerie Adrien Maeght, Paris. © 1993 ARS, New York / ADAGP, Paris. *Page 182*

Jacques-André Boiffard, *Untitled,* 1929. Silver print, 9½ x 7⅞ inches. Musée National d'Art Moderne, Paris. *Page 187*

Jacques-André Boiffard, *Untitled,* 1929. Silver print, 5 x 3 inches. Private collection, Paris. *Page 188*

Roberto Otero, photograph of Picasso's living room at Notre Dame de Vie, Mougins, from *Forever Picasso* (New York: Abrams, 1982), p. 147. *Page 199*

Pablo Picasso, *Bather with Beach Ball,* Boisgeloup, 30 August 1932. Oil on canvas, 57⅝ x 45⅛ inches. Partial gift of an anonymous donor and promised gift of Ronald S. Lauder to the Museum of Modern Art, New York. © 1993 ARS, New York / SPADEM, Paris. *Page 200*

Pablo Picasso, *Three Musicians,* Fontainebleau, summer 1921. Oil on canvas, 79 x 87¾ inches. The Museum of Modern Art, New York, Mrs. Simon Guggenheim Fund. © 1993 ARS, New York / SPADEM, Paris. *Page 203*

Max Ernst, *A Little Girl Dreams of Taking the Veil,* 1930: "Dans mon colombodrome." © 1993 ARS, New York / SPADEM / ADAGP, Paris. *Page 204*

Zootrope, *La Nature* (1888), p. 12. *Page 207*

Bronze figures representing eleven successive positions of a pigeon in flight, *La Nature* (1888), p. 12. *Page 208*

Stereoscopic projections, *La Nature* (1891), p. 49. *Page 211*

Reynaud's projective praxinoscope, *La Nature,* (1882), p. 357. *Page 212*

Pablo Picasso, *Déjeuner sur l'herbe d'après Manet,* 10 July 1961. Oil on canvas, 44½ x 57 inches. Staatsgalerie Stuttgart. © 1993 ARS, New York / SPADEM, Paris. *Page 223*

Pablo Picasso, *Déjeuner sur l'herbe d'après Manet,* 13 July 1961. Oil on canvas, 23⅝ x 28¾ inches. Musée Picasso, Paris. © 1993 ARS, New York / SPADEM, Paris. *Page 224*

Pablo Picasso, *Déjeuner sur l'herbe d'après Manet Sketchbook,* 4 July 1961 I. 10⅝ x 16½ inches. Private collection. © 1993 ARS, New York / SPADEM, Paris. *Page 227*

Pablo Picasso, *Déjeuner sur l'herbe d'après Manet Sketchbook,* 4 July 1961 II. 10⅝ x 16½ inches. Private collection. © 1993 ARS, New York / SPADEM, Paris. *Page 228*

Pablo Picasso, *Raphaël et la Fornarina,* 4 September 1968 I. Etching, 5⅞ x 8⅛ inches. Galerie Louise Leiris, Paris. © 1993 ARS, New York / SPADEM, Paris. *Page 231*

Pablo Picasso, *Déjeuner sur l'herbe d'après Manet Sketchbook,* 2 August 1962 I. Pencil and crayon, 9 x 12⅝ inches. Private collection. © 1993 ARS, New York / SPADEM, Paris. *Page 232*

Pablo Picasso, *Déjeuner sur l'herbe d'après Manet Sketchbook,* 2 August 1962 II. Pencil and crayon, 9 x 12⅝ inches. Private collection. © 1993 ARS, New York / SPADEM, Paris. *Page 233*

Pablo Picasso, *Untitled,* 15 November 1966 VI. Aquatint and etching, 8⅞ x 12¾ inches. Galerie Louise Leiris, Paris. © 1993 ARS, New York / SPADEM, Paris. *Page 234*

Pablo Picasso, *Untitled,* 14 August 1962. Ceramic tile, 6½ × 7½ inches. © 1993 ARS, New York / SPADEM, Paris. *Page 237*

Sketch made by the Wolf Man, from Sigmund Freud, "From the History of an Infantile Neurosis," p. 30. *Page 238*

Jackson Pollock, *Out of the Web: Number 7,* 1949. Oil and Duco on masonite, 47⅞ x 96 inches. Staatsgalerie, Stuttgart. © 1993 Pollock-Krasner Foundation / ARS, New York. *Page 249*

Jackson Pollock, *Echo: Number 25,* 1951. Enamel on canvas, 91⅞ x 86 inches. Museum of Modern Art, New York, Acquired through the Lillie P. Bliss Bequest and the Mr. and Mrs. David Rockefeller Fund, 1969. © 1993 Pollock-Krasner Foundation / ARS, New York. *Page 250*

Cy Twombly, *Untitled,* 1956 (New York City). Oil and graphite on canvas, 46 x 69 inches. Private collection. Photo by Rudolph Burckhardt. *Page 257*

Brassaï, *Graffiti,* 1930. Silver print, 11¾ x 8¼ inches. Private Collection, Paris. *Page 258*

Jackson Pollock, *Galaxy,* 1947. Oil and aluminum on canvas, 43½ x 34 inches. Jocelyn Museum, Omaha, Nebraska. © 1993 Pollock-Krasner Foundation / ARS, New York. *Page 261*

Jackson Pollock, *Number 1, 1948,* 1948. Oil on unprimed canvas, 68 x 104 inches. The Museum of Modern Art, New York. © 1993 Pollock-Krasner Foundation / ARS, New York. *Page 262*

Thomas Hart Benton, diagrams, published in "Mechanics of Form Organization in Painting," *The Arts* (November 1926), p. 288. *Page 263*

Cy Twombly, *Panorama,* 1955 (New York City). House paint and crayon on canvas, 101 x 233 inches. Courtesy Thomas Ammann, Zurich. Photo by Geoffrey Clements. *Page 264*

Cy Twombly, *The Italians,* 1961. Oil, pencil, and crayon on canvas, 78⅝ inches

x 102¼ inches. The Museum of Modern Art, New York, Blanchette Rockefeller Fund. Photo by Rudolph Burckhardt. *Page 267*

Andy Warhol, *Do It Yourself (Flowers),* 1962. Synthetic polymer paint and Prestype on canvas, 69 x 59 inches. Courtesy Thomas Ammann, Zurich. *Page 268*

Installation view, *Andy Warhol,* Institute of Contemporary Art, Philadelphia, 1965. *Page 271*

Andy Warhol, *Piss Painting,* 1961. Urine on canvas, 48 x 80 inches. *Page 272*

Hans Namuth, *Jackson Pollock,* 1950. Silver print. Estate of the artist. © 1991 Hans Namuth Ltd. *Page 273*

Andy Warhol, *Oxidation Painting,* 1978. Mixed mediums on copper metallic paint on canvas, 78 x 204½ inches. Courtesy Thomas Ammann, Zurich. *Page 274*

Pablo Picasso, *Girl before a Mirror,* Boisgeloup, 14 March 1932. Oil on canvas, 64 x 51¼ inches. The Museum of Modern Art, New York, Gift of Mrs. Simon Guggenheim. © 1993 ARS, New York / SPADEM, Paris. *Page 279*

Jackson Pollock, *Masqued Image,* c. 1938–1941. Oil on canvas, 40 x 24⅛ inches. The Modern Art Musum of Fort Worth, purchase through the Anne Burnett and Charles Tandy Foundation. © 1993 Pollock-Krasner Foundation / ARS, New York. *Page 280*

Jackson Pollock, *Sea Change,* 1947. Oil and pebbles on canvas, 57⅞ x 44⅛ inches. Seattle Museum of Art, gift of Peggy Guggenheim. Photo by Paul Macapia. © 1993 Pollock-Krasner Foundation / ARS, New York. *Page 285*

Jackson Pollock, *Stenographic Figure,* 1942. Oil on linen, 40 x 56 inches. The Museum of Modern Art, New York, Mr. and Mrs. Walter Bareiss Fund. *Page 286*

Illustration in André Breton's "Message Automatique," *Minotaure* (1933). *Page 287*

Jackson Pollock, *The She Wolf,* 1943. Oil, gouache, and plaster on canvas, 41⅞ x

67 inches. The Museum of Modern Art, New York. *Page 288*

Morris Louis, *Saraband,* 1959. Acrylic resin on canvas, 100⅛ inches x 149 inches. The Solomon R. Guggenheim Museum, New York. *Page 291*

Jackson Pollock, *Full Fathom Five,* 1947. Oil on canvas with nails, tacks, buttons, key, coins, cigarettes, matches, etc., 50⅞ x 30⅛ inches. The Museum of Modern Art, New York. *Page 292*

Jackson Pollock, *One (Number 31, 1950),* 1950. Oil and enamel on canvas, 106 x 210 inches. The Museum of Modern Art, New York. *Page 295*

Robert Morris, *Untitled,* 1968. Felt, 144 x 114 inches. Collection of the artist. Photo by Rudolph Burckhardt. *Page 296*

Robert Morris, *Untitled,* 1967–1968. Felt, ⅜ inches thick. Collection Philip Johnson. Photo by Rudolph Burckhardt. *Page 297*

Hans Namuth, film strip from *Jackson Pollock,* 1950. Estate of the artist. *Page 298*

Gjon Mili, *Picasso "Drawing" with Flashlight, Vallauris,* 1949. Silver print. Life Magazine, © Time Warner Inc. *Page 299*

Jackson Pollock, *Number 7, 1951,* 1951. Enamel on canvas, 56½ x 66 inches. National Gallery of Art, Washington, D.C., Gift of the Collectors Committee. *Page 300*

Jackson Pollock, *Blue Poles,* 1952. Enamel, aluminum paint, and glass fragments on canvas, 83 x 192 inches. Australian National Gallery, Canberra. *Page 305*

Jackson Pollock, *Convergence,* 1952. Oil on canvas, 93½ x 155 inches. Albright-Knox Art Gallery, Buffalo, The Martha Jackson Collection. *Page 306*

Diagram for *Convergence,* from Matthew Rohm, *Visual Dynamics in Jackson Pollock* (Ann Arbor: UMI Research Press, 1987). *Page 306*

Eva Hesse, *Hang Up,* January 1966. Acrylic paint on cloth over wood; acrylic paint on cord over steel tube, 72 x 84 x 78 inches. The Art Institute of Chicago, Gift of Arthur Keating and Mr. and Mrs. Edward Morris by exchange. *Page 311*

Eva Hess, *Untitled,* 1967. Ink wash and pencil on paper on board with nylon string, 14⅞ x 14⅞ inches. Collection Mrs. Victor W. Ganz. *Page 312*

Eva Hesse, *Untitled,* completed March 1970. Latex over rope, string, and wire, height of three units 144, 126, and 90 inches; width varies with installation. Whitney Museum of American Art, New York. Photo by Geoffrey Clements. *Page 317*

Eva Hesse, *Right After,* 1969. Fiberglass, 60 x 156 x 48 inches. Milwaukee Art Museum, Gift of Friends of Art. Photo by P. Richard Eells. *Page 318*

Index